W9-BHE-065

DISCARDED BY
MEMPHIS PUBLIC LIBRARY

DISCARDED BY
MEMPHIS PUBLIC LIBRARY

AE20303
12.95
m-26

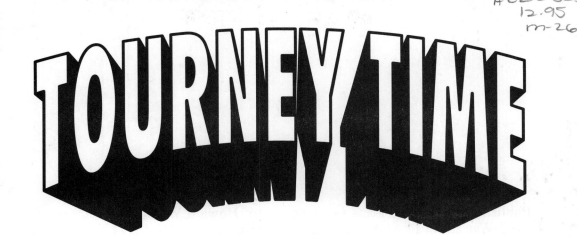

TOURNEY TIME

IT'S AWESOME BABY!

DISCARDED BY
MEMPHIS PUBLIC LIBRARY

Dick Vitale
with
Mike Douchant

MASTERS PRESS
SPORTS PUBLISHER

A Division of Howard W. Sams & Co.

Published by Masters Press (a subsidiary of Howard W. Sams)
2647 Waterfront Pkwy E. Dr, Suite 300, Indianapolis, IN 46214

©1993 Dick Vitale

All rights reserved.
Published 1993

Printed in the United States of America

No part of this publication may be reproduced, stored in a retrieval system, or transmitted, in any form or by any means, electronic, mechanical, photocopying, recording, or otherwise, without the prior permission of Masters Press.

Library of Congress Cataloging-in-Publication Data
Vitale, Dick.

    Tourney time--it's awesome baby / Dick Vitale with Mike
Douchant.
      p.   cm.
    Includes Index.
    ISBN 0-940279-84-3 : $12.95
    1. National College Athletic Association Tournament-
Miscellaneous. I. Douchant, Mike, 1951-   II. Title.
GV885.49.N37V48   1993   93-41953
796.323'63.973--dc20   CIP

Cover design: Lynne Annette Clark
Cover photographs: Stephen Baker and Brian Spurlock
Illustrations: Terry Varvel
Production assistance: Christy Pierce, Julie Biddle, Leah Marckel,
                 and Matthew K. Floyd
Special thanks to Sacino's Formal Wear for use of the tuxedo and to
the college sports information departments for use of the photographs.

CONTENTS

FOREWORD

I love baseball, and I've attended the Super Bowl, but let me tell you something: Eat your heart out, Tommy Lasorda; eat your heart out, Sparky Anderson; eat your heart out, John Madden. I mean are you kidding me? No sports event is more special than the NCAA Tournament. People can't wait to find out about the pairings and fill out their tourney brackets. It's excitement galore, wherever you are. Every store, every shop, every restaurant, every workplace, you better believe it, people are talking about college basketball during March Madness. The pressure of a one-game elimination scenario yields a hoop hysteria full of intensity and emotion. There is flat-out nothing like the jubilation of the Big Dance. The tourney is uno number one, baby.

Back in 1977, when I was coaching at the University of Detroit, it was a thrill to receive that phone call from the committee notifying us that we were invited to the tournament. It made all the blood, sweat, and tears worth it. Remember, we weren't a marquee school, and we didn't have the luxury of an automatic bid because we were an independent. But we had one heck of a team led by three guys that went on the play in the NBA – Terry Tyler, Terry Duerod, and John Long.

It wasn't because of any genius that I possessed, but we won 25 games and lost only four that season. Nevertheless, for us to get a chance to play in the tournament we had to pull a knockout punch. I'll never forget we had won 20 in a row going to Marquette and the pressure was on to beat Al McGuire's Warriors at Milwaukee so we could be assured of getting that lovely tournament bid. Well, it's a one-point game in the closing seconds. I switch from man-to-man to a halfcourt pressure zone defense, and we knock the rock loose. I was really trying to get a timeout, but my player looked at me and said, "Hey, I'm not going to let him get a T.O. He'll screw it up with some strategy." So Dennis Boyd takes off downcourt, shakes and bakes and hits the J at the buzzer. It's a 64-63 victory for U of D and that means that there's no way in the world that the committee could look at our credentials and say, "You're out of the tourney, baby!"

It's just incredible to be part of the action as a player or coach. My Titans lost a heartbreaker to Michigan in my last game on the sideline in 1977. It was in Lexington, Kentucky in the Mideast Regional semifinals. That's right, I coached there before you did, Rick Pitino. I coached there, but I had a big "L" baby, losing against the number one team in the nation.

I might have been the wackiest that ever walked the sideline. If I was coaching today I'd be a household name, because I was absolutely bananas along that sideline. Well, I was really going crazy by the time we had our matchup against mighty Michigan. I teased Wolverines coach Johnny Orr by calling him Muhammad Ali and labeling myself Chuck Wepner. I said, "Johnny, you're Ali, baby! You're the king! You're the champ! You guys are the amazing maize and blue. I'm just Chuck Wepner. I bleed and I cut, but we are going to scrap and claw, and we are going to give Michigan all they can handle." And we did just that before losing 86-81. But I really believe that we took so much out of Michigan that night emotionally and physically that they had nothing left when they were upset in the regional final by UNC Charlotte's Cornbread Maxwell and Company. I was really looking forward to watching the replay of that game because the greatest coach of all time, Johnny Wooden, was working as a television analyst. I was anxious to hear what he had to say about me and the program. I watched that game over and over, but we came up short everytime. It was Heartbreak Hotel!

If we had beaten Michigan, we would have been on such a high that we would've beaten UNCC, and then we would've defeated you a second time, Big Al. And if Marquette could defeat North Carolina in the final, then we could have, and I'd have been holding the gold trophy and wearing the gold ring, not you, Al baby! Oh, I like to dream, Al, I like to dream.

Despite not making it to the Final Four as a coach I have such a passion and love for the game of basketball, and I know what it's done for me in my life. My moments coaching at junior high, high school, college, and the professional levels and my years as a broadcaster have provided me with opportunities to meet so many beautiful people. My hope now is that this book will help some of those beautiful people enjoy the tournament even more than they already do.

Postseason competition is unbelievable. But in all modesty, I believe you'll enjoy the pageantry even more by having this handy-dandy guide by your side before, during, and after *Tourney Time*. Because *it's awesome baby!*

ACKNOWLEDGMENTS

Eternal thanks to my wife Lorraine and my daughters Terri and Sherri for their devotion and support in helping make this project become a reality. Also, to my partner, Mike Douchant, for his countless hours of research, and to Mark Montieth, editor at Masters Press, for helping bring the project together.

And, none of this would have ever been possible if not for the beautiful people at ESPN and ABC for giving me an open forum to share my views with the fantastic fans.

Dick's Top 5

Solid Gold Tourney Dynasties

1. **UCLA** — Made 15 consecutive appearances from 1967-81 when the field ranged from 23 to 48 teams, winning 10 titles in a 12-year span, including seven in a row.

2. **Indiana** — Only school to win the NCAA championship in four different decades - 1940, 1953, 1976 and 1987.

3. **North Carolina** — Only school to participate in the NCAA Tournament every year since conferences were first permitted to have more than one representative in 1975.

4. **Kentucky** — Only school to have a minimum of four coaches direct teams to the NCAA Tournament and each of them compile a winning playoff record with that university.

5. **Kansas** — Only school to reach the Final Four under five different coaches.

TEAMS THAT KNEW HOW TO Rock 'N Roll

I used to be so much in awe of legendary coach John Wooden that I'd turn to putty and become virtually incoherent when I was around him — not that some people don't think I'm incoherent at times anyway. But I'm more comfortable in his presence now, and it should give many coaches hope that better days are ahead if they'd examine the Wizard of Westwood's early mark in postseason play.

UCLA's record in the NCAA Tournament under Wooden was an anemic 3-9 from 1950 through 1963 before the Bruins captured an unprecedented 10 national titles in 12 years from 1964 through 1975. Wooden's first Final Four team (18-11 record in 1962) was the only national semifinalist in 20 years from 1960 through 1979 to finish a season with double-digit defeats.

"For the most part, we had no home court (until Pauley Pavilion was built in time for the 1965-66 season)," Wooden once said. "We practiced in a multi-purpose gymnasium that had just two baskets to practice on. We had a big floor with gymnastics practice going on at one side and practice for other sports going on at the other side. We played more games on the road than at home.

"We won our first two national championships under those conditions. To me, that's the absolutely most remarkable thing about all the championships we won, that we were able to win two without having a real home court to play on. The greatest help to our program was getting Pauley Pavilion. The main thing was the advantages it gave us in practice, more than having a homecourt advantage for

1

TOURNEY TIME

games (149-2 record at Pauley under Wooden). It really helped us in so many ways, such as recruiting."

Incredibly, his 10 championship teams lost a total of 10 regular-season games and never trailed at halftime in an NCAA Tournament final. The only one of 20 Final Four contests in which the 10 UCLA champions were behind at halftime was the 1975 national semifinal against Louisville, which led the Bruins by four points (37-33) at the break.

Wooden's UCLA teams won 38 consecutive NCAA playoff games between their 1963 losses to Arizona State (79-75 in overtime in West Regional semifinal) and San Francisco (76-75 in regional third-place game) until a 1974 loss to North Carolina State (80-77 in double overtime in national semifinals).

The Bruins, failing to participate in the 1966 playoffs after compiling an 18-8 record, won eight of the games in Los Angeles during their incomparable streak. They didn't pick on patsies despite winning 28 of the 38 games by more than 10 points (16.4-point average margin of victory overall). Thirty of the 38 opponents had lost fewer than seven games before playing UCLA. Among the notable coaches to lose at least twice to the imperial Bruins during their playoff streak were Jerry Tarkanian (Long Beach State), Lou Henson (New Mexico State), Guy Lewis (Houston), Don Donoher (Dayton) and Stan Watts (Brigham Young).

Six of UCLA's seven consecutive national champions from 1967 through 1973 won their playoff games by an average margin of at least 16 points. The closest result for the Bruins during their 38-game winning streak was in the 1971 West Regional final when they erased an 11-point deficit and overcame 29 percent field goal shooting (18 of 62) to edge Long Beach State (57-55). The 38 victims had combined to win almost 84 percent of their games before they were eliminated by UCLA. As a means of comparison, Duke was 32-5 in seven years from 1986 through 1992 against teams combining to win 78 percent of their games before meeting the Blue Devils in the playoffs.

Starting with UCLA's first championship team in 1964, 11 schools have generated more than two Final Four appearances in a 29-year span through 1993 (number after slash indicates Final Four appearances in the school's history):

13/14: UCLA (1964-65-67-68-69-70-71-72-73-74-75-76-80)

9/11: North Carolina (1967-68-69-72-77-81-82-91-93)

9/10: Duke (1964-66-78-86-88-90-90-91-92)

6/10: Kansas (1971-74-86-88-91-93)

6/ 6: Louisville (1972-75-80-82-83-86)

6/ 6: Michigan (1964-65-76-89-92-93)

5/10: Kentucky (1966-75-78-84-93)

5/ 7: Indiana (1973-76-81-87-92)

5/ 5: Houston (1967-68-82-83-84)

4/ 4: UNLV (1977-87-90-91)

3/ 4: Georgetown (1982-84-85)

REPEAT AFTER ME

I remember how disheartening it was in my first year as athletic director at the University of Detroit (1977-78) when we had a 24-3 record but didn't earn a repeat appearance to the NCAA playoffs. In my final season as a college coach the previous season (25-4 mark), I became the only Titans coach to win an NCAA Tournament game when future NBA players Terry Duerod, John Long and Terry Tyler sparked us to a 93-76 victory over Middle Tennessee State in the 1977 Mideast Regional before we lost to top-ranked Michigan (86-81) in the next round. It's difficult enough to make consecutive appearances in the tourney, not to mention win back-to-back NCAA titles.

Georgetown was the first NCAA Tournament champion since the UCLA teams of 1975-76 to return to the Final Four the following season (returned in 1985 after defeating Houston, 84-75, in 1984 final) until UNLV and Duke achieved the feat in 1991 and 1992, respectively. Georgetown came close to capturing three crowns in four years during the Patrick Ewing era but lost two finals by a total of three points (63-62 against North Carolina in 1982 and 66-64 against Villanova in 1985).

The Hoyas and Carolina's titlist in 1982 were the only two defending champions in a 14-year span from 1976-89 to compile a winning NCAA playoff record the year after capturing the crown. Six of the champions in that stretch didn't participate in the tourney the next year — Indiana '76, Kentucky '78, Michigan State '79, North Carolina State '83, Louisville '86 and Kansas '88. Marquette '77, Louisville '80 and Indiana '87 lost their opening playoff games the next year, Indiana '81 lost in the second round the next year, and Villanova '85 and Michigan '89 lost in the regional semifinals the next year.

In 1992, Duke became the first school to win back-to-back national titles since UCLA captured seven in a row from 1967 through 1973, as well as the first school since UCLA in 1973 to be in three consecutive national championship games. A common link among the last four schools — San Francisco, Cincinnati, UCLA and Duke — to repeat as national champion is their perseverance enduring troubled times in the valley not too many years before ascending to Hoops Heaven. Consider the following lulls before they created dynasties:

- San Francisco suffered three consecutive losing seasons from 1951 through 1953.

- Cincinnati was a total of six games below .500 in three seasons from 1952 through 1954.

- UCLA averaged exactly 10 defeats per year from 1958 through 1962.

- Duke was a total of 13 games below .500 in ACC competition in 1982 and 1983, with a total of 17 losses each season.

Here is a capsule look at the seven times a school successfully defended its major college championship:

SCHOOL	COACH	CHAMPIONSHIP SEASONS
Oklahoma A&M*	Henry Iba	1944-45 and 1945-46

Comment: Seven-footer Bob Kurland averaged 18.3 points per game as the Aggies compiled a two-year record of 58-6. Kurland outscored centers Dolph Schayes of NYU and Bones McKinney of North Carolina by a total of 34 points (45-11) in the two title games. Kurland was the only Aggie to reach double figures in any of the Aggies' three playoff games in 1946.

Kentucky　　　　　**Adolph Rupp**　　　　　**1947-48 and 1948-49**

Comment: Alex Groza and Ralph Beard were the only double-digit scorers each season as the Wildcats posted a two-year mark of 68-5. Groza, a 6-7 center, was the leading scorer in each of the four Final Four games. Beard's backcourt mate in 1948 was Ken Rollins, the lone senior among Rupp's "Fabulous Five." Rollins held standout guard Bob Cousy, the leading scorer for defending champion Holy Cross, to just five points in the 1948 semifinals. Kentucky's titlists had tremendous maturity inasmuch as Groza, Rollins, Dale Barnstable, Jim Line and Cliff Barker were World War II service veterans. Barker, a ballhawk extraordinaire, was in a German prisoner-of-war camp for 16 months.

San Francisco　　　　**Phil Woolpert**　　　　**1954-55 and 1955-56**

Comment: Bill Russell and K.C. Jones helped the Dons win 57 of 58 games in the two-year span, including their last 55. Russell retrieved 25 rebounds in the 1955 final while defensive specialist Jones, 6-1, held La Salle's three-time consensus first-team All-America Tom Gola, 6-6, without a basket during one 21-minute stretch and outscored him, 24-16. Jones was ineligible for the 1956 playoffs because he had played one game two years earlier before an appendectomy ended his season, but USF still became the first undefeated champion in NCAA history when Russell grabbed a Final Four-record 27 rebounds in the title game against Iowa.

Cincinnati　　　　**Ed Jucker**　　　　**1960-61 and 1961-62**

Comment: Paul Hogue, Tom Thacker and Tony Yates were regulars both seasons as the well-balanced Bearcats won 56 of 61 games. Yates, a former serviceman, was the floor general. Four Cincinnati players scored in double figures in both championship contests against intrastate and favored rival Ohio State. Hogue, a 6-9 center who hit just 54.2 percent of his free throw attempts for the two title teams, sank only two of 10 foul shots in his two previous games before putting Cincinnati ahead to stay with a pair of free throws in overtime in a 70-65 championship game victory in 1961. In the 1962 national semifinals against UCLA, he was 12 of 17 from the charity stripe and scored 14 consecutive points for the Bearcats down the stretch to finish with 36 before Thacker's desperation long-range basket, his only points of the game, gave them a 72-70 win.

SCHOOL	COACH	CHAMPIONSHIP SEASONS
UCLA	John Wooden	1963-64 and 1964-65

Comment: Guard Gail Goodrich was the leading scorer each season as the Bruins won 58 of 60 games without a regular taller than 6-7. Goodrich outscored consensus second-team All-America Jeff Mullins of Duke, 27-22, in the 1964 final and outscored unanimous first-team All-America Cazzie Russell of Michigan, 42-28, in the 1965 final.

UCLA	John Wooden	1966-67 through 1972-73

Comment: Centers Lew Alcindor, Steve Patterson and Bill Walton boosted the Bruins to a 205-5 record over the seven-year streak of NCAA crowns. The trio combined to average 29.3 points, 15.1 rebounds and hit 71.2 percent of their field-goal attempts in the seven title games. Alcindor averaged 30.3 points and 18 rebounds and shot 71.7 percent from the floor in three title games from 1967 through 1969. Patterson averaged 23 points and 9.5 rebounds and shot 63.6 percent from the floor in two finals in 1970 and 1971. Walton averaged 34 points and 16.5 rebounds and shot 76.9 percent from the floor in two championship games in 1972 and 1973. Four of the champions had nine different players score in the title contest (1967, 1968, 1969 and 1973).

Duke	Mike Krzyzewski	1990-91 and 1991-92

Comment: Christian Laettner became the NCAA Tournament's all-time leading scorer and teammate Bobby Hurley became the tourney's all-time leader in assists as the Blue Devils posted a two-year mark of 66-9. Laettner scored 28 points in a 79-77 victory over previously undefeated UNLV in the 1991 semifinals to avenge a 30-point loss against the Rebels in the 1990 final. Hurley took up the slack with 26 points when Laettner was limited to eight points in an 81-78 decision over Indiana in the 1992 national semifinals. Laettner closed out his college career with a game-high 19 points in the 1992 championship game against Michigan.

*School now known as the Oklahoma State Cowboys.

NOBODY'S LOOKING OUT FOR NO. 1

There's enough pressure on a team entering postseason play without it also being ranked No. 1 in the country. That's why I think Duke's handling of that No. 1 ranking two years ago is so special. Coach Mike Krzyzewski was able to get the Blue Devils to accept that challenge and they really proved something when they defied a recent trend by becoming the first top-ranked team in 10 years entering the NCAA Tournament to win the national title. The previous five top-ranked teams failed to reach the championship game, a fate suffered by Indiana last year. UNLV lost twice in the national semifinals (1987 and 1991) and Temple '88, Arizona '89 and Oklahoma '90 failed to reach the Final Four.

Temple, a 63-53 loser to Duke in the 1988 East Regional final, and Kansas State, an 85-75 loser to Cincinnati in the 1959 Midwest Reginal final, are the only teams ranked No. 1 by both AP and UPI entering the tourney to lose by a double-digit margin before the Final Four.

The school gaining the sweetest revenge against a top-ranked team was St. John's in 1952. Defending NCAA championship Kentucky humiliated the Redmen by 41 points (81-40) early in the season. But St. John's, sparked by center Bob Zawoluk's 32 points, avenged the rout by eliminating the Wildcats (64-57) in the East Regional, ending their 23-game winning streak. The Redmen then defeated second-ranked Illinois in the national semifinals before losing to Kansas in the NCAA final.

In the 1982 championship game, North Carolina needed a basket with 16 seconds remaining from freshman Michael Jordan to nip Georgetown, 63-62, and become the only top-ranked team in 13 years from 1979 through 1991 to capture the NCAA title. It was a particularly bitter pill to swallow for six of the 10 top-ranked teams to lose in the NCAA championship game in overtime or by two or three points in regulation. Sizing up how the No. 1 teams fared in the NCAA playoffs through 1993 since the Associated Press introduced national rankings in 1949:

18 — Won national title (Kentucky '49, Kentucky '51, Indiana '53, San Francisco '55 and 56, North Carolina '57, UCLA '64, UCLA '67, UCLA '69, UCLA '71, UCLA '72, UCLA '73, North Carolina State '74, UCLA '75, Indiana '76, Kentucky '78, North Carolina '82, Duke '92).

10 — Finished as national runner-up (Bradley '50/defeated by CCNY; Ohio State '61/Cincinnati; Ohio State '62/Cincinnati; Cincinnati '63/Loyola of Chicago; Michigan '65/UCLA; Kentucky '66/Texas Western; Indiana State '79/Michigan State; Houston '83/North Carolina State; Georgetown '85/Villanova, Duke '86/Louisville).

4 — Lost in national semifinals (Cincinnati '60/California; Houston '68/UCLA; UNLV '87/Indiana; UNLV '91/Duke).

6 — Lost in regional finals (Kentucky '52/St. John's; Kansas State '59/Cincinnati; Kentucky '70/Jacksonville; Michigan '77/UNC Charlotte; Temple '88/Duke; Indiana '93/Kansas).

2 — Lost in regional semifinals (North Carolina '84/Indiana; Arizona '89/UNLV).

3 — Lost in second round (DePaul '80/UCLA; DePaul '81/St. Joseph's; Oklahoma '90/North Carolina).

1 — Lost in first round (West Virginia '58/Manhattan).

1 — Declined a berth (Kentucky '54).

FINAL FOUR LORE

Twelve universities had appeared 20 times or more in the NCAA Tournament through 1993 — Kentucky (35), UCLA (29), North Carolina (27), Notre Dame (24), Louisville (23), St. John's (23), Indiana (22), Kansas (22), Kansas State (21), Villanova (21), Syracuse (20) and DePaul (20).

Notre Dame, an independent, is the only one of the 10 schools to compile a losing NCAA playoff record (25-28) and never participate in the national championship game. The Fighting Irish managed their only trip to the Final Four in 1978 and lost in the national semifinals against Duke (90-86).

Notre Dame isn't the lone marquee school to discover how elusive the Final Four can be, however. The last time both championship final teams appeared in the tourney again the following season and lost their opening-round games was 1981, when defending champion Louisville and runner-up UCLA succumbed against Arkansas and Brigham Young, respectively. Among high-profile conferences, here is a list of five of the national champions from 1974 through 1980 to not exactly dominate NCAA playoff competition in the last decade or so:

Louisville (one Final Four appearance in 10 years from 1984-93/16-6)

Marquette (blanked 16 consecutive years from 1978-93/2-6)

Michigan State (blanked 14 consecutive years from 1980-93/6-5)

North Carolina State (one in 19 years from 1975-93/15-8)

UCLA (blanked 13 consecutive years from 1981-93/8-8)

MIXING MARCH MADNESS AND SADNESS

When is a game really an upset? For all the bitter disappointment experienced by fans of a highly-ranked team unexpectedly bowing out of the NCAA Tournament, an equal amount of euphoria emanates from supporters of the winner. The upsets and near-upsets are what make the tournament great. Everyone loves the idea of a Cinderella knocking off a Rolls Roycer.

The ultimate in March Madness materialized last year when Arizona, ranked fifth in the nation by AP, was stunned in the first round of the West Regional by Santa Clara (64-61). In terms of point spreads, it was the biggest upset in NCAA playoff history because Santa Clara was a 20-point underdog. The next largest point spread to not hold up occurred in 1986 when 17½-point underdog Arkansas-Little Rock shocked Notre Dame in the Midwest Regional (90-83).

However, upset has become perhaps the most misused word in all of college basketball. Although name schools occasionally lose before expected, many times a playoff game is mistakenly labeled an upset when it isn't anything of the sort. For example, Cleveland State's 83-79 win over Indiana in the 1986 East Regional is frequently characterized as a major upset. But the first-round game shouldn't be considered an upset of such colossal proportions because Cleveland State compiled a 29-4 record that season while Indiana lost eight games and was ranked

Upsets are what make the NCAA Tournament so great. Everybody loves to see the Davids knock off the Goliaths. The Richmond Spiders have pulled off two of the greatest upsets in tournament history. In 1988, as the 13th seed, they felled Indiana. Three years later, as the 15th seed, they killed off Syracuse (above). My, what a tangled web these Spiders weaved!

a modest 16th by AP and 14th by UPI entering the tournament. It was a surprise of parallel proportions in many quarters when No. 9 seed Texas-El Paso toppled No. 1 seed Kansas, 66-60, in the second round of the 1992 Midwest Regional. But it wasn't that huge an upset because UTEP was coming off winning the Western Athletic Conference regular-season or postseason tournament championship for the eighth time in 10 years and finished the season with a 27-7 record.

The most indisputable playoff upsets come when a team ranked in the top three or four of a national poll is eliminated before it reaches a regional semifinal. Five teams seeded No. 1 in a regional lost their opening playoff game in the first 15 years after the seeding process started in 1979. DePaul was the nation's top-ranked team in back-to-back seasons when the Blue Demons lost their opening tournament game each year (77-71 against UCLA in 1980 West Regional and 49-48 against St. Joseph's in 1981 Mideast Regional). They also lost their opening playoff game as a No. 1 seed in the 1982 Midwest Regional (82-75 against Boston College) when they were ranked second nationally behind eventual champion North Carolina. Snakebitten starters all three of those seasons for DePaul were forward Terry Cummings and guard Skip Dillard.

The two other No. 1 seeds to sustain quick KO's were North Carolina in 1979 (72-71 against Penn in East Regional) and Oregon State in 1981 (50-48 against Kansas State in West Regional). The Year of the Upset was 1981 because third-ranked Arizona State, an 88-71 loser against Kansas in the Midwest Regional, joined DePaul and second-ranked Oregon State among the top three teams to drop their playoff openers.

A championship game frequently misconstrued as an enormous upset was North Carolina's 54-53 triple-overtime victory against Wilt Chamberlain-led Kansas in 1957. After all, Carolina was undefeated that season (32-0), winning 22 games by at least nine points, and the Tar Heels' top three scorers wound up playing in the NBA, albeit briefly — forwards Lennie Rosenbluth and Pete Brennan and guard Tommy Kearns.

On the other hand, the NCAA final victories for North Carolina State '83 and Villanova '85 over Houston and Georgetown, respectively, spell upset by any definition. "The biggest upset was N.C. State-Houston," Kentucky coach Rick Pitino said. "Then there was Villanova-Georgetown and Duke-UNLV (1991 national semifinals). In one game, the better team doesn't always win."

Genuine tournament upsets are rare, but several have been forgotten because they weren't Final Four games and occurred before seeding was introduced. For instance, Dayton wasn't ranked in the UPI top twenty in 1967 when the Flyers opened the playoffs with a 69-67 overtime triumph against seventh-ranked Western Kentucky by holding Hilltoppers first-team All-America Clem Haskins, playing with his broken wrist in a cast, to eight points. Dayton also defeated two other top ten teams — Tennessee (ranked ninth by UPI) and North Carolina (third) — before getting clobbered by top-ranked UCLA in the national final.

Here is even more restrictive criteria for determining full-fledged upsets, recapping six games when a team ranked among the UPI top four was defeated before a regional final by a squad not ranked in the UPI top twenty:

YEAR	FAVORITE (UPI RANKING)	UNDERDOG TEAM (COACH)	REGIONAL (ROUND)
1958	West Virginia (1st)	Manhattan (Ken Norton)	East (first)

Comment: Jack Powers, the current executive director of the NIT, collected 29 points and 15 rebounds to carry Manhattan (16-10) to an 89-84 victory at Madison Square Garden. Jerry West scored just 10 points in his first NCAA Tournament game for West Virginia (26-2), a winner at Kentucky in December over the eventual national champion Wildcats.

1959   Kentucky (2nd)   Louisville (Peck Hickman)   Mideast (semis*)

Comment: Kentucky (24-3) hit less than one-third of its field goal attempts in blowing a 15-point lead and losing to Louisville, 76-61. Consensus first-team All-America Johnny Cox connected on just 3 of 15 shots from the floor for the Wildcats. Don Goldstein finished with game-high totals of 19 points and 13 rebounds for the Cardinals (19-12), who eventually reached the Final Four at Louisville, where they finished fourth.

1967   Louisville (2nd)   SMU (Doc Hayes)   Midwest (semis*)

Comment: Charles Beasley was limited to nine points, but fellow SWC first-team selection Denny Holman picked up the slack with 30 points, including a decisive basket with three seconds remaining, to spark SMU (20-6) to an 83-81 victory over Louisville (23-5) at Lawrence, Kan. Wes Unseld and Butch Beard combined for 32 points and 21 rebounds, but it wasn't enough for the Cardinals, who hit just 5 of their 14 free throws. Louisville, which twice defeated national runner-up Dayton by at least 15 points, suffered its five defeats by a total of just 14 points.

1973   Long Beach St. (3rd)   San Francisco (Bob Gaillard)   West (semis)

Comment: Coach Jerry Tarkanian's fourth consecutive and last tournament team at Long Beach State (26-3) succumbed against San Francisco, 77-67, in Los Angeles when two-time consensus first-team All-America Ed Ratleff hit just 4 of 18 field goal attempts for the 49ers. San Francisco (23-5) featured a balanced attack with 25 points from Mike Quick, 20 points and eight assists by Phil Smith, 17 rebounds by Eric Fernsten, and 18 points and nine rebounds by Kevin Restani.

1977   UCLA (4th)   Idaho State (Jim Killingsworth)   West (semis)

Comment: Gene Bartow departed after only two seasons as John Wooden's successor following UCLA's 76-75 setback at Idaho State. The Bruins finished with a 24-5 record when guards Roy Hamilton and Brad Holland combined to hit just 8 of 24 field goal attempts. Idaho State (25-5), prevailing despite shooting just 40.6 percent from the floor, received 27 points and 12 rebounds from Steve Hayes.

	FAVORITE	UNDERDOG TEAM	REGIONAL
YEAR	(UPI RANKING)	(COACH)	(ROUND)
1978	New Mexico (4th)	Cal State Fullerton (Bobby Dye)	West (first)

Comment: Cal State Fullerton (23-9) had four players score from 18 to 23 points and made 62.1 percent of its attempts from the floor to erase a six-point, halftime deficit and upend New Mexico, 90-85. Future Lakers standout Michael Cooper had an off-game for the Lobos (24-4), sinking just six of 15 field goal attempts as they blew an opportunity to advance to the regional semifinals and final on their homecourt in Albuquerque, N.M. In the next round, Cal State Fullerton overcame a 12-point deficit at intermission to notch a 75-72 triumph over San Francisco (ranked 11th by AP and 13th by UPI). Incredibly, the Titans almost erased a 15-point, halftime deficit in the regional final before losing, 61-58, against Arkansas (ranked 5th by AP and 6th by UPI). Fullerton fell short because of 40.3 percent field-goal shooting compared to 61.7 percent for the Razorbacks.

*Tournament opener for loser.

SHOCK TREATMENT

Teams become more conservative in the postseason, protecting the basketball a little more, looking for the high percentage shot more than ever, tightening up defensively. Defense is so vital in cutting the nets down and winning the gold.

In the first six years of the seeding process when the playoff field ranged from 40 to 53 teams, a total of 13 No. 1 and 2 seeds lost their openers. The NCAA Tournament hasn't been saturated with authentic upsets since the playoff field was expanded to 64 teams in 1985, but there has been an average of two first-round "shockers" annually. Despite the lack of genuine upsets in recent seasons, teams seeded 13th or worse defeated teams seeded among the top four in a regional a total of 18 times in the last nine years. Thirteen of the 18 surprises were decided by five points or less.

Since byes were eliminated in 1985, never have all of the top four seeds in each regional survived the opening round. The conferences most susceptible to upsets the past seven years were the ACC (four times), Big Eight (four), Pacific-10 (four) and Big Ten (three). The three schools to lose as many as two games in this category are Arizona (1992 and 1993), Indiana (1986 and 1988) and Missouri (1987 and 1990). Arizona's stunning defeat last year against Santa Clara materialized despite the Wildcats reeling off 25 unanswered points in a stretch bridging the last five minutes of the first half and the first five minutes of the second half.

Which school will be next to make me eat my words and possibly force another Austin Peay State stand-on-your-head routine? Here is a rundown of the 18 first-round knockouts by the bottom of the bracket from 1985-93:

In 1987, I promised viewers I would stand on my head if Austin Peay upset Illinois in the first round of the tournament. So, naturally, that's exactly what happened, 68-67. I was invited to Austin Peay's postseason awards banquet, where a few of the players assisted me in keeping my promise.

1985 — Navy (13th seed) over Louisiana State (4), 78-55.

1986 — Cleveland State (14) over Indiana (3), 83-79, and Arkansas-Little Rock (14) over Notre Dame (3), 90-83.

1987 — Xavier (13) over Missouri (4), 70-69; Southwest Missouri State (13) over Clemson (4), 65-60, and Austin Peay State (14) over Illinois (3), 68-67.

1988 — Murray State (14) over North Carolina State (3), 78-75, and Richmond (13) over Indiana (4), 72-69.

1989 — Middle Tennessee State (13) over Florida State (4), 97-83, and Siena (14) over Stanford (3), 80-78.

1990 — Northern Iowa (14) over Missouri (3), 74-71.

1991 — Richmond (15) over Syracuse (2), 73-69; Xavier (14) over Nebraska (3), 89-84, and Penn State (13) over UCLA (4), 74-69.

1992 — East Tennessee State (14) over Arizona (3), 87-80, and Southwestern Louisiana (13) over Oklahoma (4), 87-83.

1993 — Santa Clara (15) over Arizona (2), 64-61; Southern (13) over Georgia Tech (4), 93-78.

PLAYOFFS FREQUENTLY KNOCK WIND OUT OF WIN CROWD

Of the first 17 teams to enter an NCAA Division I Tournament undefeated, just seven went on to win the championship. Four of the seven "perfect examples" were coached by John Wooden, the architect guiding UCLA to the national crown each time the quintessential Bruins entered postseason competition with an unblemished record.

San Francisco's Phil Woolpert (1956) was the first coach to spearhead an undefeated NCAA champion. Indiana's Bob Knight (1976) is the only coach other than Wooden in the last 35 years to have a team enter the tournament unbeaten and emerge unscathed.

When we talk about the greatest teams of all-time, I have a special affection for Indiana's team of '76. I really feel they epitomized what I believed in as a coach. Quinn Buckner was a true prototype point guard, Kent Benson was a true low post center, Scott May was a deluxe shooter, Bobby Wilkerson was a great multidimensional player and Tom Abernethy was a textbook role player who defended and rebounded well. I think one of the greatest achievements ever was the Hoosiers going undefeated in back-to-back years (1975 and 1976) in a rigorous league like the Big Ten. It might never be done again.

Indiana had all the ingredients and the Hoosiers knew how to win the close game. They may not have been the greatest athletic team of all-time, but from the purist standpoint —team-oriented basketball emphasizing cutting, screening, passing, and defense — they were the best.

Indiana had to overcome a six-point deficit at intermission to defeat Michigan in the '76 championship game. The only other time a team erased a halftime deficit of more than three points in the final to capture the crown was in 1963, when Loyola of Chicago defeated Cincinnati (60-58 in overtime) after trailing by eight points at intermission (29-21) and 15 points with 12 minutes remaining.

Four of the unbeaten titlists won a tournament game by fewer than six points and four of the previously undefeated teams suffered their initial setback by at least 16 points. Ten teams entered the tourney without a defeat in a 10-year span from 1967-76. Here is a brief summary of what happened to teams entering the NCAA playoffs undefeated:

YEAR	SCHOOL (COACH)	REGULAR-SEASON WON-LOSS RECORD	PLAYOFF RECORD
1951	Columbia (Lou Rossini)	21-0	0-1

NCAA Performance: Ivy League champion blew seven-point, halftime lead and lost in the first round of East Regional against eventual national third-place finisher Illinois (79-71). The Lions' John Azary was outscored by the Illini's Don Sunderlage (25-13) in a battle of All-America candidates.

1956	San Francisco (Phil Woolpert)	25-0	4-0

NCAA Performance: Won national championship by an average of 14 points after winning all but two of its regular-season games by double-digit margins. Marquette, 13-11 that season, came closest to USF in a 65-58 decision on a neutral court in the DePaul Invitational. Unanimous first-team All-America Bill Russell averaged 22.8 points in four tournament games as the Dons won each of them by more than 10 points.

1957	North Carolina (Frank McGuire)	27-0	5-0

NCAA Performance: Won national championship by an average of 8.4 points after winning five of its final 11 games against ACC competition by five points or less. The Tar Heels didn't outscore their opponents in both halves of any of their five playoff victories, but Lennie Rosenbluth bailed them out by scoring at least 20 points in each game. Rosenbluth was Carolina's leading scorer in 27 of their 32 games, although the Tar Heels won a triple-overtime NCAA final against Kansas after he fouled out with 1:45 remaining in regulation.

1961	Ohio State (Fred Taylor)	24-0	3-1

NCAA Performance: Lost national final against Cincinnati (70-65 in overtime) after almost getting upset in opening playoff game at Louisville. Three-time unanimous first-team All-America Jerry Lucas registered game highs of 27 points and 12 rebounds for the Buckeyes in the championship contest while teammate John Havlicek was limited to four points.

YEAR	SCHOOL (COACH)	REGULAR-SEASON WON-LOSS RECORD	PLAYOFF RECORD
1964	UCLA (John Wooden)	26-0	4-0

NCAA Performance: Won national championship by an average of 7.5 points after gifted guards Gail Goodrich and Walt Hazzard sparked the Bruins to 12 double-digit margin victories in their last 13 regular-season games. Despite shooting a meager 40.3 percent from the floor and 52.9 percent from the free-throw line, UCLA overcame a 13-point deficit to end San Francisco's 19-game winning streak (76-72) in the West Regional final. Eight of their 30 victories were by seven points or less, including a 58-56 triumph at California.

1967	**UCLA (John Wooden)**	**26-0**	**4-0**

NCAA Performance: Won national championship by a record average of 23.75 points. The Bruins' toughest test was in the West Regional final, where Pacific trailed by fewer than 10 points in the closing minutes until UCLA pulled away to win by 16 (80-64) behind Lew Alcindor's 38 points. They won 26 of their 30 games by at least 15 points with the only contest in doubt being a 40-35 overtime triumph at Southern Cal in mid-season.

1968	**Houston (Guy Lewis)**	**28-0**	**3-2***

NCAA Performance: Lost national semifinal against UCLA (101-69) when the Cougars' Elvin Hayes, averaging 37.6 points per game entering the Final Four, was restricted to 10 as the Bruins employed a diamond-and-one defense with Lynn Shackelford assigned to cover Hayes. Houston entered the '68 Final Four undefeated although forward Melvin Bell, the third-leading scorer and second-leading rebounder for the '67 Final Four team, missed the season after undergoing knee surgery.

1968	**St. Bonaventure (Larry Weise)**	**22-0**	**1-2***

NCAA Performance: Lost East Regional semifinal against North Carolina (91-72) despite 23 points and nine rebounds by consensus second-team All-America Bob Lanier of the Bonnies. The Tar Heels' Larry Miller collected 27 points and 16 rebounds while teammate Charlie Scott chipped in with 21 points.

1971	**Marquette (Al McGuire)**	**26-0**	**2-1**

NCAA Performance: Lost Mideast Regional semifinal against Ohio State (60-59) after the Warriors' playmaker, unanimous first-team All-America Dean (The Dream) Meminger, fouled out with five minutes left. Teammate Allie McGuire, the coach's son, committed a costly turnover in the closing seconds before Buckeyes' guard Allan Hornyak hit two crucial foul shots. Jim Cleamons led Ohio State with 21 points.

Year	School (Coach)	Regular-Season Won-Loss Record	Playoff Record
1971	Penn (Dick Harter)	26-0	2-1

NCAA Performance: Lost East Regional final to Villanova (90-47) when none of the Quakers players scored more than eight points. Final Four Most Outstanding Player Howard Porter scored 35 points for the Wildcats to more than double the output (16) of three Penn players who wound up in the NBA — Corky Calhoun, Phil Hankinson and Dave Wohl.

1972	UCLA (John Wooden)	26-0	4-0

NCAA Performance: Won national championship by an average of 18 points. Although the Bill Walton-led Bruins trailed Florida State by a season-high seven points in the first half and the final margin of the championship game was just five (81-76), the outcome was never really in doubt. They won only one other game all season by fewer than 13 points (by six at Oregon State).

1973	UCLA (John Wooden)	26-0	4-0

NCAA Performance: Won national championship by an average of 16 points. The Bruins' Bill Walton erupted for a championship game-record 44 points in an 87-66 triumph over Memphis State in the final after he was outscored by fellow center Steve Downing, 26-14, in a 70-59 victory over Indiana in the national semifinals. They won 26 of their 30 games by a double-digit margin with the closest results being six-point victories against league rivals Oregon State and Stanford.

1975	Indiana (Bob Knight)	29-0	2-1

NCAA Performance: Lost Mideast Regional final to Kentucky (92-90) despite Kent Benson's 33 points and 23 rebounds. Scott May, Indiana's scoring leader before sustaining a broken arm, returned to the lineup against the Wildcats, but scored just two points. Knight said he erred by playing an offensive-minded player (John Laskowski) substantially more minutes (33 to 3) than defensive standout Tom Abernethy. Kentucky won despite 6 of 19 field goal shooting by leading scorer Kevin Grevey. UK guards Jimmy Dan Conner and Mike Flynn combined to outscore Indiana counterparts Quinn Buckner and Bobby Wilkerson, 39-22.

1976	Indiana (Bob Knight)	27-0	5-0

NCAA Performance: Scott May and Kent Benson combined for 40.8 points and 16.5 rebounds per game for team winning national championship by an average of 13.2 points. The Hoosiers kept their perfect record intact despite trailing in the second half of three of their five tournament games, including Mideast Regional contests against Alabama and Marquette accounting for two of the 11 contests they won by single-digit margins. The closest result was a two-point triumph at Ohio State in their Big Ten Conference opener. Knight's alma mater finished in the Big Ten basement that season with a 2-16 league record.

1976	Rutgers (Tom Young)	28-0	3-2*

NCAA Performance: Lost national semifinal against Michigan (86-70) when the Scarlet Knights' top three scorers for the season — forward Phil Sellers and guards Mike Dabney and Eddie Jordan — combined to shoot 31.4 percent from the floor (16 of 51). John Robinson posted game highs of 20 points and 16 rebounds for the Wolverines.

1979	Indiana State (Bill Hodges)	29-0	4-1

NCAA Performance: Lost national final against Michigan State (75-64) when the Sycamores' Larry Bird, who hit 53.2 percent of his field-goal attempts on the season, made just one-third of his shots from the floor (7 of 21). Magic Johnson scored a game-high 24 points for the Spartans.

1991	UNLV (Jerry Tarkanian)	30-0	4-1

NCAA Performance: Lost national semifinal against Duke (79-77) when All-Americas Larry Johnson and Stacey Augmon combined for just 19 points, a total representing less than half of their combined season average of 39.2 points per game. Christian Laettner scored a team-high 28 points for the Blue Devils to help them overcome UNLV's 40-26 edge in rebounding.

*The three teams with two tournament defeats also lost in NCAA playoff consolation games.

NOTES: Loyola of Chicago '39 (lost to Long Island in final), Seton Hall '41 (lost to Long Island in semifinals and CCNY in third-place game) and Alcorn State '79 (lost at Indiana in second round) entered the National Invitation Tournament unbeaten before losing. Incidentally, a group of the same Alcorn State players (E.J. Bell, Willie Howard, Joe Jenkins, Larry Smith and Clinton Wyatt) also were involved in victories in the 1977 NAIA Tournament and the 1980 NCAA Tournament under coach Davey Whitney.

THE WAY WE WERE

Wow! I occasionally receive some good-natured ribbing from my family members when they look at photos of me in my coaching days, when I wore the thick glasses and wild K-Mart special outfits. Admittedly, it was a pretty ugly sight. Maybe I should have gone looking for Rick Pitino, Pat Riley and Chuck Daly hand-me-downs. But I wasn't hired because I looked like Robert Redford.

It's also been pretty ugly regarding the pressure on the six UCLA coaches guiding the Bruins to the NCAA playoffs after John Wooden departed. The only other school to have seven different coaches direct teams to the national tournament is Seattle, a university no longer classified Division I. The Chieftains came close to winning the NCAA title in 1958, but they blew an 11-point lead in the final and lost against Kentucky.

Seattle (1953 through 1956) and Long Beach State (1970 through 1973) are the only schools to participate in the national tournament each of their first four seasons after moving up from the small-college ranks to Division I status. Later, fans were sleepless in Seattle when the school became the only one to appear in the playoffs three consecutive years under three different coaches — Vince Cazzetta (1962), Clair Markey (1963) and Bob Boyd (1964). Oddly, Boyd-coached Seattle was UCLA's first victim when the Bruins started their streak of 38 consecutive tournament victories from 1964-74. Boyd subsequently was Southern Cal's coach when the Trojans handed UCLA back-to-back setbacks (46-44 in 1969 and 87-86 in 1970) to account for two of the total of five defeats sustained by the Bruins during their stretch of seven consecutive national championships from 1967 through 1973.

The last of the seven Seattle playoff coaches was Portland Trail Blazers executive Morris (Bucky) Buckwalter, who took the Chieftains to their 11th and final NCAA Division I Tournament in 1969. Four years later, court jester Abe Lemons steered Oklahoma City to its 11th and final Division I playoff before the school de-emphasized its program in the next decade.

Seattle and Oklahoma City are among 16 schools that no longer are or never were classified as major colleges, but previously exhibited sufficient skill to participate in the NCAA Division I Tournament. Three of the former major colleges reached the Final Four a total of five times — City College of New York (finished fourth in 1947 and won championship in 1950), New York University (second in 1945 and fourth in 1960) and Seattle (second in 1958). NYU defeated Duke, 74-59, in the 1960 East Regional final before the Blue Devils reached the Final Four in 1963 and 1964. Two additional similar triumphs of note materialized in 1956 when Wayne State defeated DePaul, 72-63, in the Midwest Regional and Oklahoma City mauled Memphis State, 97-81, in the West Regional.

In 1953, George (Rinso) Marquette, the first-year coach at Lebanon Valley (Pa.), guided the Flying Dutchmen to the NCAA Tournament. They received a bid after La Salle and Seton Hall chose to go to the NIT. Lebanon Valley's "Seven Dwarfs" — no player was taller than 6-1 — won the Middle Atlantic Conference and led the nation in field-goal shooting (47.2 percent). They flogged Fordham, 80-67, in the first round of the East Regional before bowing to Bob Pettit-led LSU, an eventual Final Four team. Lebanon Valley, with a current enrollment of 900 after having 425 students in 1953, remains the smallest school ever to play in the tournament. The leading scorer for Lebanon Valley was Howie Landa, who went on to coach nationally-ranked Mercer County (N.J.) Community College and then serve as an assistant to both the men's and women's teams at UNLV.

An alphabetical list of the 16 current small colleges to previously appear in the NCAA Division I playoffs:

School (Playoff Appearances)	NCAA Playoffs Years	W-L	Last Season Division I	Current Status
Cal State Los Angeles (1974)	1	0-1	1975	Div. II
Catholic (1944)	1	0-2	1981	Div. III
CCNY (1947-50)	2	4-2	1953	Div. III
Hardin-Simmons, Tex. (1953-57)	2	0-2	1990	NAIA
Houston Baptist (1984)	1	0-1	1989	Div. II
Lebanon Valley, Pa. (1953)	1	1-2	DNA*	Div. III
Loyola, La. (1954-57-58)	3	0-3	1972	NAIA
NYU (1943-45-46-60-62-63)	6	9-9	1971	Div. III
Oklahoma City (1952-53-54-55-56-57-63-64-65-66-73)	11	8-13	1985	NAIA
Seattle (1953-54-55-56-58-61-62-63-64-67-69)	11	10-13	1980	NAIA
Springfield, Mass. (1940)	1	0-1	DNA*	Div. II
Trinity, Tex. (1969)	1	0-1	1973	Div. III
Tufts, Mass. (1945)	1	0-2	DNA*	Div. III
Wayne State, Mich. (1956)	1	1-2	1950*	Div. II
West Texas State (1955)	1	0-1	1986	Div. II
Williams, Mass. (1955)	1	0-1	DNA*	Div. III

*Prior to the arrival of the College Division (now Division II), the NCAA Tournament Committee had the option of selecting teams without major-college status. Wayne State's participation in the Division I Tournament came six years after it left the major-college ranks.

Some Smooth Sailing, But Mainly a Rugged Road

When you talk about North Carolina's chances of repeating, it is as real as can be. If the NCAA Tournament was a four-out-of-seven series like the NBA, put the gold trophy in Chapel Hill today. But in a one-game scenario, it is not Lock City for the Tar Heels to win it all, although all the preseason prognosticators, including yours truly, had them as a prohibitive favorite. History shows it won't be easy for them.

Nine NCAA champions through 1993 won all of their playoff games by double-digit margins, but most titlists are severely tested at least once on the treacherous tournament trail. Thirty-three champions won a minimum of one playoff game by three points or less, including 16 titlists to win at least one game by just one point. Wyoming '43 would have become the only champion to trail at halftime in every tournament game if the Cowboys didn't score the last three baskets of the first half in the national final to lead Georgetown at intermission (18-16). Three titlists trailed at intermission in both of their Final Four games — Kentucky '51, Louisville '86 and Duke '92.

UCLA '67, the first varsity season for Lew Alcindor (now Kareem Abdul-Jabbar), set the record for largest average margin of victory for a champion when the Bruins started a dazzling streak of 10 consecutive Final Four appearances. They won their 12 NCAA playoff games with Alcindor manning the middle by an average margin of 21.5 points.

No player has dominated the NCAA Tournament like Kareem Abdul-Jabbar (left), whose name was Lew Alcindor in college. He was the Final Four's MVP three straight years when UCLA won the title in 1967, '68 and '69. Guard Mike Warren (above) played on the 1967 and '68 teams. He's since gone on to a successful acting career.

Which of John Wooden's 10 national champion UCLA teams did the Wizard of Westwood perceive as his best?

"I've never come out and said it," Wooden said, "but it would be hard to pick a team over the 1968 team. I will say it would be the most difficult team to prepare for and play against offensively and defensively. It created so many problems. It had such great balance. "We had the big center (Alcindor) who is the most valuable player of all time. Mike Warren was a three-year starter who may have been the most intelligent floor leader ever. Lucius Allen was a very physical, talented individual who was extremely quick. Lynn Shackleford was a great shooter out of the corner who didn't allow defenses to sag on Jabbar. Mike Lynn didn't have power, but he had as fine a pair of hands around the boards as I have ever seen."

The roster for UCLA's 1968 national champion included six players with double-digit season scoring averages, but senior forward Edgar Lacey dropped off the team with an 11.9-point average following a dispute with Wooden after a ballyhooed mid-season defeat against Houston before 52,693 fans at the Astrodome. Lacey, assigned to defend Cougars star Elvin Hayes early in the game, was annoyed with Wooden for singling him out following Hayes' 29-point first-half outburst. Lacey, the leading rebounder for the Bruins' 1965 NCAA titlist when he was an All-Tournament team selection, missed the 1966-67 campaign because of a fractured left kneecap.

The three Alcindor-led UCLA teams rank among the seven NCAA champions with average margins of victory in a tournament of more than 19 points per game. It's no wonder a perceptive scribe wrote the acronym NCAA took on a new meaning during the plunderous Alcindor Era — "No Chance Against Alcindor." Here is a breakdown of the point differential and average margin of victory in the NCAA playoffs for the first 55 national champions:

CHAMPIONSHIP TEAM	COACH	G.	-MARGIN OF VICTORY- LARGEST	SMALLEST	AVERAGE MARGIN
UCLA '67	John Wooden	4	49	15	23.75
Loyola of Chicago '63	George Ireland	5	*69	2	23.0
Indiana '81	Bob Knight	5	35	13	22.6
UCLA '68	John Wooden	4	32	9	21.25
Michigan State '79	Jud Heathcote	5	34	11	20.8
Ohio State '60	Fred Taylor	4	22	17	19.5
UCLA '69	John Wooden	4	38	3	19.5
UNLV '90	J. Tarkanian	6	30	2	18.67
Oklahoma State '45	Hank Iba	3	27	4	18.67
UCLA '70	John Wooden	4	23	11	18.0
UCLA '72	John Wooden	4	32	5	18.0
Kentucky '58	Adolph Rupp	4	33	1	17.5
Kentucky '49	Adolph Rupp	3	29	10	17.33
Indiana '40	B. McCracken	3	24	9	17.0
UCLA '73	John Wooden	4	21	11	16.0
Kentucky '48	Adolph Rupp	3	23	8	15.67

CHAMPIONSHIP TEAM	COACH	G.	-MARGIN OF VICTORY- LARGEST	SMALLEST	AVERAGE MARGIN
North Carolina '93	Dean Smith	6	45	6	15.67
UCLA '65	John Wooden	4	24	8	15.5
Oregon '39	Howard Hobson	3	18	13	15.33
Kansas '52	Phog Allen	4	19	4	14.75
N.C. State '74	Norman Sloan	4	28	3	14.25
Duke '91	Mike Krzyzewski	6	29	2	14.0
San Francisco '56	Phil Woolpert	4	18	11	14.0
San Francisco '55	Phil Woolpert	5	23	1	13.8
Indiana '76	Bob Knight	5	20	5	13.2
Cincinnati '62	Ed Jucker	4	20	2	12.75
Duke '92	Mike Krzyzewski	6	26	1	12.5
Cincinnati '61	Ed Jucker	4	23	5	12.0
Louisville '86	Denny Crum	6	20	3	11.83
Oklahoma State '46	Hank Iba	3	17	3	11.67
Holy Cross '47	Doggie Julian	3	15	8	11.33
California '59	Pete Newell	4	20	1	11.25
La Salle '54	Ken Loeffler	5	16	2	11.2
Stanford '42	Everett Dean	3	15	6	10.67
Indiana '87	Bob Knight	6	34	1	10.5
Michigan '89	Steve Fisher	6	37	1	9.83
Georgetown '84	John Thompson	5	14	1	9.8
Kentucky '51	Adolph Rupp	4	16	2	9.75
Louisville '80	Denny Crum	5	20	2	9.2
Kentucky '78	Joe B. Hall	5	22	3	9.0
Kansas '88	Larry Brown	6	13	3	8.83
UCLA '71	John Wooden	4	18	2	8.5
North Carolina '57	Frank McGuire	5	16	1	8.4
Marquette '77	Al McGuire	5	15	1	8.0
UCLA '64	John Wooden	4	15	4	7.5
UCLA '75	John Wooden	5	14	1	7.4
Indiana '53	B. McCracken	4	13	1	7.25
Utah '44	Vadal Peterson	3	10	2	7.0
Texas-El Paso '66	Don Haskins	5	15	1	6.4
Wyoming '43	Everett Shelton	3	12	3	6.33
N.C. State '83	Jim Valvano	6	19	1	5.33
Villanova '85	Rollie Massimino	6	12	2	5.0
North Carolina '82	Dean Smith	5	10	1	4.6
Wisconsin '41	Bud Foster	3	6	1	4.0
CCNY '50	Nat Holman	3	5	1	3.0

*All-time tournament record (111-42 first-round victory over Tennessee Tech).

NOTES: Twelve teams participated in a total of 16 overtime games en route to national titles — Utah (1944), North Carolina (two triple overtime Final Four games in 1957), Cincinnati (1961), Loyola of Chicago (1963), Texas-El Paso (two in 1966, including a double overtime), N.C. State (double overtime in 1974), UCLA (two in 1975), Louisville (two in 1980), N.C. State (double overtime in 1983), Michigan (1989), Duke (1992) and North Carolina (1993).

Dr. Jekyll and Mr. Hyde

One of the things a coach strives for is consistency. Loyola of Chicago, overcoming 27.4 percent field-goal shooting by committing just three turnovers, won the 1963 final against Cincinnati (60-58 in overtime) after trailing at halftime by eight points (29-21). No team has won the NCAA championship by overcoming a double-digit halftime deficit in the title game although North Carolina came close in 1977. The Tar Heels erased a 12-point deficit at intermission by scoring 18 points in the first 6:12 of the second half against Marquette before sputtering and bowing against the Warriors (67-59).

The emotional roller coaster was routine stuff for Marquette. The Warriors overcame halftime deficits to win their first three playoff games in 1977 against Cincinnati, Kansas State and Wake Forest before trailing most of the second half against UNC Charlotte in the national semifinals.

More than half of the NCAA Tournament championship games (28 of 55) were decided by at least 10 points. But it wasn't easy for some of those teams. For example, Kentucky didn't gain its first lead in the 1958 title game against Seattle until slightly more than six minutes remained. The seven titlists to win a national final by a double-digit margin after trailing at halftime:

CHAMPION	TURNAROUND IN TOURNAMENT TITLE GAME
Wyoming '43	Trailed Georgetown 16-13 at halftime before winning 46-34
Holy Cross '47	Trailed Oklahoma 31-28 before winning 58-47
Kentucky '51	Trailed Kansas State 29-27 before winning 68-58
La Salle '54	Trailed Bradley 43-42 before winning 92-76
Kentucky '58	Trailed Seattle 39-36 before winning 84-72
Indiana '76	Trailed Michigan 35-29 before winning 86-68
Duke '92	Trailed Michigan 31-30 before winning 71-51

Close Encounters

Excluding Georgetown's nine-point victory over Houston in the 1984 NCAA championship game, the other seven title games from 1982 through 1989 were decided by an average of two points. What an unbelievable stretch of finals!

In 1992, Duke became the 18th NCAA Tournament champion to win at least two playoff games by fewer than six points when the Blue Devils edged Kentucky (104-103 in overtime in East Regional final) and Indiana (81-78 in national semifinals). North Carolina's first two titlists are among the following champions to win by the fewest total of points in their two Final Four games:

Michigan '89 (total of three points with final in O.T./opponents were Illinois in national semifinals and Seton Hall in final)

Indiana '87 (five/UNLV and Syracuse)

North Carolina '57 (five with both games in triple overtime/Michigan State and Kansas)

North Carolina '82 (six/Houston and Georgetown)

Mine Eyes Have Seen the Glory — and Gory

I'll never forget UNLV's performance in the 1990 Final Four. It was poetry in motion. I mean, it had to be an incredible machine to blow away outstanding teams such as Georgia Tech and Duke. Jerry Tarkanian hardly had to chew his towel at all, because it was showtime for the Runnin' Rebels.

It wasn't a pleasant sight for fans of other Final Four teams running smack into squads playing at the peak of their game. Four of UCLA's 10 champions (1965, 1967, 1968 and 1973) won their two Final Four games by a total of at least 30 points. The six titlists to scorch their semifinal and championship game opponents by a total of more than 35 points:

UCLA '68 (victory margin total of 55 points as Lew Alcindor collected a total of 53 points and 34 rebounds in the two Final Four games against Houston in national semifinals and North Carolina in final)

Michigan State '79 (45-point victory margin as Magic Johnson and Greg Kelser combined for 100 points against Penn and Indiana State)

Ohio State '60 (42-point victory margin as Jerry Lucas collected 35 points and 23 rebounds against NYU and California)

Kentucky '49 (39-point victory margin as Alex Groza scored 52 points against Illinois and Oklahoma State)

UNLV '90 (39-point victory margin as four players — Greg Anthony, Stacey Augmon, Anderson Hunt and Larry Johnson — scored at least 27 points against Georgia Tech and Duke)

Kansas '52 (36-point victory margin as Clyde Lovellette scored 33 points in each game against Santa Clara and St. John's)

Ohio State '60 is the only one of these six schools to be among the five teams to win their NCAA final by at least 20 points — UNLV over Duke (103-73 in 1990), UCLA over Memphis State (87-66 in 1973), Ohio State over California (75-55 in 1960), UCLA over Purdue (92-72 in 1969) and Duke over Michigan (71-51 in 1992). UNLV's rout when the Rebels became the only team to score more than 100 points in a final game was a record for margin of victory.

Defending champion North Carolina's cakewalk over Rhode Island in the second round last year represented the sixth-highest margin of victory in any round of the NCAA Tournament. Here is a rundown of the six runaways:

Margin	Teams and Result	Year (Regional/Round)
69	Loyola (Chi.) 111, Tennessee Tech 42	1963 (Mideast/first)
49	UCLA 109, Wyoming 60	1967 (West/semifinals)
49	Syracuse 101, Brown 52	1986 (East/first)
47	Duke 101, Connecticut 54	1964 (East/final)
47	DePaul 99, Eastern Kentucky 52	1965 (Mideast/first)
45	North Carolina 112, Rhode Island 67	1993 (East/second)

SAD STATE OF AFFAIRS

Three states — Alaska, North Dakota and South Dakota — do not have any NCAA Division I institutions. Of the 47 states and the District of Columbia with major university members, 14 have never had a school reach the national semifinals of the Division I Tournament. There were 15 states in this category until the Sean Elliott-led Arizona Wildcats reached the Final Four in 1988.

Many thought the Grand Canyon state possessed a team with the ability to advance to the Final Four in 1981. Arizona State, ranked third by AP entering the playoffs with a 24-3 record, had the door open to a possible national title when No. 1 seeds DePaul and Oregon State lost their playoff openers at the buzzer. But the Sun Devils, featuring four upperclassmen who combined for a total of more than 35 seasons in the NBA (guards Fat Lever and Byron Scott, center Alton Lister and forward Sam Williams), became one of the biggest busts in tourney history.

The door to the Final Four was also slammed shut on them in their opener by Kansas (88-71 in Midwest Regional) when they fell behind by 16 points at intermission. Arizona State had defeated Iowa by eight points early in the season before the Hawkeyes twice upended eventual national champion Indiana in Big Ten Conference competition. Of the 14 No. 1 or 2 seeds to drop their playoff opener since seeding started in 1979, the only top two seed other than Arizona State to succumb by more than seven points was Missouri, a 77-63 loser against Iowa in the 1983 Midwest Regional when Tigers star center Steve Stipanovich was limited to six points.

Six of the 14 wistful states shut out of the Final Four currently have more than three colleges classified as Division I — South Carolina (nine Division I schools), Maryland (seven), Alabama (six), Mississippi (six), Connecticut (five) and Missouri (five).

South Carolina's "Trail of Tears" includes perhaps the finest team in the state's history and what some observers believe was the nation's best squad in 1970. The South Carolina Gamecocks went unbeaten in ACC competition during the regular season and finished a league-record five games ahead of their closest rival. The ACC selected its representative to the NCAA playoffs at the time through its own postseason tourney and seven of the eight previous winners reached the Final Four. But the Gamecocks, featuring a starting lineup with only one senior (current Georgia Tech coach Bobby Cremins), lost to North Carolina State in the ACC Tournament final (42-39 in double overtime).

After ranking sixth in both of the final wire-service polls for the second consecutive season in 1971, South Carolina joined Furman in becoming the first schools from the palmetto state to participate in the NCAA Tournament. They promptly lost their opening games in the East Regional by a total of 46 points. Consensus second-team All-America guard John Roche scored a school-record 56 points for South Carolina against Furman that year. But Roche combined with teammates Tom Riker and Kevin Joyce to constitute a trio of future NBA first-round draft choices shooting 26.8 percent from the floor (11 of 41) in a 79-64 setback against Penn in the Gamecocks' playoff debut.

In 1974, South Carolina was led by future pros Mike Dunleavy, Alex English and Brian Winters when the Gamecocks won more than 20 games for the sixth consecutive season but lost to Furman in the first round of the East Regional (75-67) for the Paladins' only playoff victory in eight contests.

Taking a more stately approach, Pennsylvania has had the most different universities reach the Final Four with eight. Joining Philadelphia's Big Five (La Salle, Penn, St. Joseph's, Temple and Villanova) in advancing to the national semifinals from the "Quaker State" are Duquesne, Penn State and Pittsburgh. Only three other states — California (six), New York (five) and Texas (five) — have had more than four different schools advance to the Final Four. The state of North Carolina produced the last three national champions and a total of seven, tying it for second with Kentucky on the all-time list of states with multiple titlists. California is first, with 14.

The only times two teams from the same state met in the championship game were when Cincinnati defeated top-ranked Ohio State in 1961 and 1962 by a total of 17 points. The two victories gave Cincinnati three wins in four years against teams ranked No. 1 entering the tournament. In 1959, the Bearcats beat Bob Boozer-led Kansas State in the Midwest Regional final (85-75).

We Shall Return

I got a strong work ethic from my second-generation Italian parents, John and Mae Vitale. They were garment workers all their lives and knew the meaning of resiliency. My father fought back when his women's clothing company had financial difficulties, and my mom overcame tuberculosis and a stroke.

That's why I'm fond of the teams that try, try again! Of the schools to fail to capture a national championship in their first appearance at the Final Four, here are the eight institutions to go more than 20 years before finally realizing their dream of winning an NCAA Tournament title:

School	Initial Final 4	First Title	Time Lapse	Tournament Appearances During Long Time Lapse
Villanova	1939	1985	46 years	15
Georgetown	1943	1984	41 years	7
Duke	1963	1991	28 years	12
Michigan	1964	1989	25 years	10
N.C. State	1950	1974	24 years	6
Michigan State	1957	1979	22 years	2
Louisville	1959	1980	21 years	10
Ohio State	1939	1960	21 years	4

Rattling Skeletons

College presidents finally seem to be paying more than just lip service to proposals for upright athletic programs. But the well-worn cliche "cheaters never prosper" isn't quite valid.

Kentucky won the 1978 NCAA Tournament while the Wildcats were on NCAA probation. Likewise, Kansas was the 1991 playoff runner-up although the Jayhawks were damaged goods after slipping into a similar category because of NCAA rules violations.

Presumably, NCAA sanctions were worth it for this chronological list of eight shrewd schools to reach the Final Four in the year immediately after an NCAA probation ended as a result of previous transgressions:

SCHOOL	LAST YEAR OF NCAA PENALTY	FINAL FOUR RESULT THE NEXT SEASON
Bradley	1953	Lost '54 national final vs. La Salle
Louisville	1958	Lost '59 national semifinal vs. West Virginia
West Virginia	1958	Lost '59 national final vs. California
Cincinnati	1959	Lost '60 national semifinal vs. California
St. Bonaventure	1969	Lost '70 national semifinal vs. Jacksonville
Florida State	1971	Lost '72 national final vs. UCLA
Kansas	1973	Lost '74 national semifinal vs. Marquette
N.C. State	1973	Captured '74 national championship.

GREAT EXPECTATIONS

The pressure to excel in postseason competition was particularly intense for Michigan's prodigies last year after the Wolverines had reached the championship game in 1992 before bowing to Duke. Four of the Fab Five — Jalen Rose (107 points), Chris Webber (98), Jimmy King (83) and Juwan Howard (82) — rank among the top six freshman scorers in a single tournament in the last 13 years. The only other yearlings to score at least 75 points in that span were Louisville's Pervis Ellison (93 in 1986) and Georgia Tech's Kenny Anderson (124 in 1990).

If Michigan's quintet had become the Fraud Five by losing its opening playoff game in 1993 instead of reaching the national final again, it would have been the biggest bust for a team to return a Final Four squad intact since Duke lost its East Regional opener against St. John's (80-78) as a No. 2 seed in 1979.

Three players who finished their Blue Devil careers with more than 2,000 points (Gene Banks, Mike Gminski and Jim Spanarkel) each compiled lower scoring averages in 1979 than they manufactured the previous year, when Duke was national runner-up. In 1978, Banks, Gminski and Spanarkel became the only trio to each score at least 20 points in both Final Four games (total of 71 points in 90-86 victory over Notre Dame in the semifinals and 63 in 94-88 setback against Kentucky in the championship game). Duke is the only national runner-up to score more than 85 points in an NCAA final. Banks, Gminski and Spanarkel all scored at least 16 points when they combined to shoot 53.5 percent from the floor against St. John's in 1979, but none of their teammates managed more than seven points as the Blue Devils blew a five-point halftime lead.

Other teams returning the nucleus of a Final Four team have proved to be disappointing as well. Defending champion North Carolina doesn't want to join the following three teams who, since the tournament field expanded to 25 entrants in 1969, reached the national final one year but didn't win a playoff game the next season despite losing no more than one starter who wasn't the leading scorer for the Final Four squad:

Title Game Team (Record)	W-L Mark Next Year	Key Player Loss
Jacksonville '70 (27-2)	22-4	Rex Morgan

1971 NCAA Performance: The Dolphins blew a 14-point halftime cushion and lost in the first round of the Mideast Regional against eventual Final Four team Western Kentucky (74-72). Western Kentucky's Jim McDaniels outscored Jacksonville's Artis Gilmore, 23-12, in a battle of seven-foot first-team All-Americas.

North Carolina State '74 (30-1)	22-6	Tom Burleson

1975 NCAA Performance: Despite the presence of national player of the year David Thompson, the ACC Tournament runner-up Wolfpack did not compete in the NCAA playoffs after losing twice against regular season champion Maryland in league play.

Marquette '77 (25-7)	24-4	Bo Ellis

1978 NCAA Performance: The Warriors, making their eighth of 10 consecutive tournament appearances, wasted a five-point halftime lead and lost in the first round of the Mideast Regional against Miami of Ohio (84-81 in overtime). Current Ohio State coach Randy Ayers collected 20 points and 10 rebounds for the Redskins to help offset national player of the year Butch Lee's 27 points for Marquette.

NOTES: Jacksonville '71 (Tom Wasdin succeeded Joe Williams) and Marquette '78 (Hank Raymonds succeeded Al McGuire) had new coaches. North Carolina State's coach both seasons was Norman Sloan. . . . The five schools other than Marquette to participate in the NCAA playoffs as defending champions but lose their opening-round game were Indiana '87 (defeated by Richmond in East Regional the next year), Louisville '80 (Arkansas in Midwest Regional), Kentucky '58 (Louisville in Mideast Regional), Indiana '53 (Notre Dame in East Regional) and Utah '44 (Oklahoma State in Western Regional).

Twice Wasn't Enough

Illinois coach Lou Henson's hair (the Lou-do) was really in bad shape after his sensational team suffered a hairline loss to Michigan (83-81) in the 1989 national semifinals at Seattle. The Fighting Illini had whipped the Wolverines by a double-digit margin in both of their Big Ten Conference contests. It must be hair-raising memories for Illinois and other teams thinking about what might have been after twice defeating an opponent to later win the NCAA Tournament.

The first 38 NCAA national champions, from Oregon (29-5 record in 1938-39) through Indiana (the last unbeaten team with a 32-0 mark in 1975-76), averaged barely over two defeats per season. None of the titlists sustained more than six losses until Marquette's Al McGuire-coached squad was 25-7 in 1977.

However, McGuire's swan song was a sign of things to come as six of the 11 championship teams from 1981 through 1991 finished with at least seven losses. Two of the six — Villanova '85 and Kansas '88 — are the only champions to enter the playoffs not ranked in a wire-service final top 20 from the time AP and UPI began conducting polls in 1951.

Villanova '85 and Kansas '88 joined North Carolina State '83 and Michigan '89 as the four titlists in a seven-year span to each lose at least twice to two different opponents during their championship season. St. John's holds the distinction of being the only school to defeat a team (Villanova '85) three times in a season the opponent wound up capturing the NCAA crown. St. John's also defeated Villanova three times the next year when the Wildcats were the defending national champion. Here is a look at the seven champions to lose to a team at least twice during their championship season:

YEAR	CHAMPION (RECORD)	TEAM(S) DEFEATING TITLIST AT LEAST TWICE
1954	La Salle (26-4)	Niagara (24-6) defeated the Explorers twice by 27 points total before finishing third in the NIT.
1981	Indiana (26-9)	Iowa (21-7) defeated the Hoosiers twice by 16 points total before losing NCAA playoff opener.
1983	N.C. State (26-10)	Maryland (20-10) defeated the Wolfpack twice by 14 points total before losing in the second round to eventual national runner-up Houston. Virginia (29-5) defeated the Wolfpack twice by 19 points total before losing to N.C. State by one point in the West Regional final.
1985	Villanova (25-10)	St. John's (31-4) defeated the Wildcats three times by a total of 22 points before losing to Georgetown in the national semifinals. Georgetown (35-3) defeated the Wildcats twice by nine points total before losing to Villanova by two points in the national final.
1986	Louisville (32-7)	Kansas (35-4) defeated the Cardinals twice by seven points total before losing to Duke in the national semifinals.
1988	Kansas (27-11)	Kansas State (25-9) defeated the Jayhawks twice by 26 points total before losing to KU in the Midwest Regional final. Oklahoma (35-4) defeated the Jayhawks twice by 16 points total before to KU by four points in the national final.
1989	Michigan (30-7)	Illinois (31-5) defeated the Wolverines twice by 28 points total before losing to Michigan by two points in the national semifinals. Indiana (27-8) defeated the Wolverines twice by two points total before losing to Seton Hall in the West Regional semifinals.

I absolutely love this picture, because it typifies what the NCAA Tournament is all about. Take a look at the unadulterated innocence and joy on the face of Bill Russell, who obviously was "having a ball" when San Francisco returned home after winning the championship in 1955. That's K.C. Jones, who like Russell later played for and coached the Boston Celtics, standing in front of Russell. K.C. was ineligible the following year, but Russell led the Dons to another title.

SPOILERS

Duke '92 came close to becoming the eighth NCAA champion to go unde-feated. The Blue Devils' two losses were by a total of just six points (ACC road games against North Carolina and Wake Forest to start and end a stretch in which they played five of six contests away from home.

A couple of other national champions incurring two defeats to come even closer to perfect records were Kentucky '51, a loser of two neutral court games (St. Louis and Vanderbilt) by a total of five points, and Cincinnati '62, a loser in two Missouri Valley Conference road games (at Wichita State and Bradley) by a total of three points.

Not surprisingly, UCLA accounted for four of the first seven unbeaten titlists. The Bruins also had three championship teams in four years from 1968 through 1971 each suffer just one loss and were responsible for the only setback suffered by two national titlists (San Francisco '55 and North Carolina State '74).

Indiana, the 1953 champion, lost three games by a total of five points on field goals scored with fewer than five seconds remaining. Of the six NCAA champions to lose just one game, here is a look at the setback that prevented them from compiling an unblemished record:

YEAR	CHAMPION (RECORD)	LONE DEFEAT
1955	San Francisco (28-1)	47-40 at UCLA in USF's 3rd game of the season
1966	Texas-El Paso (28-1)	74-72 at Seattle in 24th game
1968	UCLA (29-1)	71-69 at Houston in Astrodome in 14th game
1969	UCLA (29-1)	46-44 at home against USC in 26th game
1971	UCLA (29-1)	89-82 at Notre Dame in 15th game
1974	N.C. State (30-1)	84-66 against UCLA at St. Louis in 3rd game

FAULTY FIGURES

It is absurd to look at margins of victories and make logical deductions. It's like comparing tennis scores and projecting that if I lost to someone 6-1 and he lost to someone else 6-3, then that means I'm two games better than the third party. Forget about it. You've got to play it on the court.

For example, Wake Forest is the only school to defeat the last three NCAA champions — Duke '91 (86-77), Duke '92 (72-68) and North Carolina '93 (88-62). But that doesn't mean the Demon Deacons could have or should have won the national championship.

Last season, Wake Forest also won at Temple by 37 points (106-69) and had a 28-point halftime lead en route to a blowout at Georgia Tech (81-58). Temple led Michigan for much of the West Regional final before losing (77-72). Michigan went on to defeat Kentucky in the national semifinals before bowing to North Carolina in the title game. Carolina had lost to Georgia Tech in the ACC Tour-nament final. Judging from these scores, you could have projected Wake Forest as a big winner when it met Kentucky in the playoffs. But Kentucky eliminated the Demon Deacons by 34 points in the Southeast Regional semifinals (103-69).

If that doesn't seem to add up when you compare previous scores, then two of the mighty Wildcats' games against Tennessee really don't make any sense. Kentucky lost at Tennessee just 16 days before trouncing the Volunteers by 61 points (101-40) in the quarterfinals of the SEC Tournament.

Yes, you can prove just about anything you want by comparing scores to measure the strength of teams. If one assesses squads solely on the results of selected games, then lightweights could be considered among the nation's elite.

For example, Kentucky's last championship team in 1978 lost just two games (against LSU and Alabama). Taking those two defeats to an extreme, the following are vivid examples of college basketball's unpredictability and the profound danger of emphasizing comparative scores:

Shouldn't the City College of New York, winner of both the NCAA and NIT crowns in 1950, have been hailed as an impact school in 1978? After all, Division III CCNY had a 14-11 record that season and defeated Cornell, which defeated Yale, which defeated Fordham, which defeated Georgetown, which defeated Alabama, which defeated national champion Kentucky.

How about Georgia State, which was 5-21 that season? The Panthers defeated Old Dominion, which defeated SMU, which defeated Houston, which defeated Arkansas, which defeated LSU, which defeated Kentucky.

And shouldn't Louisiana College, an NAIA institution with a 13-16 record that year, have been deemed a viable power after winning at Texas-El Paso, which defeated Kansas State, which defeated SMU, which defeated Houston, which defeated ..., which defeated ..., which ...

Far more than 300 schools have won an NAIA Tournament game, but Louisiana College isn't one of them. So much for the significance of comparing scores.

Putting Things in Proper Perspective

Rebounding from adversity certainly is a bench mark of a champion. For example, defending champion North Carolina lost back-to-back ACC games last season by a total of 40 points (at Wake Forest and Duke). Following are more teams to overcome temporary snags en route to a national championship:

- Five NCAA titlists (UCLA '65, UCLA '75, Villanova '85, Duke '91 and North Carolina '93) lost a regular season or conference tournament game by more than 20 points.

- Michigan '89 lost on a neutral court against obscure Alaska-Anchorage and suffered defeats in five of 10 Big Ten games in one span.

- Kansas '88 lost five games by double-digit margins. The Jayhawks went almost a month without a victory against a Division I opponent as their only win in a mid-season, six-game stretch was against Hampton (Va.).

- Louisville '86 lost six of 15 games during the first half of the season.

Villanova '85 lost four of five Big East Conference games in one span before losing its regular-season finale by 23 points at Pittsburgh.

North Carolina State '83 lost six of eight games in one span. Five of the Wolfpack's six ACC losses were by at least eight points, including back-to-back defeats by 18 points apiece.

Indiana '81 got off to a modest 7-5 start, including a defeat on a neutral court against Pan American.

Louisville '80 lost two of three games in late December, including a 13-point defeat on a neutral court against Illinois, which finished with a losing record in Big Ten competition.

Michigan State '79 required two overtime victories at home to avoid compiling six Big Ten losses in a seven-game span. Four of the Spartans' five Big Ten defeats were to second-division teams, including an 18-point setback against conference cellar dweller Northwestern.

Marquette '77 lost five home games, including its last three, to register the Warriors' worst record in 10 years. They lost those home games in Milwaukee Arena, where during one period coach Al McGuire's teams were 145-7, including an 81-game winning streak.

Cincinnati '61 lost three times by a total of 44 points in a five-game stretch early in the season, including the Bearcats' first two Missouri Valley Conference contests.

Kentucky '58 lost three times in a four-game span in mid-December.

La Salle '54 lost twice by a total of 32 points in a stretch of three games.

Indiana '53 lost two of its first three games prior to starting Big Ten competition.

Most observers thought City College of New York '50 was out of the playoff picture after the Beavers lost three of five games late in the season.

Holy Cross '47 suffered its three defeats in successive early-season games. The Crusaders' first two setbacks were by a total of 26 points.

Last year, North Carolina lost at Wake Forest by 26 points (88-62), but the worst defeat for a team to later win a national championship was UCLA's 110-83 loss to Illinois at the start of the 1964-65 season. The Bruins lost just one game the remainder of the season to finish with a 28-2 record. Ten years later, UCLA captured its 10th NCAA title in 12 years despite losing 103-81 at Washington, a second-division team in the Pacific-8 Conference. The defeat against the Huskies made the Bruins the only national champion to lose a conference game by more than 20 points against a team with a losing league record.

Seven consecutive national champions lost at least one game by 12 points until Duke broke the streak in 1992, when it dropped two ACC road games by six points, total. Through 1993, 33 national champions have lost a total of 51 games by double-digit margins, proof positive that many of the titlists were far from invincible. More often, teams get hot at the right time, receive an opportune break or two, secure a favorable playoff bracket, or capitalize on plain old luck.

Dreams Still Come True

I love to dream. It would be Fantasyland if I was picked for best commentary by *USA Today* every week during the season when Rudy Martzke, the newspaper's television sports critic, announces his picks each Monday. Maybe I'll get on Martzke's good side by giving his alma mater, Wisconsin, some extra pub. Then I'll put myself in position to win a coveted Rudy Award for top analyst instead of it always being Lock City for my friend Billy Packer.

Wisconsin fans, after watching the Badgers raise their overall record to 12-5 with a Big Ten Conference mark of 5-3 midway through last season, were hopeful of ending a couple of droughts and resurrecting NCAA playoff success from long ago. But despite encouraging improvement from Stu Jackson's team, they stumbled down the stretch and finished 14-14 overall and 7-11 in the Big Ten — the school's 19th consecutive losing mark in league play.

But this could be a big year for Wisconsin, which has the Big Ten's best winning percentage in the NCAA playoffs despite not having a 20-victory season since winning the national championship in 1941. The Badgers are 4-1 in tournament play, but haven't participated in the event since 1947. They capitalized on a home-court advantage to overcome halftime deficits in the first two rounds of the 1941 national tourney on their way to the championship.

In 1940, Wisconsin finished ninth in the Big Ten and the Badgers' overall record of 5-15 represented their worst mark since joining the Big Ten in 1906. Amazingly, after losing their 1941 conference opener by 17 points at Minnesota when they failed to make a single field goal in the second half, the Badgers swept undefeated through the remainder of their league schedule and the playoffs. The only other school to compile a losing mark one season and capture the national title the next year is Utah, which went from 10-12 in 1943 to 22-4 in 1944.

Two other champions — Ohio State '60 and Louisville '86 — compiled unassuming records the season before winning a national title. Each of these four schools benefited from the arrival of an athlete named Final Four Most Outstanding Player. A summary of their turnarounds:

Champion (W-L Mark)	Previous Season	Games Improved	Key New Player, Pos., Cl.
Wisconsin '41 (20-3)	5-15	+13 1/2	John Kotz, F, Soph.
Louisville '86 (32-7)	19-18	+12	Pervis Ellison, F-C, Fr.
Ohio State '60 (25-3)	11-11	+11	Jerry Lucas, C, Soph.
Utah '44 (22-4)	10-12	+10	Arnie Ferrin, F, Fr.

THE YOUNG AND THE FEARLESS

Who says you need experience to win a title? Duke's first championship team in 1991 included three underclassmen starters — freshman forward Grant Hill and sophomore guards Bobby Hurley and Thomas Hill. After repeating as champion in 1992 and losing to California in the second round last year, Grant Hill had compiled a 13-1 NCAA playoff record while Hurley and Thomas Hill were 18-2.

Others teams have won the championship with freshmen and/or sophomores dominating the lineup. The one kingpin in this group most likely to be overlooked is City College of New York, an unranked "Cinderella" squad that won the 1950 crown by defeating three teams ranked in the AP top five, although five of its six leading scorers were sophomores. Midnight struck for the Beavers following their storybook season when four CCNY regulars and other New York-based players were indicted in a point-shaving scandal rocking the sport the following year. After the investigation revealed scholastic records were falsified to allow several recruits admission to CCNY, the school de-emphasized its program in 1953.

A summary of what materialized the next couple of years for the eight NCAA titlists other than Duke and CCNY to have at least three underclassmen starters:

**CHAMPION
(RECORD/COACH)**   **UNDERCLASSMEN STARTERS**
**North Carolina '82   C Sam Perkins (Soph.), G Michael Jordan (Fr.),
(32-2)/Dean Smith   F Matt Doherty (Soph.)**

Comment: The Tar Heels compiled a 56-11 record the next two seasons with at least a share of the ACC regular-season crown each year. But they didn't reach the ACC Tournament final in 1983 and 1984 and had a modest 3-2 NCAA playoff record in that span despite being a No. 2 and No. 1 seed, respectively. Jordan declared early for the NBA draft after his junior year.

**Louisville '80   F Derek Smith (Soph.), F Rodney McCray (Fr.),
(33-3)/Denny Crum   C Wiley Brown (Soph.), G Jerry Eaves (Soph.)**

Comment: The Cardinals compiled a 44-19 record the next two seasons, winning the Metro Conference title in 1981 and finishing second to Memphis State in 1982. In the NCAA playoffs, they lost their opener in 1981 on a "Hail Mary" basket by Arkansas' U.S. Reed and lost to Georgetown in the 1982 national semifinals. McCray helped them reach the national semifinals again in 1983 before they lost to Houston.

**UCLA '72   C Bill Walton (Soph.), F Keith Wilkes (Soph.),
(30-0)/John Wooden   G Greg Lee (Soph.)**

Comment: The Bruins went 30-0 again in the 1972-73 season and 26-4 in 1973-74 with a Pacific-8 title despite losing back-to-back games at Oregon State and Oregon. North Carolina State, avenging an 18-point loss on a neutral court earlier in the 1973-74 season, snapped UCLA's 38-game tourney winning streak (80-77 in the Final Four, in two overtimes).

CHAMPION (RECORD/COACH)	UNDERCLASSMEN STARTERS
UCLA '67 (30-0)/John Wooden	C Lew Alcindor (Soph.), G Lucius Allen (Soph.), F Lynn Shackelford (Soph.),

Comment: The Bruins went 29-1 each of the next two seasons with both of the losses by two points (against Houston in 1968 and USC in 1969). After winning two more national titles, Alcindor & Co. had 12 victories in as many NCAA Tournament games by an average margin of 21.5 points.

Ohio State '60 (25-3)/Fred Taylor	C Jerry Lucas (Soph.), G Mel Nowell (Soph.), F John Havlicek (Soph.)

Comment: The Buckeyes compiled a 53-3 record the next two seasons with their only Big Ten defeat in that span against 1962 conference runner-up Wisconsin (86-67). Their other two setbacks were both in national championship games against intrastate rival Cincinnati when Havlicek and Nowell combined for just 33 points on 29.5 percent field-goal shooting in the two finals.

La Salle '54 (26-4)/Ken Loeffler	F Charles Singley (Soph.), F Frank Blatcher (Soph.), G-F Fran O'Malley (Soph.),

Comment: The Explorers compiled a 41-15 record the next two seasons. After losing to San Francisco in the 1955 national final and with three-time first-team All-America Tom Gola graduating, Loeffler left for Texas A&M and was replaced as coach by former Stanford sensation Jim Pollard, who notched a 15-10 mark in his first year.

Holy Cross '47 (27-3)/Alvin Julian	F-C George Kaftan (Soph.), F Dermie O'Connell (Soph.), G-F Bob Cousy (Fr.), F-G Andy Laska (Fr.), G Joe Mullaney (Soph.), C-F Frank Oftring (Fr.)

Comment: The Crusaders compiled a 45-12 record the next two seasons. Their bid to repeat as national champion was ended in the 1948 national semifinals by eventual titlist Kentucky (60-52). After Julian left to coach the Boston Celtics, they were 19-8 in Buster Sheary's first season as coach in 1948-49. Cousy and Oftring were co-captains as seniors in the 1949-50 season when Holy Cross won its first 26 games to earn the No. 1 ranking nationally by the AP. But the Crusaders lost four of their last five contests, including both outings in the NCAA playoffs.

CHAMPION	
(RECORD/COACH)	UNDERCLASSMEN STARTERS
Utah '44	F Arnie Ferrin (Fr.), G-F Herb Wilkinson (Fr.),
	G Bob Lewis (Fr.), F-C Wat Misaka (Fr.),
(22-4)/V. Peterson	C Fred Sheffield (Soph.), F-G Dick Smuin (Fr.)

Comment: Ferrin, Misaka and Sheffield were the only three of this group of players to earn any more letters with the Utes, loser of both of their NCAA playoff games in 1945. Ferrin was a second-team consensus All-America in 1947, when Utah won the NIT as Misaka, a 5-8 center, restricted unanimous first-team All-America Ralph Beard to two points in a 49-45 triumph over Kentucky in the championship game.

THE LONG AND SHORT OF IT

The only school to reach the Final Four in its one and only NCAA Tournament appearance was Larry Bird-led Indiana State in 1979. Bird collected a total of 54 points and 29 rebounds in two Final Four games, but he also committed a Final Four-record total of 17 turnovers when Indiana State edged DePaul in the national semifinals, 73-71, before bowing to Michigan State in the final, 75-64.

Indiana State's coach for the 33-1 season was current Mercer coach Bill Hodges, who was named interim coach after Bob King suffered a stroke in the preseason. The Sycamores, who moved up to Division I status in 1972, haven't had a winning season since they finished 16-11 under Hodges in 1979-80.

Unlike the oblivion befalling Indiana State, numerous schools regularly participate in the NCAA Tournament. But even an illustrious institution such as North Carolina isn't immune to playoff pitfalls. Carolina's current amazing streak of 13 consecutive appearances in a regional semifinal (round of 16) came on the heels of three consecutive opening-round tournament defeats during the Mike O'Koren/Al Wood era (losses to San Francisco '78, Penn '79 and Texas A&M '80 although none of the trio was ranked in a Top 10 poll entering the tourney).

Here are the 11 all-time longest appearance streaks with a minimum of nine consecutive appearances in the tourney:

SCHOOL	NO.	YEARS (PLAYOFF RECORD IN THAT SPAN)
North Carolina	19	1975-93 (45-17)
UCLA	15	1967-81 (49-7 until NCAA probation in 1982)
Georgetown	14	1979-92 (28-13 until appearing in 1993 NIT)
Duke	10	1984-93 (34-8)
Louisiana State	10	1984-93 (9-10)
Marquette	10	1971-80 (17-10 until appearing in 1981 NIT)
Syracuse	10	1983-92 (16-10 until NCAA probation in 1993)
Arizona	9	1985-93 (9-9)
Arkansas	9	1977-85 (10-9 until losing season record in 1986)
Georgia Tech	9	1985-93 (13-9)
UNLV	9	1983-91 (23-8 until NCAA probation in 1992)

Two Doses of Silver Don't Measure Up to One of Gold

North Carolina coach Dean Smith took a lot of heat for years about winning *only* one national title. But think about what it might have been for the Tar Heels if Bob McAdoo, James Worthy, Michael Jordan and J.R. Reid hadn't left school early for the NBA. Let me tell you, the gold in Carolina would have been blinding had Smith's star players stayed for their entire four seasons of eligibility.

Duke, Kansas, Michigan and North Carolina are the only four universities to lose an NCAA championship game as many as four times.

Duke and North Carolina also are among the four schools to reach the Final Four three consecutive seasons without winning a national title — Duke (1988, 1989 and 1990), Houston (1982, 1983 and 1984), North Carolina (1967, 1968 and 1969) and Ohio State (1944, 1945 and 1946). After finishing national runner-up the past two years, Michigan could become the fifth school in this category in 1994. Ohio State and Houston also had teams lose two consecutive NCAA Tournament finals. Here is a summary of the three back-to-back bridesmaids:

Runner-up (Years)	Coach	Key Players on Both Second-Place Teams
Ohio State ('61 & '62)	Fred Taylor	Jerry Lucas, John Havlicek, Mel Nowell, Bob Knight, Gary Gearhart, Richard Reasbeck

Comment: Lucas' game-high 27 points and 12 rebounds weren't enough to prevent a 70-65 setback against Cincinnati in 1961. The next year, he was hampered by a knee injury and hit just 5 of 17 field goal attempts when the Buckeyes bowed to the Bearcats again, 71-59. Havlicek, inducted into the Naismith Memorial Basketball Hall of Fame after becoming a 13-time NBA All-Star, had a modest total of 15 points in the two title game defeats for Ohio State.

Houston ('83 & '84)	Guy Lewis	Michael Young, Alvin Franklin, Hakeem Olajuwon, Reid Gettys, Benny Anders

Comment: Young, the Cougars' leading scorer each season, shot just 35.5 percent from the floor (11 of 31) in the championship game defeats against North Carolina State (54-52) and Georgetown (84-75). Houston's poor free throw shooting also reared its ugly head in both finals as the Cougars combined to hit just 56.1 percent of their foul shots (23 of 41).

**Michigan ('92 & '93) Steve Fisher   Chris Webber, Jalen Rose,
                                              Juwan Howard, Ray Jackson,
                                              Jimmy King, Eric Riley**

Comment: The Wolverines led at halftime in the 1992 final against Duke before becoming the only team to have such a lead in the championship game and lose by at least 20 points (71-51). They led by eight midway through the second half last year against North Carolina before unraveling down the stretch, including Webber's infamous call for a timeout the team didn't have left in the closing seconds of a 77-71 loss. The bloom came off in the finals for Rose, who committed a total of 10 turnovers in the two championship games and hit 5 of 12 from the floor in each contest.

One Shining Moment

Wilt Chamberlain's final season at Kansas in 1958 included one of the most amazing turnarounds in NCAA history. Nebraska, in the midst of 15 consecutive losing seasons, was clobbered at Kansas by 56 points (102-46) before upsetting the Jayhawks (43-41) four games later in Omaha. I was surprised to learn that Nebraska has never won an NCAA Tournament game, making the Cornhuskers treasure the moment even more when they defeated NCAA champion-to-be Kansas in the regular season in 1988.

Cincinnati, compiling just one winning record in Metro Conference competition (8-6 in 1985) in 12 years from 1978 through 1989, is the only school to register a losing record in a season it won a road game against a conference rival that later became NCAA champion. The 12-16 Bearcats, notching a 5-7 Metro mark, won at Louisville (84-82) midway through the 1985-86 season after overcoming a 13-point second-half deficit. The Cardinals recovered from their only home-court loss that year to win the NCAA title.

Most observers don't remember the defect, but four Big Ten Conference second-division teams defeated Magic Johnson-led Michigan State in 1979. One of Michigan State's setbacks was by 18 points against perennial cellar dweller Northwestern, which has 25 consecutive losing league records and finished in the Big Ten basement 12 times in the last 16 years. Following is a brief look at Northwestern and the five other schools at least four games under .500 in conference play to capitalize on a home-court advantage and defeat a league rival that went on to win the NCAA Tournament (conference in parentheses):

Second-Division Team	League Record	Overall Record	Upset Against Eventual NCAA Champion
Oregon State '39 (PCC)	6-10	13-11	Beavers defeated Oregon, 50-31
Oregon '59 (PCC)	3-13	9-16	Ducks defeated California, 59-57
Illinois '79 (Big Ten)	7-11	19-11	Illini defeated Mich. State, 57-55
Northwestern '79 (Big Ten)	2-16	6-21	Wildcats defeated Mich. St., 83-65
Wisconsin '79 (Big Ten)	6-12	12-15	Badgers defeated Mich. State, 83-81
Nebraska '88 (Big Eight)	4-10	13-18	Cornhuskers defeated Kansas, 70-68

The Good, the Bad and the Ugly

The only year all of the Final Four teams won their conference tournaments was 1983 — North Carolina State (ACC), Houston (SWC), Georgia (SEC) and Louisville (Metro). On the flip side, the only year as many as three Final Four teams finished third or lower in their regular-season league standings was 1980 — UCLA (fourth in Pacific-10), Purdue (third in Big Ten) and Iowa (fourth in Big Ten). Here is a breakdown of Final Four team won-loss records a keen observer should know from one end of the spectrum to the other end:

Good — The best composite winning percentage when four teams arrived at the Final Four was in 1970 when UCLA (26-2), New Mexico State (26-2), Jacksonville (26-1) and St. Bonaventure (25-1) combined for a 103-6 record (.945). . . . The only other time four teams converged at the national semifinals with a total of fewer than 10 losses was in 1960 when Ohio State (23-3), California (27-1), Cincinnati (27-1) and New York University (22-3) combined for a 99-8 record (.925). . . . The only time a group of teams arrived at the Final Four with a total of at least 125 victories was in 1986 when Louisville (30-7), Duke (36-2), Kansas (35-3) and LSU (26-11) combined for a 127-23 record (.847). . . . Last year came close to becoming the first time each Final Four team won at least 30 games, but Kansas finished with a 29-7 record when the Jayhawks lost to eventual champion North Carolina in the national semifinals. Carolina finished with a 34-4 mark after winning the NCAA final against Michigan (31-5). The Wolverines defeated Kentucky (30-4) in the other national semifinal.

Bad — The worst composite winning percentage when four teams arrived at the national semifinals was in 1954 when La Salle (24-4), Bradley (18-12), Penn State (17-5) and Southern California (19-12) combined for a 78-33 record (.703). . . . The only other time four teams converged at the Final Four with a total of more than 25 defeats was in 1980 when Louisville (31-3), UCLA (21-9), Purdue (22-9) and Iowa (23-8) combined for a 97-29 record (.770) to become the only group of national semifinalists since 1954 to win fewer than 80 percent of their games. . . . The two winningest teams for a single season in NCAA history — Duke (37-3 record in the 1985-86 season) and UNLV (37-2 in 1986-87) — both reached the Final Four, but neither of them captured the national title those years.

Ugly — Southern Cal lost both of its Final Four games in 1954 (against Bradley and Penn State) to become the only national semifinalist with as many as 14 defeats. Bradley lost the 1954 championship game against La Salle to become one of only three Final Four squads to finish a season with more than a dozen defeats. . . . The only other time a national title game featured two teams with a total of as many as 16 defeats like the La Salle-Bradley matchup was in 1981 when Indiana (25-9 entering final) opposed North Carolina (29-7). . . . The worst winning percentage for a Final Four team was compiled by Baylor, which finished with a 14-13 record (.519) in the 1949-50 season after losing both of its Final Four games (against Bradley and North Carolina State).

Behind the Scenes

Did you know . . . ?

The only teams to finish national runner-up one year and then capture the title the next year were **North Carolina** (runner-up in 1981 and champion in 1982) and **Duke** (runner-up in 1990 and champion in 1991).

Ten schools captured the NCAA title in their first appearance in the playoffs. The most recent school to achieve the feat was **Loyola of Chicago** in 1963. Loyola, in its first ever playoff game, set an all-time tournament record for victory margin (69 points) with a 111-42 trouncing of **Tennessee Tech**. The Ramblers also won their next three games by double-digit margins to reach the national championship game, where they overcame a 15-point deficit with less than 14 minutes remaining to defeat top-ranked **Cincinnati** (60-58 in overtime). Only two other first-time tournament entrants — **Jacksonville** and **UNC Charlotte** — defeated the nation's top-ranked team entering the playoffs since the AP introduced national rankings in 1949. Jacksonville kayoed **Kentucky** (106-100) in the 1970 Mideast Regional final and UNC Charlotte shocked **Michigan** (75-68) in the 1977 Mideast Regional final.

The only school to play in as many as three overtime games in a single tournament was **Syracuse**, which finished in fourth place in 1975 when the Orangemen lost to **Louisville** (96-88 in OT). In earlier rounds, Syracuse won overtime games against **La Salle** and **Kansas State**. Four national champions — **North Carolina** '57, **Texas-El Paso** '66, **UCLA** '75 and **Louisville** '80 — had to win two overtime games in the playoffs. Five NCAA finals were decided in overtime: 1944 — **Utah** over **Dartmouth** (42-40); 1957 — **North Carolina** over **Kansas** (54-53 in triple OT); 1961 — **Cincinnati** over **Ohio State** (70-65); 1963 — **Loyola of Chicago** over **Cincinnati** (60-58), and 1989 — **Michigan** over **Seton Hall** (80-79). North Carolina's national semifinal game in 1957 against **Michigan State** was also in triple overtime. It was survival of the fittest as the Tar Heels became the only school to play back-to-back triple-overtime games in the playoffs.

Indiana is the only school to win the NCAA championship in four different decades (1940, 1953, 1976 and 1987).

The only Final Four squad to have as many as six players finish with double-digit season scoring averages was **UNLV** '77 — forwards **Eddie Owens** (21.8 points per game) and **Sam Smith** (14.8); guards **Glen Gondrezick** (14.6), **Reggie Theus** (14.5) and **Robert Smith** (12.8), and center **Lewis Brown** (10.2). The Rebels, averaging 107.1 points as a team on their way to a national third-place finish, also had two other players come close to a double-figure scoring average — guard **Tony Smith** (9 ppg) and center **Larry Moffett** (8). Tony Smith was the only one of the eight players in UNLV's regular rotation to never appear in an NBA game.

Dick's Top 5

Best Final Four Sites

1. **New Orleans** — How can you not like the food, jazz and party atmosphere on Bourbon Street?

2. **Indianapolis** — When you talk about basketball mania, you better believe they have it in Hoosierland.

3. **Seattle** — The Emerald City environment shined.

4. **Lexington** — Loved all of the gorgeous Kentucky horse farms and having the hotel so close to the arena.

5. **Dallas** — Enjoyed going out to Southfork where J.R. Ewing and company did their thing.

The Final Four had changed a great deal between my first visit in 1967 and my second one in 1983. A good friend of mine, Tom Ramsden, and I used to sit for hours in Ross' Diner on Route 46 in Elmwood Park, N. J., diagramming plays on napkins and using salt and pepper shakers as players. Tom is a master of the Xs and Os, and really helped me when I was getting started as a coach. We were having another one of our strategy sessions when, at a moment's notice, we decided to drive to Louisville to watch Lew Alcindor and UCLA in the Final Four.

My next Final Four appearance came when ESPN sent me to Albuquerque, 16 years later. I had never attended the coaches' convention at the Final Four in the 1970s because I always thought I could use that time to gain a competitive edge by hitting the recruiting trail while many of my peers were out hobnobbing. I couldn't believe how big both ESPN and the tournament were becoming.

The NCAA Tournament is definitely a thrill, but certainly not a cheap thrill. Consider that the average price per playoff ticket in 1978 was under $8. Less than 15 years later, the cost of an average ticket escalated almost 175 percent to about $22. In 1991, ticket sales generated $14,400,000.

The first public draw to fill oversubscribed orders for Final Four tickets was used for the 1974 championship. The public "lottery" for the drawing of Final Four tickets regularly receives more than 100,000 applications, with a high of 267,498 for the 1994 Final Four in Charlotte, nearly doubling the previous high of 143,829 for Indianapolis in 1991. In all, 533,193 tickets were requested for Charlotte, and a computer selected the winners of the 2,014 public tickets.

Of the 267,498 general public applications for this year's Final Four, hoops-crazy North Carolina led the way with 53,977 applications. North Carolina's figure represents more Final Four ticket applications from one state than what was received by the NCAA from the entire country in 1980 when Indianapolis was host to the event. Approximately nine percent of the 1994 tickets, costing $65 each, were allocated to the general public in the Charlotte Coliseum (seating capacity of 22,500).

What a difference a few years can make as the Final Four continues to increase in popularity! The NCAA received 131,378 applications for last year's Battle of New Orleans after receiving 15,600 applications for the first Superdome Final Four in 1982.

The NCAA's luck of the draw includes selecting only one application per household. Applicants can apply as many times as they want, but only one application will be selected. Applicants can only request one or two tickets. Mail orders must be received (not postmarked) by no later than midnight April 30. Applicants can also use a 900 telephone number from March 1 to April 30. Interest income generated by ticket application funds are used to support NCAA youth programs and drug education efforts.

But the NCAA can't control the scalping of Final Four tickets. One drastic option discussed is eliminating the lottery and just giving the tickets to the four participating institutions, coaches attending their national convention, NCAA membership and the host organizing group. The National Association of Basketball Coaches (NABC) Board of Directors has adopted a policy to try to curb abuse of Final Four tickets among its members.

Charlotte should be sweet to scalpers in 1994, especially if North Carolina or Duke — or both — get there again. Scalpers seem to be everywhere at the Final Four festival, and stand out as the sole snag in the NCAA's sure-footed system. The crafty profiteers relish their role, thinking they have a perfect job with great pay, flexible hours, no licenses, no dress code, no heavy lifting, and no real responsibility other than protecting the most precious pieces of small cardboard in all of sports.

What credentials do you require to excel at the scalpers' paradise? No special skills, just access to tickets, a keen sense of seat location and scalping regulations, and the ability to repeat a three-word question: "Need a ticket?"

The demand for Final Four tickets is principally for the semifinals on Super Saturday. Championship game tickets aren't as much of a problem for out-of-towners to procure because a good percentage of disgruntled fans from the two losing teams on Saturday leave before the final on Monday evening. Scalping will still be a problem despite the NCAA going exclusively to larger domed stadiums. The top 5,000 or so lower-level seats in domes command as much money as tickets in smaller arenas in cities such as Dallas (1986), Kansas City (1988) and Denver (1990). Selling tickets above face value in North Carolina is illegal, but a pair of premium tickets will go as high as $2,000 to $2,500.

EXPANDING FIELD OF DREAMS

I think 64 teams is the proper number of entrants for the NCAA Tournament. I know some people support opening up the tourney to everybody and eliminating any politicking that goes on behind closed doors. Forget about it. I think the NCAA Division I Committee has done a solid job in selecting teams. You're always going to have No. 65 and No. 66 complaining. Almost everyone gets a shot anyway, with all of the postseason conference tournaments.

In 1950, 145 schools were classified as major colleges. Forty years later, the number of NCAA Division I institutions had more than doubled. The NCAA Tournament bracket never included more than 25 entrants until it expanded to 32 teams in 1975, when teams other than the conference champion could be chosen on an at-large basis from the same league for the first time.

Four of the last six NCAA champions — Kansas '88, Michigan '89, Duke '91 and North Carolina '93 — wouldn't have been invited to participate in the playoffs prior to 1975 because they did not win their conference or conference tournament.

A look at the tourney's growth from eight teams to 64 (the number of schools classified as Division I at the time are in parentheses for designated years):

PLAYOFF ENTRANTS	YEARS (NUMBER OF DIVISION I SCHOOLS)
8 teams	1939 through 1950 (145 major colleges)
16 teams	1951 (153) and 1952 (156)
22-25 teams	1953 (158) through 1974 (233)
32 teams	1975 (233) through 1978 (254)
40 teams	1979 (257)
48 teams	1980 (261) through 1982 (272)
52 teams	1983 (274)
53 teams	1984 (276)
64 teams	since 1985 (282)

WHERE THE ACTION IS

The NCAA Tournament is the greatest sporting event we have. No doubt about it. Even the jaded, supposedly unbiased media members get excited about it. And who can blame them, after enduring the hyped-up Super Bowl and its 20-point average margin of victory from 1980 through 1993?

The number of media credentials is normally an accurate barometer to determine the popularity of a sports event. A total of 64 newspaper writers, the largest media group up to that time, assembled for the 1957 NCAA finals in Kansas City. In recent years, the robust Final Four regularly has in the neighborhood of 1,000 media representatives with credentials.

Media purists frequently bemoan the cosmetic appearance of games conducted in cavernous domed stadiums, but the magnitude of the playoffs is such the NCAA doesn't have much of an option. A recent NCAA decision to abandon intimate settings and establish a minimum seating capacity of 30,000 for Final Four sites reduces the field of potential candidates to nine because there is limited hotel lodging near Syracuse's Carrier Dome. The following nine facilities are eligible: Atlanta's Georgia Dome, Houston's Astrodome, Indianapolis' Hoosier Dome, New Orleans' Louisiana Superdome, Minneapolis' Metrodome, Pontiac (Mich.) Silverdome, St. Petersburg's Florida Suncoast Dome, San Antonio's Alamodome and Seattle's Kingdome.

The only one of the nine domes not slated to host the Final Four through 2002 is the Silverdome. The only year the Astrodome played host to the event was 1971.

If you have an opportunity to attend a Final Four in a domed stadium, risk pulling a leg muscle and take a stroll to the nosebleed section to watch the ants play. You'll gain an appreciation for the people who love the game so much they just want to be in the same building as the teams. They can't possibly enjoy what they're not seeing, but want to be there to absorb the atmosphere. It's akin to attending the World's Fair and enduring lousy accommodations just so you can say you were there. "Announcing the sites through 2002 precludes the possibility of devoting time to adding new sites until late this decade," said Duke Athletic Director Tom Butters, chairman of the NCAA Division I Committee. "We have time now to just get ready for each event. It's pretty hard to tinker with something that has been so successful. I think we'll stay at 64 teams."

Following is the Division I Committee's designation of sites from 1994 through 2002: 1994 — Charlotte Coliseum, Charlotte, NC (April 2 and 4); 1995 — Kingdome, Seattle (April 1 and 3); 1996 — Meadowlands Arena, East Rutherford, NJ (March 30 and April 1); 1997 — Hoosier Dome, Indianapolis (March 29 and 31); 1998 — Alamodome, San Antonio (March 28 and 30); 1999 — Florida Suncoast Dome, St. Petersburg (March 27 and 29); 2000 — Hoosier Dome, Indianapolis (April 1 and 3); 2001 — Metrodome, Minneapolis (March 31 and April 2); 2002 — Georgia Dome, Atlanta (March 30 and April 1).

Kansas City benefited from being closest to the NCAA home office. But Kansas City and the other two cities to be host to the Final Four the most times — New York and Louisville — don't measure up to the new seating capacity standard. Here are the seven cities which will have been the host site of the Final Four the most years by 2002:

10 — Kansas City (1940, 1941, 1942, 1953, 1954, 1955, 1957, 1961, 1964, 1988)

7 — New York (1943, 1944, 1945, 1946, 1947, 1948, 1950)

6 — Louisville (1958, 1959, 1962, 1963, 1967, 1969)

5 — Seattle (1949, 1952, 1984, 1989, 1995)

4 — Indianapolis (1980, 1991, 1997, 2000)

3 — Minneapolis (1951, 1992, 2001)

3 — New Orleans (1982, 1987, 1993)

HOME FREE?

Perhaps no sport is influenced more by the location of a game than basketball. Therefore, the site of contests has had an incalculable impact on NCAA Tournament history. Consider the following questions:

Would City College of New York, a loser in three of five games in a late-season swoon, have been able to become the only school to win the NIT and NCAA playoffs in the same season if both of the national postseason tournaments weren't staged in New York in 1950?

Would Kentucky's storied "Fiddlin' Five," a team equaling the most defeats (six) of any Wildcats squad in the previous 15 seasons, have won the 1958 title if it didn't enjoy a home-state edge throughout the playoffs (Mideast Regional at Lexington and Final Four at Louisville)? Didn't a highly partisan crowd give them an emotional lift in the national semifinals when they trailed Temple by four points and the Owls had the ball with less than a minute and half remaining?

Would UCLA have won seven consecutive titles from 1967 through 1973 if eight of the Bruins' playoff games weren't played in the friendly confines of Los Angeles?

Would North Carolina State have been the 1974 kingpin if the Wolfpack didn't play at home (East Regional at Raleigh) and nearby Greensboro, where it ended UCLA's 38-game playoff winning streak with an 80-77 double overtime triumph in the national semifinals?

Would Indiana have won championships in 1981 (Mideast Regional at Bloomington) and 1987 (Midwest Regional first and second round at Indianapolis) if its road to the Final Four didn't include stops in the Hoosiers' backyard?

Would North Carolina have captured the 1982 crown if the Tar Heels hadn't won three games, two of them by a total of just seven points, in fa-miliar surroundings (second round at Charlotte and East Regional at Raleigh)?

Would Duke's spurt of six Final Four appearances from 1986-92 be quite so impressive if the Blue Devils didn't benefit from three years of playing the first and second round of the East Regional close to home along Tobacco Road (at Greensboro in 1986 and 1989 and at Chapel Hill in 1988)?

Naturally, it's impossible to unequivocally answer those questions. It wasn't fair for the NCAA to permit a playoff team a primrose path by playing on its home court or remaining close to home. But until the event became more national in scope, the movers and shakers frequently rationalized their provincial stance by indicating it was necessary to spur ticket sales.

Most people don't remember, but three of the finest teams in college basketball history — San Francisco '55, Kansas '57 and Ohio State '61 — almost didn't advance to the Final Four after meeting playoff opponents on their home-courts. But USF and Ohio State each pulled off one-point victories in those "road" games to hand foes their eighth defeat of the season and Kansas frustrated homestanding Southern Methodist in overtime (73-65). Here is a recap of those three contests:

The first of San Francisco's back-to-back champions survived a scare in a West Regional and won by one point at Oregon State (57-56). The Beavers would have avenged a 26-point defeat earlier in the season against the Bill Russell-led Dons if they hadn't missed a last-second shot. A 60-34 verdict over Oregon State was the first of USF's 60 consecutive victories, the longest winning streak in major-college history until UCLA won 88 games in a row from 1971-74.

In 1957, Wilt Chamberlain-led Kansas was fortunate Southern Methodist shot just 32.1 percent from the floor in their Midwest Regional opener at Dallas. Long before Georgetown tried to minimize distractions, the Jayhawks stayed 30 miles out of town, but some bigots still burned a cross in a yard across from their lodging quarters. And narrow-minded fans at the game punctuated the contest with racial slurs. KU went on to lose the NCAA championship game in triple overtime to North Carolina.

Ohio State won 54 of 55 games in one stretch from 1960-62 during the Jerry Lucas/John Havlicek era. In 1961, the defending NCAA champion Buckeyes entered the playoffs undefeated, but needed to overcome a five-point deficit with less than three minutes remaining to escape with a 56-55 triumph at Louisville in the Mideast Regional semifinals. They eventually lost the national final game in overtime against Cincinnati.

More recently, Duke and Indiana joined a contingent including Syracuse '87, Kansas '86 and Louisiana State '86 as the five Final Four teams in a two-year span to enjoy a homecourt advantage en route to the national semifinals. Facing mounting criticism for allowing such unfair advantages, the NCAA began using neutral courts in 1989 for all rounds of the championship. In 1986, the tourney had begun having regional competition played at neutral sites. If an institution selected to host a regional was a participant, it was bracketed in another regional.

The definition of "homecourt advantage" was amended in 1991 to include playing no more than three games of a regular-season schedule, excluding league tournaments, in one arena. But Kansas doubtlessly had a "Rock Chalk Jayhawk" edge in the 1986 Midwest Regional at Kansas City and would have enjoyed a similar benefit two years ago if not upset by Texas-El Paso in the second round at Dayton. In the same vein, Xavier faced insurmountable odds when it lost by just three points against Indiana in the Hoosier Dome in Indianapolis in the second round of the Midwest Regional last year.

All teams don't capitalize on desirable sites, however. Kansas lost three consecutive title games in Kansas City (1940, 1953 and 1957) before winning there in 1988, and NYU lost the national final at New York in 1945. Several teams have lost regional games in their hometowns. Alabama-Birmingham, in fact, has lost three times in Birmingham (1982, 1984 and 1987) by an average of 15 points.

How much will Duke or North Carolina benefit if one or both of the ACC powers reach the Final Four in Charlotte this year? Following is an assessment of highly-ranked teams where the site was a key factor since the tournament started seeding teams and expanded the field to at least 40 teams in 1979:

Raw Draw — No. 3 seed St. John's lost in 1980 Mideast Regional second round against #6 Purdue (87-72) at West Lafayette. . . . #2 Kentucky lost in 1981 Mideast Regional second round against #7 seed Alabama-Birmingham (69-62) at Birmingham. . . . #3 Iowa blew an 11-point halftime lead and lost in 1981 Midwest Regional second round against #6 Wichita State (60-56) at Wichita. . . . #2 Illinois lost in 1984 Mideast Regional final against #1 Kentucky (54-51) at Lexington. . . . #3 Memphis State lost in 1986 Southeast Regional second round against #11 LSU (83-81) at Baton Rouge.

Home Sour Home — No. 1 seed Notre Dame lost in 1979 Mideast Regional final against #2 seed Michigan State (80-68) at Indianapolis. . . . #1 North Carolina lost in 1979 East Regional second round against #9 Penn (72-71) at Raleigh. . . . #1 Kentucky lost in 1980 Mideast Regional semifinals against #4 Duke (55-54) at Lexington. . . . #2 Missouri lost in 1982 Midwest Regional semifinals against #6 Houston (79-78) at St. Louis. . . . #2 Georgia Tech lost in 1986 Southeast Regional semifinals against #11 LSU (70-64) at Atlanta. . . . #2 Syracuse lost at home in 1986 East Regional second round against #7 Navy (97-85).

Overcoming the Odds — North Carolina has been the most successful school in coping with site disadvantages. The Tar Heels were seeded No. 2 or 3 when they won four such games from 1981 through 1986. Carolina defeated #3 Utah (61-56) in 1981 West Regional semifinals at Salt Lake City, #7 Notre Dame (60-58) in 1985 Southeast Regional second round at South Bend, #11 Auburn (62-56) in 1985 Southeast Regional semifinals at Birmingham, and #14 Utah (84-72) in 1986 West Regional first round at Ogden.

VIEWERS' CHOICE

When it's pressure-cooker time, I feel a little out of place sitting in the stands while CBS is on the sideline covering the NCAA Tournament. Yes, Mr. Packer, I'm eating my heart out. I'm watching Billy P. at courtside in the best seat in the house while I'm up at about the 40th row wondering why I can't get just one shot at broadcasting the Final Four. Oh well, you're the surf and turf guy, Billy P. You're steak and all we are is the appetizer. But that's OK, I have a lot of fun up in the crowd, cheering and going bananas with the real people.

CBS' 22.2 rating for last year's NCAA title game between North Carolina and Michigan was down two percent from its boffo rating in 1992. But with a total of 55 million viewers, the 1993 final ranks as the second most-watched basketball game in U.S. history.

The highest television rating in the history of the NCAA Tournament came in 1979, when Larry Bird and Indiana State (left) squared off against Magic Johnson (right) and Michigan State in the championship game. About 745,000 households were tuned in as the Magic Man's Spartans prevailed by 11 points. It's a shame these guys couldn't make it in the pros, huh?

The 1992 NCAA championship game between Duke and Michigan was the most-watched basketball game in television history. An estimated 53 million viewers took in all or part of the final in the United States' TV homes covered by the Nielsen ratings. CBS estimated an additional 10 percent of the total audience watched the 1992 final away from home — in taverns, dormitories and other venues Nielsen doesn't survey. That's more than 100 times the initial viewing audience estimated at 500,000 in 1946, when the championship game (Oklahoma State defeated North Carolina, 43-40) was televised locally for the first time in New York by WCBS-TV.

CBS began a new seven-year, $1 billion contract in 1991, including live coverage of all sessions of the tournament. In three previous three-year contracts, CBS was awarded the rights for 16 exposures (starting in 1982), 19 exposures (1985) and all regional semifinal games carried in prime time (1988).

When CBS gained exclusive rights to the playoffs in 1990, an era came to a close at ESPN. The cable network, the home of early-round tournament games since 1980, developed a cult following of sorts and many believe the increased exposure given Cinderella teams helped revolutionize recruiting, making it easier for coaches at lesser-known schools to lure high school prospects. But the bonanza dollars put on the table by CBS knocked ESPN out of the picture.

Television rights exceeded $1 million for the first time in 1973, when the Thursday-Saturday format for semifinals and final was changed to Saturday-Monday, allowing the championship game to be televised in prime time by NBC. Television rights exceeded $500,000 for the first time in 1969, when NBC was awarded the rights to televise the championship. The first major network television announcer was Curt Gowdy, the radio broadcaster for Oklahoma State's 50-station state network for the aforementioned 1946 title game.

A syndication, Sports Network, was involved in the first six live national telecasts of the NCAA Tournament from 1963 through 1968 for rights totaling $140,000. The announcer for the first six national broadcasts was Bill Flemming, a fixture on ABC's Wide World of Sports. "NCAA Executive Director Walter Byers pleaded with (syndicator) Dick Bailey to carry the tournament," Flemming said. "Certainly, Roone Arledge was the pioneer of the Olympics. But Bailey was the same way for college basketball. What got the event over the hump was the 1968 (national semi-finals) rematch between Houston and UCLA in Los Angeles after the Bruins had their long (47-game) winning streak snapped by the Cougars earlier in the season at the Astrodome. We had 253 stations pick up the semifinals and final that year (compared to an 11-station network in 1957)."

The worth of one rating point, the percentage of television households overall, escalated to 930,000 TV households in the fall of 1992 compared to 745,000 homes in 1979, when the ballyhooed matchup between Indiana State's Larry Bird and Michigan State's Magic Johnson aroused fans and generated the largest ever TV share. A share is the percentage of televisions in use at the time.

Here is a look at the 10 highest-rated televised college basketball games, all NCAA playoff finals, and a brief story line explaining why the title games were so attractive to audiences:

YEAR	CHAMPIONSHIP GAME (RANKING BY HOMES)	NETWORK	RATING /SHARE
1979	Indiana State vs. Michigan State (8)	NBC	24.1/38

Comment: All-Americas Magic Johnson and Larry Bird have ultimate head-to-head duel.

1985	Georgetown vs. Villanova (3)	CBS	23.3/33

Comment: Villanova has to shoot 80 percent from the floor to win.

1992	Duke vs. Michigan (1)	CBS	22.7/35

Comment: Fab Five Freshman attempt to keep Duke from repeating as champion.

1983	Houston vs. North Carolina State (5)	CBS	22.3/32

Comment: N.C. State goes after title despite double-digit losses.

1993	North Carolina vs. Michigan (2)	CBS	22.2/33

Comment: Fab Five turned Gab Five try to silence critics after shaky West Regional.

1982	Georgetown vs. North Carolina (10)	CBS	21.6/31

Comment: Big John attempts to keep the Dean of coaches from his first NCAA title.

1989	Michigan vs. Seton Hall (4)	CBS	21.3/33

Comment: New Michigan Coach Steve Fisher wins title after six games.

1975	Kentucky vs. UCLA (18)	NBC	21.3/33

Comment: John Wooden pursues 10th title in his farewell season.

1986	Duke vs. Louisville (9)	CBS	20.7/31

Comment: "Never Nervous" Pervis Ellison becomes first freshman MVP in more than 40 years.

1981	Indiana vs. North Carolina (14)	NBC	20.7/29

Comment: Diversion from depressing news of President Reagan being shot that morning.

THE GOOD THEY DIE YOUNG

"Has anybody here seen my old friend ----? Can you tell me where he's gone?
. . . . I just looked around and he's gone."

The words of that ballad ring true for the Final Four, as time passes so quickly. It seems like just yesterday that Jim Valvano was bringing a smile to everyone he met with his special sense of humor. His gift as a master communicator and motivator helped catapult North Carolina State to the 1983 NCAA championship.

V's legacy grew during his battle with the Big C. His courageous fight against inoperable cancer was inspirational to so many before the dreaded disease took his life. Jimmy V's message should never be forgotten. "Don't give up," he said. *"Don't ever, ever give up!"*

Another shock jolted the basketball world last summer when Boston Celtics captain Reggie Lewis died from a heart ailment. Most fans don't remember his consistently productive NCAA playoff performances because he attended a relatively obscure school (Northeastern). But Lewis averaged at least 22 points per game in four tourneys from 1984 through 1987, including first-round games against No. 3 and No. 4 seeds his last three years.

The following Final Four players also died before their time:

- Three of Oregon's starting five on the first NCAA championship team in 1939 — guards Bobby Anet and Wally Johansen and center Slim Wintermute — all died in their 40s.

- Gary Bradds, a backup to national player of the year Jerry Lucas for Ohio State's 1962 NCAA runner-up before earning the same award himself two years later, died of cancer in July 1983 at 40. Bradds was principal of an elementary school in Bowersville, Ohio at the time of his death.

- Bill Buntin, the leading rebounder and second-leading scorer (behind Cazzie Russell) for Michigan's Final Four teams in 1964 and 1965, died during an informal workout one day after his 26th birthday in May, 1968.

- Ken Spain and Theodis Lee, starters for Houston's team that entered the 1968 Final Four undefeated, died of cancer. Spain, who was first diagnosed with cancer in 1977, died from it 13 years later in October, 1990 when he was 44. Lee, who played for the Harlem Globetrotters, was 33 when he passed away in March 1979, one week after the illness was diagnosed.

- Danny Knight, the leading scorer and rebounder for Kansas' 1974 Final Four team, was 24 when he died in June 1977, three weeks after falling down the steps at home. Knight had been suffering headaches for some time and doctors attributed his death to an aneurysm in the brain.

- All 11 regulars on Pittsburgh's 1941 Final Four team served in World War II, and one of them, guard Bob Artman, was killed in action.

DUNKING FOR DOLLARS

Has the NCAA Tournament taken on too much importance? Stanford coach Everett Dean took home a meager check for $93.75 to cover his team's stay in Kansas City after the Cardinal (they were the Indians then) won the 1942 title. That was an era when the NCAA playoffs had more naivete and were, above all, an opportunity to compete against the best squads across the nation. As time passed, the postseason competition lost its innocence and became a trip to the bank. Has the tourney gotten too big?

John Wooden, the UCLA coach who won 10 championships between 1964 and 1975, thinks so.

"Television has been the worst thing that's happened to intercollegiate basketball, but there's two sides to it," he said. "It's also been the savior of women's sports and other intercollegiate sports. But it causes too much time missed from school, too many games and too much showmanship — not only from the players but from the coaches and from the fans, too.

"My coach at Purdue, Ward Lambert, who had higher principles than anyone I knew, would be upset with all the games played off campus today. He always felt intercollegiate athletics were for the students and the alumni. He wouldn't take his team (to the postseason tourney) in 1940 even though it won the Big Ten. Indiana (which handed the Boilermakers their only two league losses that year) went and won the NCAA title although it had finished second in the conference."

The rapid growth of the national tournament since television became a key factor and the revenue a school can generate is staggering. Each Final Four participant in 1990 received more than $1.47 million, a whopping increase of about 2,870 percent in just 20 years.

Trying to minimize emphasis on the intrinsic dollar value of "six-figure shots" taken by players, the NCAA implemented a new revenue-sharing formula, beginning with the 1990-91 tournament competition.

Of the following three major pools of money for the distribution plan, the sum of the first two elements equals the third:

1. More than $10 million is distributed to schools based on the number of sports they sponsor.

2. More than $20 million is distributed to schools based on the number of athletic scholarships they award.

3. More than $30 million is distributed to conferences based on their members' performance in the immediate past six years of the playoffs.

Although reaching the Final Four isn't worth as much monetarily now as it had been, the impact of winning to produce more revenue still exists. Here is the cumulative payout in five-year increments from 1970 through 1990 to each Final Four school before the revenue-sharing plan was introduced:

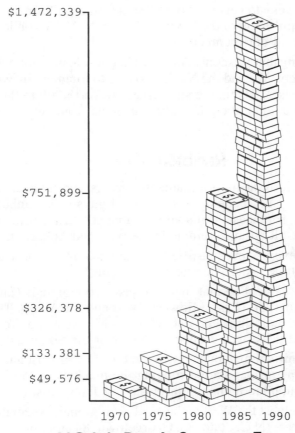

$1,472,339—

$751,899—

$326,378—

$133,381—

$49,576—

1970 1975 1980 1985 1990

NCAA DIDN'T START THE FIRE

The NCAA's crown jewel, the Division I Men's Basketball Tournament, wasn't the NCAA's idea. It was literally dumped into the governing body's lap by the National Association of Basketball Coaches.

A collection of New York sportswriters staged the first major college tournament, the National Invitation Tournament in 1938 in New York. But a group of NABC members, especially coaches from the Midwest, felt if there was to be national tourney, it should be sponsored by a collegiate organization and not scribes, particularly those with a "biased" Eastern influence.

Harold Olsen, a former Wisconsin player and coach at Ohio State, is given much of the credit for bringing the NCAA Tournament to the American sports scene. The first NCAA Tournament was conducted in 1939, sponsored not by the NCAA but by the NABC. Oddly, Olsen's Ohio State team reached the final of the eight-team event (one from each district) before losing to Oregon, 46-33.

Total attendance for the inaugural NCAA playoff was a paltry 15,025, and the venture produced $2,531 worth of red ink. Because the NABC was out of funds, it asked the NCAA to assume responsibility.

"We were darn lucky to get out of debt," said former Wisconsin coach Harold (Bud) Foster, a past president of the NABC. "When the NCAA bailed us out, they provided tickets for all our members.

"It was interesting that Wisconsin played a major role in pulling the basketball tournament out of debt. We had the NCAA boxing tournament in Madison in '39 and drew packed houses. The university turned over $18,000 to the NCAA, and that was the biggest amount the NCAA had received from any source up to that time."

REGIONAL VIEW

Sometimes you look at the tournament pairings and wonder if the NCAA Selection Committee isn't made up of a bunch of guys who flunked geography. East, west, midwest, southeast — it's all the same at tourney time, when UCLA might play in the East Regional, Temple in the West and Auburn in the Midwest.

I just don't believe it's ever justified to move teams around like that. What about missed class time? And what about their fans?

The NCAA Tournament format included just two regionals (East and West) until going to four in 1956 (East, Midwest, West and Far West). The next year, the four regionals were designated East, Mideast, Midwest and West and stayed that way until the Mideast was dropped in favor of the Southeast in 1985.

The national semifinal matchups pitted the East vs. Mideast and Midwest vs. West until the playoff format started rotating the brackets in 1973. Each of the four regionals has supplied a champion in the last five years.

Recent trends suggest the West is the weakest regional, especially after three champions in four years (N.C. State '83, Georgetown '84 and Louisville '86) were teams from other parts of the country funneled through the West Regional to balance the bracket.

Whether the "West is Worst" theory is accurate or not, you can't dispute the "East is Least" axiom. No Eastern school has won its natural regional and the national title in the same season since the event went to four regionals. The five national champions to come out of the East Regional since the start of the four-regional format were all ACC members (North Carolina '57, N.C. State '74, North Carolina '82, Duke '92 and North Carolina '93). Here is how the regional winners fared against each other in Final Four games since 1957 (national third-place games through 1981 are included):

	FINAL FOUR WON-LOSS MARKS		----NATIONAL TITLES----	
REGIONAL	SINCE 1957	SINCE 1973	SINCE '57	SINCE '73
West	43-26 (.623)	22-15 (.595)	15	5
Mideast/Southeast	36-31 (.537)	19-16 (.543)	9	7
Midwest	29-38 (.433)	16-19 (.457)	8	5
East	28-41 (.406)	15-22 (.405)	5	4

Standing Out Among Standouts

The only honors team I should be on is the All-Lobby team. During the Final Four, you'll find me in the hotel lobbies doing what I do best: talking! I love the whole scene, with all the fans and coaches and excitement.

As far as the real award winners, Michigan forward Chris Webber last year became the fourth player to be named All-Tournament in back-to-back seasons without winning a national championship. The first three players to fall into this undesirable category were Iowa forward Carl Cain (1955 and 1956), Cincinnati forward Oscar Robertson (1959 and 1960) and Houston center Hakeem Olajuwon (1983 and 1984).

UNLV guard Freddie Banks, Houston forward Elvin Hayes and Penn forward Tony Price probably wondered what they had to do to earn a spot on an All-Tournament team. Banks scored more points than any player in a Final Four game without being selected to the All-Tournament team (38 in a 97-93 defeat in the 1987 national semifinals against eventual champion Indiana). Hayes led the 1968 tournament in scoring (167 points) and rebounding (97 rebounds) by wide margins for the fourth-place Cougars. Excluding Hayes, Price is the highest scorer in a tourney for a Final Four team to fail to be named All-Tournament. He led the 1979 playoffs with 142 points for the fourth-place Quakers.

The last time a champion had just one representative on the All-Tournament team was 1973, when center Bill Walton was the only player representing UCLA. Two other title teams previously had just one representative — Texas-El Paso guard Bobby Joe Hill in 1966 and Loyola of Chicago center Les Hunter in 1963. These three national runners-up earned three spots on an All-Tournament team:

- Cincinnati '63 — Ron Bonham (36 points in two Final Four games on 14 of 15 free throw shooting), Tom Thacker (27 points and 26 rebounds) and George Wilson (34 points and 26 rebounds).

- Houston '84 — Alvin Franklin (game-high 21 points in final), Olajuwon (10 of 14 field goal shooting and 20 rebounds in two Final Four games) and Michael Young (35 points and 12 rebounds in two Final Four games).

- Duke '86 — Mark Alarie (24 points and 14 rebounds in two Final Four games), Tommy Amaker (13 assists and 10 steals) and Johnny Dawkins (48 points).

Vital(e) Statistics

Here's a look at some of the individual record holders in NCAA Tournament competition:

- The most blocked shots in a playoff game were 10 by Brigham Young freshman **Shawn Bradley** in 1991 against Virginia (West Regional first round) until LSU's **Shaquille O'Neal** rejected 11 shots the next year against Bradley's team (West Regional first round) when the Cougars were without Bradley, a 7-7 center on a Mormon mission.

Here's two of the most dominating players in NCAA Tournament history. LSU's Shaquille O'Neal holds the record for blocked shots in a game with 11, while Houston's Elvin Hayes owns the record for most rebounds in a playoff series. Neither played for a championship team, however.

Notre Dame guard **Austin Carr**, who scored a playoff record 61 points in 1970 against Ohio University (Southeast Regional first round), accounted for half of the eight games in NCAA Tournament history of more than 46 points. His 52-point outburst against Kentucky in 1970 when the Wildcats' **Dan Issel** tallied 44 points (Southeast Regional semifinals) represents the most points in one playoff game by two opposing players. After scoring just six points in his first tournament game (against Miami of Ohio) as a sophomore, Carr averaged 47.2 points in his last six playoff games to finish with a record 41.3-point average. The Fighting Irish won just two of the seven games, however.

The most three-point field goals in a playoff game were 11 by Loyola Marymount guard **Jeff Fryer** in his senior season in 1990 against Michigan (West Regional second round). Fryer also has the most playoff three-pointers in a career with 38. He averaged almost 14 three-point attempts per game as the Lions won four of seven playoff contests. Photo page

The most rebounds in a playoff game were 34 by Temple's **Fred Cohen** in a 65-59 victory over Connecticut (1956 East Regional semifinals). Cohen had just five rebounds in the Owls' next game, a 60-58 win over Canisius.

The most assists in a playoff game were 18 by UNLV playmaker **Mark Wade** in 1987 in a 97-93 loss against Indiana (national semifinals). Wade also established the record for most assists in a single playoff series that season with 61 in five games. He had at least nine assists in each of the five contests while scoring a total of just 13 points.

Michigan forward **Glen Rice** holds the records for most three-point baskets and points in a playoff series (27 treys and 184 points in six games in 1989). The senior forward hit 12 of 17 three-pointers on his way to a total of 66 points in Southeast Regional semifinal and final victories over North Carolina (92-87) and Virginia (102-65). Rice's liberal use of the three-pointer enabled him to become the only player from a national champion to average more than 25 points per game (25.6) since **David Thompson** finished with a 26-point average for North Carolina State in 1974.

Houston's **Elvin Hayes** holds the records for most rebounds in a playoff series (97 in five games as a senior in 1968) and career (222 in 13 games). He had five games with at least 24 rebounds, including the first three playoff games in 1968, before being held to five in a 101-69 national semifinal loss against UCLA. Hayes also holds the record for most playoff field goals in a career with 152. He averaged almost 24 field goal attempts per game in helping the Cougars win nine of 13 contests.

Navy's **David Robinson** holds the record for most blocked shots in a playoff series (23 in four games in 1986) and Georgetown's **Alonzo Mourning** holds the mark for most rejections in a playoff career (37 from 1989 through 1992).

Princeton's **Bill Bradley**, a U.S. Senator (D-N.J.), holds the career playoff record for highest free throw percentage (minimum of 50 attempts). He was 89 of 96 from the foul line (90.6 percent) from 1963 through 1965. In five of his nine playoff games, Bradley made at least 10 free throws while missing no more than one attempt from the charity stripe. He made 16 of 16 free throws against St. Joseph's in the first round of the 1963 East Regional and 13 of 13 foul shots against Providence in the 1965 East Regional final to become the only player to twice convert more than 12 free throws without a miss in a playoff game. Bradley also holds the record for most points in a single Final Four game (58 against Wichita State in 1965 national third-place game). The Rhodes Scholar scored 39 points in the second half of the consolation game.

Oklahoma's **Mookie Blaylock** holds the record for most steals in a playoff series (23 in six games in 1988). He had seven steals as a junior guard in an 83-79 championship game loss against Kansas.

Christian Laettner's high game for Duke en route to a playoff career record 407 points was 31 against Kentucky in a 104-103 victory in the 1992 East Regional final. Laettner capped a flawless offensive performance, hitting all 10 of his field goal attempts and all 10 of his free throws against the Wildcats, by scoring Duke's last eight points in overtime, including a stunning 18-foot turnaround jumper at the buzzer after catching a pass from the baseline on the opposite end of the court.

THE NAME GAME

Who says you need two good eyes to be a great shooter? You can watch me stroke the J before games. I'm almost automatic shooting the rock, especially when no one is guarding me.

That leads me to a new hero of mine — Marvin (Bucky) Bolyard. Who is Bucky? He was a teammate of Jerry West and Ronnie Retton, Mary Lou's father, on West Virginia's 1959 Final Four team. Bucky, a guard, was the third-leading scorer for the Mountaineers although he was blind in his left eye from a childhood accident. I really admire what Bucky was able to achieve because I have impaired vision from a childhood accident, too.

I also enjoy players with nifty nicknames, like the ones belonging to these players and coaches from past Final Fours:

Forrest C. (Phog) Allen, coach/Kansas '40, '52 and '53
Forrest (Forddy) Anderson, coach/Bradley '50, '54, and Mich. St. '57
Paul (Curly) Armstrong, forward/Indiana '40
Justin (Sam) Barry, coach/Southern California '40
Richard (Scooter) Barry, guard/Kansas '88
Daron (Mookie) Blaylock, guard/Oklahoma '88
Ulysses (Junior) Bridgeman, guard-forward/Louisville '75

"Butch" Lee

"Slick" Leonard

"Doggie" Julian

"Bones" McKinney

Forrest (Frosty) Cox, coach/Colorado '42

Charles (Chick) Davies, coach/Duquesne '40

William (Tippy) Dye, coach/Washington '53

Dwight (Dike) Eddleman, forward/Illinois '49

Maurice (Bo) Ellis, forward/Marquette '77

Eric (Sleepy) Floyd, guard/Georgetown '82

Harold (Bud) Foster, coach/Wisconsin '41

Amory (Slats) Gill, coach/Oregon State '49 and '63

H.C. (Bully) Gilstrap, coach/Texas '43

Jack (Goose) Givens, forward/Kentucky '78

E.O. (Doc) Hayes, coach/SMU '56

George (Jud) Heathcote, coach/Michigan State '79

Bernard (Peck) Hickman, coach/Louisville '59

Earvin (Magic) Johnson, guard/Michigan State '79

Wallace (Wah Wah) Jones, forward/Kentucky '48 and '49

Alvin (Doggie) Julian, coach/Holy Cross '47 and '48

Bill (Pickles) Kennedy, guard/Temple '58

David (Big Daddy) Lattin, center/Texas-El Paso '66

Alfred (Butch) Lee, guard/Marquette '77

Horace B. (Bebe) Lee, coach/Colorado '55

Bob (Slick) Leonard, guard/Indiana '53

Durand (Rudy) Macklin, forward/LSU '81

Slater (Dugie) Martin, guard/Texas '47

Cedric (Cornbread) Maxwell, forward/UNC Charlotte '77

Carlton (Scooter) McCray, forward/Louisville '82 and '83

Billy (The Hill) McGill, center/Utah '61

Horace (Bones) McKinney, coach/Wake Forest '62

Frank (Bucky) O'Connor, coach/Iowa '55 and '56

Robert Luther (Lute) Olson, coach/Iowa '80 and Arizona '88

V.C. (Buck) Overall, forward/Texas '43

Richard (Digger) Phelps, coach/Notre Dame '78

C.M. (Nibs) Price, coach/California '46

Tom (Satch) Sanders, center/New York University '60

Nevil (The Shadow) Shed, forward-center/Texas-El Paso '66

Willem (Butch) van Breda Kolff, coach/Princeton '65

Ernest (Kiki) Vandeweghe, forward/UCLA '80

Keith (Silk) Wilkes, forward/UCLA '72, '73 and '74

Donald (Duck) Williams, guard/Notre Dame '78

Urgel (Slim) Wintermute, center/Oregon '39

Bob (Zeke) Zawoluk, center/St. John's '52

1994 NCAA Tournament Schedule

First and Second Rounds

East: Nassau Veterans Memorial Coliseum (phone number at host institution for tickets is 516/794-9300), Uniondale, NY (March 17 and 19, 1994). Capital Centre (301/350-1500), Landover, MD (March 18 and 20, 1994).

Southeast: Rupp Arena (606/257-1818), Lexington, KY (March 17 and 19, 1994). Florida Suncoast Dome (813/825-3334), St. Petersburgh, FL (March 18 and 20, 1994).

Midwest: Kansas Coliseum (316/689-3267), Wichita, KS (March 17 and 19, 1994). The Myriad (405/236-5000), Oklahoma City (March 18 and 20, 1994).

West: Dee Events Center (801/626-6222), Ogden, UT (March 17 and 19, 1994). Arco Arena (209/946-2474), Sacramento, CA (March 18 and 20, 1994).

Regionals

East: Miami Arena (800/462-2637), Miami (March 25 and 27, 1994).

Southeast: Thompson-Boling Arena (615/974-2491), Knoxville, TN (March 25 and 26, 1994).

Midwest: Reunion Arena (214/637-4667), Dallas (March 25 and 27, 1994).

West: Los Angeles Sports Arena (213/740-4672), Los Angeles (March 24 and 26, 1994).

Final Four

Charlotte Coliseum, Charlotte, NC (April 2 and 4, 1994).

1995 NCAA Tournament Schedule

First and Second Rounds

East: Knickerbocker Arena, Albany, NY. Baltimore Arena, Baltimore.

Southeast: The Pyramid, Memphis, TN. Tallahasee-Leon County Civic Center, Tallahassee, FL.

Midwest: Frank Erwin Special Events Center, Austin, TX . Dayton Arena, Dayton, OH.

West: Boise State University Pavilion, Boise, ID. Jon M. Huntsman Center, Salt Lake City.

Regionals

East: Meadowlands Arena, East Rutherford, NJ.

Southeast: Birmingham-Jefferson Civic Center, Birmingham, AL.

Midwest: Kemper Arena, Kansas City.

West: Oakland-Alameda County Coliseum, Oakland, CA.

Final Four

Kingdome, Seattle, WA (April 1 and 3, 1995).

NCAA TOURNAMENT FINAL FOUR RESULTS

YEAR	CHAMPION (COACH)	SCORE	RUNNER-UP
1939	Oregon (Howard Hobson)	46-33	Ohio State
1940	Indiana (Branch McCracken)	60-42	Kansas
1941	Wisconsin (Bud Foster)	39-34	Washington State
1942	Stanford (Everett Dean)	53-38	Dartmouth
1943	Wyoming (Everett Shelton)	46-34	Georgetown
1944	Utah (Vadal Peterson)	42-40 (OT)	Dartmouth
1945	Oklahoma State (Henry Iba)	49-45	New York University
1946	Oklahoma State (Henry Iba)	43-40	North Carolina
1947	Holy Cross (Doggie Julian)	58-47	Oklahoma
1948	Kentucky (Adolph Rupp)	58-42	Baylor
1949	Kentucky (Adolph Rupp)	46-36	Oklahoma State
1950	CCNY (Nat Holman)	71-68	Bradley
1951	Kentucky (Adolph Rupp)	68-58	Kansas State
1952	Kansas (Phog Allen)	80-63	St. John's
1953	Indiana (Branch McCracken)	69-68	Kansas
1954	La Salle (Ken Loeffler)	92-76	Bradley
1955	San Francisco (Phil Woolpert)	77-63	La Salle
1956	San Francisco (Phil Woolpert)	83-71	Iowa
1957	North Carolina (Frank McGuire)	54-53 (3OT)	Kansas
1958	Kentucky (Adolph Rupp)	84-72	Seattle
1959	California (Pete Newell)	71-70	West Virginia
1960	Ohio State (Fred Taylor)	75-55	California
1961	Cincinnati (Ed Jucker)	70-65 (OT)	Ohio State
1962	Cincinnati (Ed Jucker)	71-59	Ohio State
1963	Loyola, Ill. (George Ireland)	60-58 (OT)	Cincinnati
1964	UCLA (John Wooden)	98-83	Duke
1965	UCLA (John Wooden)	91-80	Michigan
1966	Texas Western (Don Haskins)	72-65	Kentucky
1967	UCLA (John Wooden)	79-64	Dayton
1968	UCLA (John Wooden)	78-55	North Carolina
1969	UCLA (John Wooden)	92-72	Purdue
1970	UCLA (John Wooden)	80-69	Jacksonville
1971	UCLA (John Wooden)	68-62	Villanova
1972	UCLA (John Wooden)	81-76	Florida State
1973	UCLA (John Wooden)	87-66	Memphis State
1974	N.C. State (Norman Sloan)	76-64	Marquette
1975	UCLA (John Wooden)	92-85	Kentucky
1976	Indiana (Bob Knight)	86-68	Michigan
1977	Marquette (Al McGuire)	67-59	North Carolina
1978	Kentucky (Joe B. Hall)	94-88	Duke
1979	Michigan State (Jud Heathcote)	75-64	Indiana State
1980	Louisville (Denny Crum)	59-54	UCLA
1981	Indiana (Bob Knight)	63-50	North Carolina
1982	North Carolina (Dean Smith)	63-62	Georgetown
1983	N.C. State (Jim Valvano)	54-52	Houston
1984	Georgetown (John Thompson)	84-75	Houston
1985	Villanova (Rollie Massimino)	66-64	Georgetown
1986	Louisville (Denny Crum)	72-69	Duke
1987	Indiana (Bob Knight)	74-73	Syracuse
1988	Kansas (Larry Brown)	83-79	Oklahoma
1989	Michigan (Steve Fisher)	80-79 (OT)	Seton Hall
1990	UNLV (Jerry Tarkanian)	103-73	Duke
1991	Duke (Mike Krzyzewski)	72-65	Kansas
1992	Duke (Mike Krzyzewski)	71-51	Michigan
1993	North Carolina (Dean Smith)	77-71	Michigan

THIRD PLACE	FOURTH PLACE	MOST OUTSTANDING PLAYER	SITE OF FINALS
*Oklahoma	*Villanova	None selected	Evanston, IL
*Duquesne	*Southern	Cal Marvin Huffman, Indiana	Kansas City
*Pittsburgh	*Arkansas	John Kotz, Wisconsin	Kansas City
*Colorado	*Kentucky	Howie Dallmar, Stanford	Kansas City
*Texas	*DePaul	Ken Sailors, Wyoming	New York City
*Iowa State	*Ohio State	Arnie Ferrin, Utah	New York City
*Arkansas	*Ohio State	Bob Kurland, Okla. State	New York City
Ohio State	California	Bob Kurland, Okla. State	New York City
Texas	CCNY	George Kaftan, Holy Cross	New York City
Holy Cross	Kansas State	Alex Groza, Kentucky	New York City
Illinois	Oregon State	Alex Groza, Kentucky	Seattle
N.C. State	Baylor Irwin	Dambrot, CCNY	New York City
Illinois	Okla. State	None selected	Minneapolis
Illinois	Santa Clara	Clyde Lovellette, Kansas	Seattle
Washington	Louisiana St.	B.H. Born, Kansas	Kansas City
Penn State	Southern Cal	Tom Gola, La Salle	Kansas City
Colorado	Iowa	Bill Russell, San Francisco	Kansas City
Temple	SMU	Hal Lear, Temple	Evanston, IL
San Francisco	Michigan State	Wilt Chamberlain, Kansas	Kansas City
Temple	Kansas State	Elgin Baylor, Seattle	Louisville, KY
Cincinnati	Louisville	Jerry West, West Virginia	Louisville, KY
Cincinnati	New York Univ.	Jerry Lucas, Ohio State	San Francisco
St. Joseph's	Utah	Jerry Lucas, Ohio State	Kansas City
Wake Forest	UCLA	Paul Hogue, Cincinnati	Louisville, KY
Duke	Oregon State	Art Heyman, Duke	Louisville, KY
Michigan	Kansas State	Walt Hazzard, UCLA	Kansas City
Princeton	Wichita State	Bill Bradley, Princeton	Portland, OR
Duke	Utah	Jerry Chambers, Utah	College Park, MD
Houston	North Carolina	Lew Alcindor, UCLA	Louisville, KY
Ohio State	Houston	Lew Alcindor, UCLA	Los Angeles
Drake	North Carolina	Lew Alcindor, UCLA	Louisville, KY
New Mexico St.	St. Bonaventure	Sidney Wicks, UCLA	College Park, MD
Western Ky.	Kansas	Howard Porter, Villanova	Houston
North Carolina	Louisville	Bill Walton, UCLA Los	Angeles
Indiana	Providence	Bill Walton, UCLA	St. Louis
UCLA	Kansas	David Thompson, N.C. State	Greensboro, NC
Louisville	Syracuse	Richard Washington, UCLA	San Diego
UCLA	Rutgers	Kent Benson, Indiana	Philadelphia
UNLV	UNC Charlotte	Butch Lee, Marquette	Atlanta
Arkansas	Notre Dame	Jack Givens, Kentucky	St. Louis
DePaul	Penn	Magic Johnson, Michigan St.	Salt Lake City
Purdue	Iowa	Darrell Griffith, Louisville	Indianapolis
Virginia	Louisiana St.	Isiah Thomas, Indiana	Philadelphia
*Houston	*Louisville	James Worthy, N. Carolina	New Orleans
*Louisville	*Georgia	Hakeem Olajuwon, Houston	Albuquerque, NM
*Kentucky	*Virginia	Patrick Ewing, Georgetown	Seattle
*St. John's	*Memphis State	Ed Pinckney, Villanova	Lexington, KY
*Kansas	*Louisiana St.	Pervis Ellison, Louisville	Dallas
*Providence	*UNLV	Keith Smart, Indiana	New Orleans
*Arizona	*Duke	Danny Manning, Kansas	Kansas City
*Duke	*Illinois	Glen Rice, Michigan	Seattle
*Arkansas	*Georgia Tech	Anderson Hunt, UNLV	Denver
*N. Carolina	*UNLV	Christian Laettner, Duke	Indianapolis
*Cincinnati	*Indiana	Bobby Hurley, Duke	Minneapolis
*Kansas	*Kentucky	Donald Williams, N. Carolina	New Orleans

*Tied for third position because there was no consolation game.

Dick's Top 5

PREMIER PLAYOFF PERFORMERS

1. **Lew Alcindor, UCLA** — Averaged 25.7 points and 18.8 rebounds in Final Four games from 1967 through 1969. Undefeated in 12 tourney games as he became the only individual selected the Final Four's Most Outstanding Player three times.

2. **Bill Russell, San Francisco** — Rebounding machine led the Dons to 9-0 tourney record and back-to-back championships in 1955 and 1956. Retrieved 50 missed shots in two Final Four games in 1956, including 27 against Iowa in championship game.

3. **Bill Walton, UCLA** — Scintillating championship-game performance against Memphis in 1973 when he hit 21 of 22 field-goal attempts. The Bruins compiled 11-1 record when he manned the middle.

4. **Jerry West, West Virginia** — Modest 6-3 tourney record wasn't his fault as he became the only player to score at least 25 points in eight consecutive tournament games.

5. **Christian Laettner, Duke** — The tourney's all-time leading scorer hit incredible game-winning baskets against Connecticut and Kentucky in two East Regional finals.

UNBELIEVABLE PTPers

You don't need me to tell you — but I'll do it anyway — that the NCAA championship game is the best thing going in sports. Why? Because it rarely lets you down. This is one big event that lives up to the hype, year after year.

More than one-fourth of the NCAA Tournament's games have been decided in overtime or in regulation by less than three points since the field expanded to 32 teams in 1975. Four riveting national finals in eight years from 1982 through 1989 featured clutch players producing in last-second situations.

The heroics down the stretch with a title in the balance usually don't come from the most likely source, however. A look at the waning moments of the nine championship games decided by a buzzer-beater field goal or tension-packed free throw shows the player supplying the decisive shot was neither a senior nor the championship team's primary scorer for the season or in the final game:

1989: Michigan 80, Seton Hall 79 (OT) — Junior guard Rumeal Robinson, a 65.6 percent free-throw shooter on the season, canned two free throws with three seconds remaining in overtime after a questionable foul call. Robinson had 21 points in the title game to finish the season with a scoring average of 14.9 points per game. Forward Glen Rice was the Wolverines' leading scorer in the final (31 points) and for the season (25.6 ppg).

1987: Indiana 74, Syracuse 73 — Junior college recruit Keith Smart, Indiana's fifth-leading scorer, tallied 12 of the Hoosiers' last 15 points, including a 15-foot jumper from the left baseline with five seconds remaining. Smart scored 21 points in the title game to finish the season with a scoring average of 11.2 points per game. Fellow guard Steve Alford was Indiana's leading scorer in the final (23 points) and for the season (22 ppg).

1983: North Carolina State 54, Houston 52 — Lorenzo Charles, a sophomore forward averaging a modest 8.1 points per game after scoring four points in the title game, converted guard Dereck Whittenburg's off-line desperation shot from well beyond the top of the free-throw circle into a decisive dunk. Forward Thurl Bailey was the Wolfpack's leading scorer in the final (15 points) and for the season (total of 601 for 16.7 ppg). Whittenburg, who missed 14 games after suffering a broken foot, led the team in scoring average (17.5 ppg).

1982: North Carolina 63, Georgetown 62 — Michael Jordan, a freshman guard who averaged 13.5 points per game, swished a 16-foot jumper from the left side with 16 seconds left for his 16th point to provide the game-winner. Georgetown guard Fred Brown's errant pass directly to Tar Heels forward James Worthy prevented the Hoyas from attempting a potential game-winning shot in the closing seconds. Worthy was Carolina's leading scorer in the final (28 points) and for the season (15.6 ppg).

1963: Loyola of Chicago 60, Cincinnati 58 (OT) — Junior forward Vic Rouse leaped high to redirect center Les Hunter's shot from the free throw line into the basket to climax Loyola's first tourney appearance. Rouse scored 15 points in the title game to finish the season with a scoring average of 13.5 points. Loyola is the only team to use just five players in the final. Hunter was Loyola's leading scorer in the final (16 points) and forward Jerry Harkness was the team's leading scorer for the season (21.4 ppg).

1959: California 71, West Virginia 70 — Two-time first-team All-America swingman Jerry West was denied an NCAA championship when Cal junior center Darrall Imhoff, West's teammate with the Los Angeles Lakers for four seasons in the mid-1960s, tipped in a basket with 17 seconds left. Imhoff scored 10 points in the title game to finish the season with a scoring average of 11.3 points. Guard Denny Fitzpatrick was the Bears' leading scorer in the final (20 points) and for the season (13.3 ppg).

1957: North Carolina 54, Kansas 53 (3 OTs) — Junior center Joe Quigg sank two free throws with six seconds left in the third overtime to tie the score and provide the decisive point. Quigg scored 10 points in the title game to finish the season with an average of 10.3 points per game. Forward Lennie Rosenbluth was the Tar Heels' leading scorer in the final (20 points) and for the season (28 ppg).

1953: Indiana 69, Kansas 68 — Junior guard Bob Leonard supplied the decisive point by hitting one of two free throws with 27 seconds remaining. Leonard scored 12 points in the title game to finish the season with a scoring average of 16.3 points per game. Center Don Schlundt was the Hoosiers' leading scorer in the final (30 points) and for the season (25.4 ppg).

1944: Utah 42, Dartmouth 40 (OT) — Freshman swingman Herb Wilkinson hit a desperation shot from beyond the top of the key with three seconds left. Wilkinson scored seven points in the title game to finish postseason competition with an average of nine points per game. Freshman forward Arnie Ferrin was the Utes' leading scorer in the final (22 points) and for postseason play (14 ppg).

VANISHING BREED

Wilt Chamberlain got all over my case when I said Kareem Abdul-Jabbar was the greatest center of all time because Kareem was multidimensional and excelled in every area for a center. Certainly, Bill Russell was the premier center on defense. But Wilt was the greatest athlete of them all. I mean, are you kidding me? No one of Chamberlain's size has ever had his combination of strength, quickness, versatility, grace and agility. He was one of a kind.

Two-sport stars in college are rare in this era of specialization, but they were the rule rather than the exception during Chamberlain's era in the 1950s and before. And many of them did more than just dabble at a second sport, as was the case with Larry Bird, who played for Indiana State's baseball team briefly his senior year. Long before multi-sport standouts Bo Jackson and Deion Sanders were hailed as jacks of all trades, there was three-sport whiz Dwight Eddleman, possibly the greatest all-around athlete to participate in the Final Four.

Eddleman was named the Big Ten's Most Valuable Player by the Chicago Tribune in 1949 when he was the leading scorer for Illinois' national third-place finisher in basketball. In football, he played both offense and defense, punted and returned kicks, and played in the 1947 Rose Bowl for a team that overwhelmed UCLA, 45-14. He returned punts 92 and 89 yards for touchdowns the next season as a junior. In his senior year, Eddleman ranked third in the nation with 42.9-yard punting average, including an 88-yarder. Eddleman, interrupting his collegiate career by joining the U.S. Army Air Corps during World War II, earned an amazing 11 varsity letters at Illinois. He won three Big Ten high jump titles. But his greatest

As a three-sport athletic star at Illinois, Dwight "Dike" Eddleman won 11 letters – enough to spell o-u-t-s-t-a-n-d-i-n-g.

athletic achievement probably was winning a silver medal in the high jump in the 1948 Olympics in London. The Olympics climaxed a scintillating academic school year for Eddleman. He also won the NCAA high jump crown and led Illinois' football and basketball teams in scoring.

Eddleman averaged 12.1 points per game in four pro seasons and appeared in the first two NBA All-Star Games (1951 and 1952). He retired in November, 1992 after 23 years of directing fund-raising efforts for his alma mater's athletic department. As executive director of the Fighting Illini Scholarship Fund, Eddleman helped raise more than $30 million for Illinois athletic scholarships and programs in the last decade.

A two-sport "money" player capable of leading his team to the 1993 national semifinals was Florida State point guard Charlie Ward, the starting quarterback for the Seminoles' highly-ranked football team. But Florida State was defeated in the Southeast Regional final by Kentucky.

Jerry Adair (baseball) and Cornell Green (football) are classic examples of versatile athletes who played exceedingly well in the NCAA Tournament before distinguishing themselves at the professional level in other sports.

Adair, who set several major-league fielding records for a second baseman in his 13-year American League career, was the second-leading scorer for Oklahoma State's 1958 NCAA Tournament team that reached the Midwest Regional final. Green, a five-time Pro Bowl defensive back during his 13-year career with the Dallas Cowboys from 1962-73, was one of the leading scorers in the 1962 NCAA Tournament with a 24.3-point average in three games for Utah State. But the Aggies, despite Green's game-high 26 points, were eliminated, 73-62, in the West Regional semifinals by John Wooden's first Final Four team at UCLA. Green played in Super Bowls V and VI.

Ward will have another opportunity in 1994 to join Chamberlain and the following chronological list of key Final Four players who also showed their extraordinary physical abilities in other athletic endeavors:

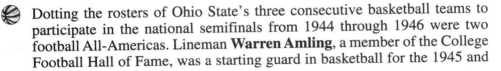

Howard (Red) Hickey, a first-team All-Southwest Conference forward for Arkansas' 1941 Final Four team, earned a spot on the Razorbacks' all-decade football team as a tackle. Hickey, a lineman for six seasons in the NFL with two different franchises from 1941 through 1948, was a member of the 1945 champion Cleveland Rams. He coached the San Francisco 49ers for five years from 1959 through 1963, compiling a 27-27-1 record.

Fred Sheffield, the starting center for Utah's 1944 champion, was the first athlete to place four consecutive years in the high jump at the NCAA nationals. He was first in 1943 with a best jump of 6-8, second in 1944, tied for first in 1945 and tied for second in 1946.

Dotting the rosters of Ohio State's three consecutive basketball teams to participate in the national semifinals from 1944 through 1946 were two football All-Americas. Lineman **Warren Amling**, a member of the College Football Hall of Fame, was a starting guard in basketball for the 1945 and

1946 squads. He is one of the few athletes to earn consensus football All-America honors at two positions (guard in 1945 and tackle in 1946). **Jack Dugger**, a starting forward in 1944 and 1945, was an end on the Buckeyes' 1944 undefeated Big Ten Conference football champion. Dugger played for three different pro football teams from 1946 through 1949.

Cecil Hankins, a forward who led Oklahoma A&M in scoring in the 1945 NCAA Tournament when the Aggies captured the national basketball title, was a two-way back and leading pass receiver for the school's football team that trounced TCU, 34-0, in the Cotton Bowl the same academic school year. He tied teammate and Final Four Most Outstanding Player Bob Kurland for most points in the national semifinals and final with 37. Hankins, who scored a touchdown in a 33-13 victory against St. Mary's (Calif.) in the 1946 Sugar Bowl, went on to play two seasons in the NBA with two different franchises.

Tom Hamilton, a forward on Texas' 1947 Final Four team that set a school record for most victories in a season with 26, was a star first baseman for the Longhorns' 1949 baseball squad that won the first of the school's four College World Series titles. Hamilton hit .474 that season to lead the Southwest Conference. He played briefly with the Philadelphia Athletics in 1952 and 1953.

Wallace Jones, a starting forward for Kentucky's back-to-back national champions in basketball (1948 and 1949), lettered as a two-way end on three college football teams coached by the legendary Bear Bryant and lettered three times for the Wildcats' baseball team. Jones averaged 10.2 points per game in three NBA seasons with the Indianapolis Olympians.

Charlie Hoag, a swingman who was one of seven Kansas players chosen for the 1952 U.S. Olympic basketball team that captured a gold medal in Helsinki after the Jayhawks won the NCAA title, earned three letters in football. He was a running back and captain of the '52 football squad.

Hal Patterson, a starting forward and second-leading rebounder for Kansas' 1953 national runner-up, was a two-year football letterman with the Jayhawks as an end and also lettered in baseball. Patterson played 14 seasons in the Canadian Football League, where he was an All-Star. He scored 54 touchdowns in the CFL and had 34 games with at least 100 yards in pass receptions. KU teammate **Gil Reich**, a starting guard who averaged eight points per game after transferring from Army, was a two-way back and kicking specialist for the Jayhawks' football squad. Reich, selected by the Green Bay Packers in the second round of the 1953 NFL draft after being named an All-America defensive back by the football writers, did not play in the NFL.

Penn State basketball center **Jesse Arnelle**, the leading scorer at the 1954 Final Four with a total of 43 points in two games, was a four-year football letterman and one of the finest ends ever to play for the Nittany Lions. The school's all-time leading scorer and rebounder in basketball also ranks 14th on the career receptions list in football. He played one season in the NBA with the Fort Wayne Pistons.

K.C. Jones, a defensive specialist who scored a game-high 24 points in the final for 1955 champion San Francisco, was selected as a receiver by the Los Angeles Rams in the 30th round of the 1955 NFL draft. Jones averaged 7.4 points and 4.3 assists per game in nine seasons with the Boston Celtics. The Hall of Famer was a member of the NBA champion his first eight years in the league.

Rick Herrscher, the top substitute for Southern Methodist's 1956 Final Four team, was a utilityman for the New York Mets in 1962.

Center **Wilt Chamberlain**, the leading scorer at the 1957 Final Four for national runner-up Kansas, was also a track athlete who participated in three events in college (high jump, triple jump and shot put). He was especially adept in the high jump, winning the 1957 Big Eight Conference outdoor title (6'5"), tying for first in the 1957 Drake Relays (6'6 1/2") and tying for first in the 1958 Big Eight indoor title with what was then a school record (6'6 3/4"). Chamberlain also played professional volleyball after spending 14 seasons in the NBA. **John Parker**, Kansas' starting point guard and co-captain of the '57 basketball team, was an accomplished javelin thrower for the Jayhawks' track squad. Chamberlain and Parker were track teammates of Al Oerter, a four-time Olympic gold-medal winner in the discus.

Bucky Bolyard and **Ronnie Retton**, guards for West Virginia's 1959 NCAA runner-up, were All-Southern Conference baseball selections. Bolyard, an outfielder-pitcher, was the third-leading scorer as a senior for the Mountaineers' Final Four team despite being blind in one eye from a childhood accident. Retton, a lefthanded hitting shortstop, batted over .270 in his first four of six seasons in the New York Yankees' farm system.

Carl Bouldin, a guard for Cincinnati's three Final Four teams from 1959-61 and the Bearcats' leading scorer in two Final Four games for their 1961 national champion, pitched four years in the major leagues with the Washington Senators from 1961 through 1964.

John Havlicek, a starting forward for Ohio State's three Final Four teams from 1960-'62, was selected as a wide receiver by the Cleveland Browns in the seventh round of the 1962 NFL draft. In the Browns' final cut before the start of the regular season, Havlicek was cut in favor of Gary Collins, a two-time All-Pro who caught a total of five touchdown passes in three NFL championship games (1964, 1965 and 1969). Hondo didn't play college football, but was a two-year letterman for the Buckeyes' baseball squad as a first baseman. He averaged 20.8 points, 6.3 rebounds and 4.8 assists per game in 16 seasons with the Boston Celtics. College teammate **Dick Furry**, a forward and first player off the bench for the 1960 national champion, was a three-year letterman as a high jumper for the school's track team.

Bill Hull and **Frank Christie**, forwards for the 1962 Wake Forest squad that finished third in the NCAA Tournament, excelled in other sports. Hull, the first athlete in ACC history to start in both football and basketball, was an All-ACC end who played one season with the Dallas Texans after being selected in the fifth round of the 1962 AFL draft. He finished among the Demon Deacons' all-time leading rebounders. Christie, who started in three consecutive ACC Tournament championship games, won seven of eight decisions as a pitcher for the school's baseball team during his junior and senior seasons.

The only football Heisman Trophy winner to play in the basketball Final Four was **Terry Baker** of Oregon State. Baker was a quarterback who won the Outstanding Player Award in the 1962 Liberty Bowl when he led the Beavers' football squad to a 6-0 victory over Villanova with a school record 99-yard run from scrimmage. He was also the basketball team's No. 2 point producer the same academic school year (13.4-point average), but was held scoreless in an 80-46 loss against eventual champion Cincinnati in the 1963 national semifinals. Baker was a quarterback/halfback with the Los Angeles Rams from 1963 through 1965. Teammate **Steve Pauly**, the second-leading rebounder and third-leading scorer for Oregon State's Final Four team, was the AAU national champion in the decathlon in 1963 after finishing third in the event the previous year.

Keith Erickson, who led 1964 champion UCLA in rebounding and scored a team-high 28 points in a 90-84 national semifinal victory over Kansas State, was a member of the U.S. Olympic volleyball team that finished ninth in a field of 10 squads in Tokyo that year. Erickson also was a starting shortstop for the school's baseball team as a sophomore. He averaged 9.5 points per game in 12 seasons in the NBA after helping the Bruins repeat as basketball champion in 1965. UCLA teammate **Fred Slaughter**, the starting center for the '64 squad as a senior, participated on the school's freshman track team as a sprinter, high jumper, discus thrower and shot putter.

Pat Riley, who led Kentucky's 1966 national runner-up in scoring (22 ppg) and rebounding (8.9 rpg), was selected as a flanker by the Dallas Cowboys in the 11th round of the 1967 NFL draft. He averaged 7.4 points per game in nine seasons with three NBA teams.

Dave Lattin, the second-leading scorer and rebounder for Texas Western's 1966 national champion, was selected as a flanker by the Kansas City Chiefs in the 17th round of the 1967 NFL draft. He averaged 7 points and 4.9 rebounds per game in five seasons in the NBA and ABA.

Ken Spain, a member of the 1968 U.S. Olympic team in Mexico City after starting at center for Houston's squad that was undefeated entering the Final Four earlier in the year, was selected as an end by the Detroit Lions in the 16th round of the 1969 NFL draft. Spain also had tryouts with the Houston

Opponents often were up in arms over the play of Oregon State's Terry Baker, who led the school's basketball team to the Final Four in 1963 after winning the Heisman Trophy for his quarterbacking prowess.

Oilers, Kansas City Chiefs and Oakland Raiders. He played briefly in the ABA with Pittsburgh in the 1970-71 season.

Drake center **Rick Wanamaker**, who blocked one of UCLA star Lew Alcindor's shots in the Bulldogs' 85-82 loss in the 1969 national semifinals, won the decathlon title in the 1970 NCAA meet, 1971 Pan American Games and 1971 National AAU meet. He finished fourth in the National AAU event in 1972 and fifth in 1974.

Dave Robisch, the leading scorer for Kansas' 1971 Final Four team, was a two-year letterman for the Jayhawks' baseball squad as a pitcher. Robisch, 6-10, was named to the All-Big Eight Conference baseball team as a sophomore. He played 13 years in the ABA and NBA with a total of eight different franchises.

Bobby Jones, the field-goal shooting (66.8 percent) leader for North Carolina's 1972 national third-place team, competed as a high jumper the same academic school year as a sophomore but did not earn a letter. Jones averaged 12.1 points and 6.1 rebounds per game in 12 seasons with the Denver Nuggets and Philadelphia 76ers.

Tim Stoddard, a starting forward for North Carolina State's 1974 national champion, pitched in the 1979 World Series for the Baltimore Orioles, one of six major league teams he played for from 1975 through 1989. Wolfpack teammate **David Thompson** participated with the track team, setting a school record in the triple jump at 49 feet, 11 inches (subsequently broken) in his first meet as a freshman. The jump qualified him for the NCAA championship meet, but he dropped off the team shortly thereafter.

Quinn Buckner, the senior playmaker and defensive stalwart for Indiana's undefeated 1976 champion, was a starting safety as a freshman for the Hoosiers' football squad, leading it in interceptions and fumble recoveries. Buckner was selected by the Washington Redskins in the 14th round of the 1976 NFL draft. He averaged 8.2 points and 4.3 assists per game in 10 seasons with three NBA teams.

Wayman Britt, a starting forward for Michigan's 1976 national runner-up, was selected as a defensive back-wide receiver by the Washington Redskins in the 13th round of the 1976 NFL draft. He played briefly with the Detroit Pistons in the 1977-78 season.

Roosevelt Barnes, a backup guard for Purdue's 1980 national third-place basketball team, also played college baseball and football. He was a linebacker who played four seasons in the NFL with the Detroit Lions after being their 10th-round draft choice in 1982.

Joe Hillman, the top guard off the bench for Indiana's 1987 champion, was an infielder-outfielder for the Hoosiers' baseball team and played two summers in the Oakland A's farm system. He hit .310 with Southern Oregon in the Northwest League in 1988.

Quinn Buckner, who took over as coach of the NBA's Dallas Mavericks this season, was a two-sport star at Indiana for two years. He started at safety on the football team as a freshman and sophomore, but gave up the gridiron for basketball. He helped lead the Hoosiers to the national championship in 1976.

Kenny Lofton, a substitute guard and integral part of Arizona's 1988 Final Four team, is a starting outfielder for the Cleveland Indians and was a leading candidate for Rookie of the Year in the American League in 1992. Lofton led the majors with 70 stolen bases last summer as an outfielder for the Cleveland Indians. In 1992, he led the American League with 66 stolen bases, a record for an AL rookie. He began his major league career with the Houston Astros. Arizona teammate **Jud Buechler**, a backup forward for the '88 Wildcats as a sophomore, played professional four-man volleyball in the summer with U.S. Olympians Bob Samuelson and Jeff Stork during his four-year career with several NBA teams.

Strings Attached?

I had a 6-10 phenom on my high school team by the name of Les Cason. There's no question Cason opened up some doors for me to big-name coaches, including a hot property by the name of Jerry Tarkanian. After Cason announced at a press conference that he was going to sign with Long Beach State, rumors circulated about me going along with him in a package deal to be Tarkanian's assistant. Actually, I left East Rutherford High after we won two state championships, with Les as our star, for Rutgers as an assistant coach, and then went to the University of Detroit as head coach. Cason ultimately enrolled at Rutgers and played for Tom Young after I left my assistant's job there. He had attended San Jacinto (Tex.) Junior College because academic shortcomings prevented him from going straight to Long Beach out of high school.

But let's face it. The lifeblood of any college program is recruiting. Occasionally, a creative coach has to do what it takes to get what he wants. Michigan coach Steve Fisher hired longtime Detroit area high school coach Perry Watson as an assistant and Watson's high school sensation, Jalen Rose, tagged along with him to Ann Arbor. Rose promptly became the leading scorer for the Wolverines' freshman-dominated Fab Five team finishing as runner-up to Duke in the 1992 NCAA Tournament. He joined Kenny Anderson (Georgia Tech '90) and Mark Aguirre (DePaul '79) as the only freshmen to score more than 100 points in a single tournament and his 17.6-point season scoring average is the highest ever compiled by a freshman for a team reaching the national championship game.

Rose averaged 15.4 points and 3.9 assists per game as a sophomore last season when Michigan lost in the national final again. After teammate Chris Webber left college early for the NBA, Rose probably will need to succeed him as a consensus All-America to prevent the Wolverines from withering. "Jalen is fearless and he expects to win," Fisher said. "It's not false bravado. He means what he says."

Watson, appointed head coach at Detroit Mercy last summer, shook off censuring from observers subscribing to the notion he got the assistant's job at Michigan only because he persuaded Rose to stay with him. "Sometimes it (the criticism) was hard, but other times I used to laugh," Watson said. "When a team is as successful as we were, people are going to take potshots at you."

The Watson/Rose connection raised questions in regard to the ethics of hiring the coach of a high school phenom, but it has been a relatively common practice.

Experts on the subject include Dave Gavitt, who had two first-team All-Americas on his Providence team that reached the 1973 Final Four, and (Daddy) Dale Brown, who recruited a total of three eligible exceptional players in this category when he coached LSU to the national semifinals in 1981 and 1986.

Thirteen Final Four teams since 1973 have featured standouts whose high school coach joined the star player as a college assistant. The only one of the 13 squads on this list to win the title was Louisville. All-America Darrell Griffith led the "Doctors of Dunk" after leaving high school along with Cardinals assistant coach Wade Houston. Said Houston: "My relationship with the school was a lot deeper than just going with Darrell. I was among the first group of minority players to play there (1963-64 season with Eddie Whitehead and Sam Smith)."

Here is a chronological list of the 13 Final Four teams that included a player/coach combination:

FINAL FOUR TEAM	STAR PLAYER	ASSISTANT COACH	HEAD COACH
Providence '73	Marvin Barnes	Jimmy Adams	Dave Gavitt

Comment: Adams joined Gavitt's staff two years after Barnes enrolled in 1970. Barnes, a first-team consensus All-America as a senior when he led the nation in rebounding, is the Friars' all-time leading rebounder and is second in scoring. Providence hung tough against Memphis State in the national semifinals after Barnes suffered a dislocated right kneecap midway through the first half, but the Tigers pulled away in the last couple of minutes to win 98-85. Barnes, the second pick overall in the 1974 NBA draft, played four seasons in the NBA with four different teams (9.2 points and 5.5 rebounds per game) after spending two years in the ABA with the Spirits of St. Louis (24.1 ppg and 13.4 rpg).

Providence '73	Ernie DiGregorio	Nick Macarchuk	Dave Gavitt

Comment: Macarchuk joined Gavitt's staff three years after DiGregorio enrolled in 1969. DiGregorio, a first-team consensus All-America as a senior, is the Friars' all-time assists leader and is fifth in scoring. With Barnes playing only 11 minutes because of a knee injury in the national semifinal against Memphis State, Ernie D shot more than he usually did and was 15 of 36 from the floor. DiGregorio, the third pick overall in the 1973 NBA draft, played five seasons in the league with three different teams (9.6 ppg and 5.1 assists per game).

Kansas '74	Norm Cook	Duncan Reid	Ted Owens

Comment: Reid joined Owens' staff directly with Cook in 1973. Cook, who declared early for the NBA draft as a hardship case after leading the Jayhawks in scoring in his junior season, still ranks among the school's top 10 in career rebounding. He was a freshman when he scored just four points in 35 minutes in a 64-51 defeat against Marquette in the national semifinals. Cook, a first-round draft choice of the Celtics in 1976, also played briefly with the Nuggets (2.4 ppg in a total of 27 games).

FINAL FOUR TEAM	STAR PLAYER	ASSISTANT COACH	HEAD COACH
Michigan '76	**Wayman Britt**	**Bill Frieder**	**Johnny Orr**

Comment: Frieder joined Orr's staff one year after Britt enrolled in 1972. Britt, the Wolverines' all-time leader in assists when his eligibility expired, was the Lakers' fourth-round draft choice in 1976 and played briefly with the Pistons in the 1977-78 season. He hit five of six field-goal attempts before fouling out in an 86-68 loss against Indiana in the championship game.

UNLV '77	**Lewis Brown**	**George McQuarn**	**Jerry Tarkanian**

Comment: McQuarn joined Tarkanian's staff three years after Brown enrolled in 1973. Brown ranks second in school history in rebounding (behind Sidney Green), but he played just seven minutes in an 84-83 setback against North Carolina in the national semifinals. He was a fourth-round draft choice of the Bucks in 1977 and played five minutes in two games with the Bullets in the 1980-81 season.

Louisville '80	**Darrell Griffith**	**Wade Houston**	**Denny Crum**

Comment: Houston joined Crum's staff directly with Griffith in 1976. Griffith, a first-team consensus All-America as a senior, is the Cardinals' all-time leading scorer. He scored a game-high 34 points in an 80-72 triumph over Iowa in the national semifinals and a game-high 23 points in a 59-54 win over UCLA in the championship game. Griffith played 10 seasons with the Jazz after he was its first-round draft choice in 1980 (16.2 ppg).

LSU '81	**Howard Carter**	**Rick Huckabay**	**Dale Brown**

Comment: Huckabay joined Brown's staff directly with Carter in 1979. Carter, the Tigers' No. 4 all-time scorer, tallied a team-high 10 points in a 67-49 loss to Indiana in the national semifinals. He was a first-round draft choice of the Nuggets in 1983 and also played briefly with the Mavericks in his two-year NBA career (5.3 ppg).

LSU '81	**Rudy Macklin**	**Ron Abernathy**	**Dale Brown**

Comment: Abernathy joined Brown's staff directly with Macklin in 1976. Macklin, a second-team consensus All-America in 1981, is the Tigers' No. 2 all-time rebounder (behind Shaquille O'Neal) and is second in career scoring (behind Pete Maravich). Macklin hit just 2 of 12 shots from the floor in a national semifinal setback against Indiana. He was a third-round draft choice of the Hawks in 1981 and also played briefly for the Knicks in his three-year NBA career (6.4 ppg).

FINAL FOUR TEAM	STAR PLAYER	ASSISTANT COACH	HEAD COACH
Virginia '81	Jeff Lamp	Richard Schmidt	Terry Holland

Comment: Schmidt joined Holland's staff directly with Lamp in 1977, but was no longer at Virginia in 1981. Lamp, a consensus second-team All-America as a senior, is the Cavaliers' all-time No. 2 scorer (behind Bryant Stith). He scored a team-high 18 points but hit just 7 of 18 field-goal attempts in a 78-65 loss against North Carolina in the national semifinals. Lamp, a first-round draft choice of the Trail Blazers in 1981, played six years in the NBA with four different teams (5.1 ppg).

Virginia '81	Lee Raker	Richard Schmidt	Terry Holland

Comment: Schmidt joined Holland's staff directly with Raker in 1977, but was no longer at Virginia in 1981. Raker, the seventh-leading point producer in school history when his eligibility expired, scored 13 points in a national semifinal setback against North Carolina. He was a fourth-round draft choice of San Diego in 1981.

LSU '86	Derrick Taylor	Gary Duhe	Dale Brown

Comment: Duhe joined Brown's staff two years after Taylor enrolled in 1981, but was no longer at LSU in 1986. Taylor, ranking among the Tigers' top 10 in career scoring and assists, scored 16 points in an 88-77 defeat against Louisville in the national semifinals. He was a fourth-round draft choice of the Pacers in 1986.

Duke '86-88-89	Danny Ferry	Mike Brey	Mike Krzyzewski

Comment: Brey, Ferry's assistant high school coach, joined Krzyzewski's staff two years after Ferry enrolled in 1985. Ferry, a first-team consensus All-America in 1989 after being a second-team selection the previous year, is the Blue Devils' No. 4 all-time leading scorer and No. 5 rebounder. After scoring a total of just 12 points in two Final Four games as a freshman, he was Duke's leading scorer in national semifinal losses against Kansas and Seton Hall his last two seasons. Ferry, the second pick overall in the 1989 NBA draft, spent one year in Italy before playing the last three seasons with the Cavaliers (7.2 ppg and 3.5 rpg).

Michigan '92 & '93	Jalen Rose	Perry Watson	Steve Fisher

Comment: Watson joined Fisher's staff directly with Rose in 1991. Rose led the Wolverines in scoring and assists as a freshman and was second in scoring last season as a sophomore.

NOTES: In addition to Watson, former assistants Frieder (Arizona State), Houston (Tennessee) and Macarchuk (Fordham) are currently serving as Division I head coaches.

Secret Agent Men: The Greatest Stories Never Told

A Final Four player isn't required to hit a decisive basket or be selected Most Outstanding Player to be a hero. He doesn't even need to get into a game. Bob Ames, a member of the Tom Gola-led La Salle teams in 1954 (national champion) and 1955 (runner-up to San Francisco), never got off the bench at the Final Four those two years.

"Our coach, Ken Loeffler, only used seven guys, and Bob was the eighth man," said Frank Blatcher, a starter for the Explorers each season and their leading scorer with a total of 42 points in the 1954 Final Four. "He had the talent. He just never got a chance to show it."

Ames, a pre-law major, did have an opportunity to show his ability in another more vital endeavor, however. He joined the Central Intelligence Agency and worked his way up the chain of command to become the Director of the CIA's Office of Analysis of the Near East and South Asia. "The Spy Who Loved Basketball" worked closely with both the Carter and Reagan administrations.

Ames was killed in Beirut in 1983. A truck loaded with TNT on a suicide mission rammed into the facility where Ames was staying while serving as a liaison trying to allay contacts among the Lebanese, Syrians and Israelis in hopes of calming the escalating discord.

"Here was a guy who turned out to have had a greater influence on our lives than just about any 1,000 other basketball players you can name," Blatcher said. "It just shows you that you don't have to be a star to accomplish something." Something like becoming a genuine American hero.

Ames wasn't the only CIA employee to have played in the NCAA Tournament. The agency's deputy director under George Bush in 1976 was Hank Knoche, the leading scorer in the Rocky Mountain Conference with a 16.4 average for Colorado's 1946 NCAA Tournament team. Knoche, the father of American University coach Chris Knoche, reputedly was the first player selected in the NBA's first college draft in 1947 after enrolling at Washington and Jefferson (Pa.) to play with two of his brothers. But he never appeared in the then-fledgling league, which doesn't have any official draft records prior to 1949. The franchise that selected him, the Pittsburgh Ironmen, folded shortly after the draft, and his rights reverted to the New York Knicks.

"I didn't know I was the first No. 1 pick until a writer from Atlanta called me several years ago for a story," Knoche said. "An NBA historian had informed him of my alleged status."

The elder Knoche, now living in the Denver area, chose not to risk playing in an uncertain situation for little money. "I never received any contact from the Ironmen," he said. "The Knicks sent a contract offer in the mail, but it was for just $3,500 and that's if I made the team (Orlando's Shaquille O'Neal earns five times that amount every quarter).

Knoche was recalled to the military during the Korean War, where he was assigned to intelligence work for the Navy and later embarked on a civilian career that led to a job with the CIA.

La Salle's championship team from 1954 featured All-America Tom Gola (15). Another player, Bob Ames (7), went on to become a high-ranking employee of the CIA, but was killed in Beirut in 1983 in the line of duty.

Indiana's undefeated 1976 NCAA championship team is one of the greatest of all time. All five starters went on to play in the NBA, including Bobby Wilkerson (20), Scott May (42), Quinn Buckner (21), Tom Abernethy (33) and Kent Benson (54). Jim Crews (45) is now the head coach at Evansville, and Bob Bender (second row, second from right), is the head coach at Washington.

Going to Knight School

I wish everyone could see Bob Knight before a game — any game. It's amazing how tense he gets, even after all these years. Every game the Hoosiers play is treated as if it were a Final Four game. He is a master motivator who sets the tone with the most unbelievably intense practices you can imagine. Naturally, that kind of intensity is going to lead to an occasional flare-up. But let me tell you something, I love to tease The General about his playing days at Ohio State. I always kid him about the fact he and Dean Smith are the only two men to play for a national championship team and then coach one. But let me tell you, big fella, you could shoot the rock, but you couldn't play a lick of defense! All you did was cheer from the bench: "Do it Lucas! Do it Hondo (Havlicek), baby!"

Knight never played or coached in the pros, but he has been closely associated with what are believed to be the only two college squads to send all five starters to the NBA — Ohio State '60 and Indiana '76.

In 1960, Knight was a backup sophomore forward for an Ohio State team that unveiled one of the greatest shooting clinics in NCAA championship game history. The fireworks climaxed a season when Ohio State became the only squad to lead the country in scoring offense and win the NCAA title in the same season. The Buckeyes, playing in the Bay Area (San Francisco) against the nation's top defensive team (California), hit a mind-boggling 84.2 percent of their first-half field goal attempts (16-19) en route to a 75-55 victory over the defending champion Bears. Keep in mind that season marked the first time a school led the major-college ranks by hitting more than half of its shots from the floor (52.1 percent by Auburn).

Ohio State's five starters — sophomores John Havlicek, Jerry Lucas and Mel Nowell, senior Joe Roberts and junior Larry Siegfried — were all high school centers. They each scored in double figures in the NCAA final before eventually playing at least two seasons in the NBA or ABA or both.

Knight, scoreless in the 1960 championship game, was coach of Indiana's 1976 NCAA titlist, the last undefeated Division I team. Four of the Indiana starters were chosen in the 1976 NBA draft and the fifth, center Kent Benson, was the first pick overall by Milwaukee in 1977. Quinn Buckner (Milwaukee), Scott May (Chicago) and Bob Wilkerson (Seattle) were first-round picks, while Tom Abernethy (L.A. Lakers) was chosen in the third round.

Benson, May and Abernethy were All-NCAA Tournament selections in 1976, while Wilkerson and Buckner also had their moments. Wilkerson collected 19 rebounds and seven assists in a 65-51 victory over UCLA in the national semifinals, then Buckner contributed 16 points and eight rebounds in the championship game against Michigan. Trailing by six points at intermission in the final and playing without Wilkerson after the guard sustained a concussion early in the game, the Hoosiers shot 60 percent from the floor in the second half to come from behind and win (86-68). May, Benson and Buckner collaborated for 36 of Indiana's first 38 points in the second half against the Wolverines, an overtime loser at Indiana in Big Ten Conference competition.

The five starters didn't have nearly as much success in the NBA, where they combined to average 8.8 points, 4 rebounds and 2.7 assists per game. Buckner, the captain of the Hoosiers' unbeaten squad, was the only one of the starting quintet to finish his NBA career with a winning playoff record and play for a championship team (Boston Celtics in 1984). Buckner's most famous teammate with the Celtics was Larry Bird, who would have been a sophomore member of the '76 Hoosiers squad if he hadn't dropped out of school shortly after enrolling there in the fall of 1974. Bird later transferred to Indiana State, where he became a two-time consensus first-team All-America and sparked the Sycamores to the 1979 NCAA Tournament championship game. In Bird's brilliant 13-year NBA career including the playoffs, he personally outscored (25,688 points to 23,781) and outrebounded (10,657 to 8,729) the entire starting lineup from Indiana's unbeaten '76 team.

LITTLE BIG MEN

Everywhere I went during the offseason, I was criticized for praising Bobby Hurley too much. But let me say this: Hurley is a winner, winner, winner. The kid can flat-out distribute the ball with his tremendous penetration and isn't afraid to take the outside jumper at crunch time. What more can a point guard do? I still believe he was one of the five best point guards in college in the last 30 to 40 years. Hurley might not become a big-time star in the NBA, but he'll be a solid pro for 10 years.

Hurley, Duke's 6-0 guard selected as the Most Outstanding Player at the 1992 Final Four, was the shortest player to earn the award since 5-11 Hal Lear helped Temple to a national third-place finish in 1956.

The only Final Four Most Outstanding Player shorter than Hurley from a championship team was 5-11 Kenny Sailors of Wyoming in 1943. Hurley shot a mediocre 41 percent from the floor in his college career, but he was the Blue Devils' linchpin as his playmaking and intangibles helped them win 18 of 20 NCAA playoff games. He holds the career record for most playoff assists (145) although his bid to become the first player to start four consecutive NCAA finals was thwarted when California upset Duke in the second round of the 1993 Midwest Regional despite Hurley's career-high 32 points.

Many coaches have an obsession with size, but Hurley wasn't the only short subject to serve as a catalyst for an NCAA Tournament team. The only player to score more than 40 points in his first NCAA playoff game was 5-8 Johnny O'Brien, who poured in 42 points to power Seattle to an 88-77 victory over Idaho State in 1953. O'Brien, a center on offense, played second base later that summer for the Pittsburgh Pirates.

Heights cited by colleges frequently are misleading. When players with pro potential are measured by NBA officials, the prospects often are discovered to actually be an inch or two shorter. So while there probably should be more mighty mites on the following list, here is a look at Hurley and seven other starters who were listed as 6-0 or shorter for NCAA titlists in the last 30 years:

| Pint-Sized Starter, NCAA Champion | Ht. | Points Per Game Average | |
		--Overall	Tourney--
Bobby Hurley, Duke '92	6-0	13.2	13.8
Sidney Lowe, North Carolina State '83	6-0	11.3	6.7
Gary McLain, Villanova '85	6-0	8.0	7.0
Tommy Curtis, UCLA '73	5-11	6.4	11.3
Mike Warren, UCLA '67 and '68	5-11	12.4	12.4
John Egan, Loyola of Chicago '63	5-10	13.7	11.2
*Bobby Joe Hill, Texas Western '66	5-10	15.0	20.2
Monte Towe, North Carolina State '74	5-7	12.8	15.5

*Hill, the shortest player to lead an NCAA champion in season scoring average, doubled his regular-season career mark of 10.1 points per game in the 1966 tournament for Texas Western, a school now known as Texas-El Paso.

All About All-Americas

It doesn't take a genius to figure out that All-America players are all-important to teams. Hey, even I know that talent makes the difference!

Six of the seven national champions from 1986 through 1992 had a player on their roster who either already was, or later became, a consensus first-team All-America. On the other hand, sheer standouts are not absolutely essential for a squad to win a national title. North Carolina State (1983) and Villanova (1985) did not have a first- or second-team consensus All-America to rely on, although they did have great talent. No one on defending champion North Carolina's roster had earned first- or second-team college All-America status through 1993, although center Eric Montross is a strong candidate this season.

Since the tournament expanded to at least 32 teams in 1975, just two consensus first-team All-Americas have not played in the NCAA playoffs — Houston's Otis Birdsong (1977) and Minnesota's Mychal Thompson (1978).

Of the first 59 two-time consensus first-team All-Americas since the NCAA Tournament started in 1939, 37 participated in the Final Four at some point in their illustrious careers. In 1992, Ohio State's Jim Jackson and LSU's Shaquille O'Neal became the 21st and 22nd two-time consensus first-team All-Americas in that span to fail to reach the national semifinals. Incidentally, LSU is the only school to have more than one player in this category. Previously declawed Tigers were guards Pete Maravich and Chris Jackson.

Terry Dischinger averaged 28.3 points per game in his three-year varsity career at Purdue, but he is the only one of the 53 two-time consensus first-team All-Americas since 1946 to never participate in the NCAA Tournament or the NIT. Dischinger went on to be named the NBA's Rookie of the Year as a member of the Chicago Zephyrs in 1962-63 despite playing in only 57 games — he skipped most of the road games to continue his education at Purdue. He stayed in the NBA for nine seasons and never played on a team to win a playoff series, but his dedication to the classroom paid off; he's now an orthodontist in Portland, Ore.

LSU's Pete Maravich (above) and Purdue's Terry Dischinger (inset) were among the premier players in the country during their college careers, but neither ever got a chance to play in the NCAA Tournament — proof that it takes five to win.

Hall of Famer Billy Cunningham averaged 24.8 points per game in his three-year varsity career at North Carolina from 1963-65, but he also never appeared in the NCAA Tournament or the NIT.

An alphabetical list of the 16 two-time consensus first-team All-Americas in the past 40 years to never reach the Final Four:

PLAYER, SCHOOL (YEARS FIRST TEAM ALL-AMERICA)	---POSTSEASON W-L RECORD---		
	NCAA	NIT	TOTAL
Adrian Dantley, Notre Dame ('75 and '76)	4-4	DNP	4-4
Terry Dischinger, Purdue ('61 and '62)	DNP	DNP	DNP
Si Green, Duquesne ('55 and '56)	DNP	6-2	6-2
Chris Jackson, LSU ('89 and '90)	1-2	DNP	1-2
Jim Jackson, Ohio State ('91 and '92)	6-3	DNP	6-3
Dwight Lamar, Southwestern La. ('72 and '73)	3-3	DNP	3-3
John Lucas, Maryland ('75 and '76)	3-2	DNP	3-2
Pete Maravich, LSU ('68, '69 and '70)	DNP	2-2	2-2
Calvin Murphy, Niagara ('69 and '70)	1-2	DNP	1-2
Shaquille O'Neal, LSU ('91 and '92)	2-3	DNP	2-3
Ed Ratleff, Long Beach State ('72 and '73)	6-3	DNP	6-3
Tom Stith, St. Bonaventure ('60 and '61)	2-1	2-3	4-4
Wayman Tisdale, Oklahoma ('83, '84 and '85)	4-3	DNP	4-3
Wes Unseld, Louisville ('67 and '68)	1-3	0-1	1-4
Chet Walker, Bradley ('61 and '62)	DNP	3-1	3-1
Jimmy Walker, Providence ('66 and '67)	2-2	1-1	3-3

UPS AND DOWNS

I always tease Dean Smith, the Michelangelo of coaches, that he was the only man capable of holding down Mr. Michael Jordan with his passing game at North Carolina. Although the odds of Jordan going scoreless in any 21-*minute* stretch were virtually nil, he would have had to be blanked in his next 21 NBA postseason games to relinquish his spot as the player with the highest scoring average in NBA playoff history. Jordan's 34.7-point NBA playoff scoring average in his nine seasons with the Chicago Bulls before retiring last fall more than doubles the NCAA Tournament scoring average he compiled for North Carolina. Jordan averaged 16.5 points per NCAA playoff game with the Tar Heels, scoring 20 or more in just two of 10 postseason games from 1982-'84.

Every serious hoops fan knows Jordan hit the game-winning basket as a freshman in the 1982 national final against Georgetown. But do you remember his inauspicious playoff debut when he collected six points, one rebound, no assists and no steals in 37 minutes of a 52-50 opening-round victory against James Madison in the East Regional? Jordan's final NCAA Tournament game before he left school early for the NBA was nothing to brag about, either. The college player of the year managed just 13 points, one rebound, one assist and one steal in 26 foul-plagued minutes when the top-ranked Tar Heels were eliminated, 72-68. Jordan was guarded for much of the game by a much slower player, Dan Dakich, who's now an assistant coach at Indiana.

Generally, the most prolific scorers in NCAA Tournament history have learned it's not a picnic in postseason play. Duke's Christian Laettner, the all-time playoff scoring leader with 407 points from 1989 through 1992, tallied fewer than 15 points in six of his first seven tournament games. Just four of the top 20 in career scoring in the NCAA playoffs accumulated more than 10 points in every tourney game they participated — UCLA's Lew Alcindor (1967-68-69), Princeton's Bill Bradley (1963-64-65), Arizona's Sean Elliott (1986-87-88-89) and Cincinnati's Oscar Robertson (1958-59-60).

Following are additional believe-it-or-not notes concerning many of the first 20 players to score more than 235 points in NCAA playoff competition:

- Elliott was the most consistent scorer. He has the lowest point differential (14) from his highest-scoring game (31) to his lowest-scoring game (17).

- The only player on this list to fail to score at least 25 points in an NCAA Tournament game is Georgetown's Pat Ewing (1982-83-84-85). Ewing's playoff high of 24 points came in a 66-57 Midwest Regional second-round defeat against Memphis State in 1983, the only one of his four years with the Hoyas they didn't reach the Final Four.

- Bill Walton's championship game-record 44 points for UCLA against Memphis State in 1973 came after the junior center scored a modest total of 23 points in his two previous contests. Walton and UNLV's Stacey Augmon are the only two of the 20 highest scorers to have fewer than 10 points in their final tournament appearance. Walton managed just six points in a 78-61 national third-place game victory over Kansas in 1974 and Augmon also had six in a 79-77 national semifinal loss to Duke in 1991.

- Augmon (three points in 1988 against Southwest Missouri State), Walton (four in 1972 against Weber State) and Ewing (seven in 1982 against Wyoming) are among eight players from this elite group to score in single digits in their tourney debuts. Other standouts to get off to shaky starts were Notre Dame's Austin Carr (six in 1969 against Miami of Ohio), Duke's Bobby Hurley (four in 1990 against Richmond), Oklahoma's Stacey King (two in 1987 against Tulsa), Kansas' Danny Manning (nine in 1985 against Ohio) and Georgetown's Reggie Williams (six in 1984 against Southern Methodist). Carr, who has the greatest point differential (55) between his low game and his best output (61), is the only player among the top 20 playoff scorers to not reach the Final Four.

- Ohio State center Jerry Lucas scored his playoff career-high 36 points in his tournament debut in 1960 (98-79 victory over Western Kentucky in Mideast Regional semifinal). Lucas was held to nine points in each of his tourney openers the next two seasons (against Louisville and Western Kentucky) when he was named national player of the year. Walton fell into a comparable trap with one playoff game of less than 10 points each of the three seasons he was national player of the year from 1972 through 1974.

The only player in this gifted group to go scoreless in a playoff game is Duke's Danny Ferry, a forward blanked as a sophomore in the Blue Devils' 58-51 first-round victory over Texas A&M in 1987. Ferry scored less than 10 points in six consecutive tournament games before averaging 20 points per game in his last 11 playoff outings. The only other player from this collection of stars to have as many as five playoff games with fewer than 10 points was Georgetown's Williams, who had four of his five single-digit totals in his first four tournament contests as a freshman (1984).

Houston's Elvin Hayes is the only player to lead a tournament in scoring by more than 60 points. Alcindor and his UCLA teammates helped hold Hayes to 10 points in the 1968 national semifinals, but the Big E finished with 167 points in five games. Alcindor was runner-up with 103 points in four games. Hayes became the only player in tournament history to collect more than 40 points and 25 rebounds in the same game when he had 49 points and 27 rebounds in a 94-76 decision over Loyola of Chicago in the first round of the Midwest Regional.

Jerry West (1958-59-60) scored at least 25 points in his last eight tournament games for West Virginia. West is the only player to rank among the top five in scoring average in both the NCAA Tournament (30.6 points per game) and NBA playoffs (29.1 ppg).

A list summarizing the playoff point production of the top 20 scorers in NCAA Tournament history:

PLAYER, SCHOOL (GAMES)	TOTAL POINTS	--BREAKDOWN OF SCORING-- 25 OR MORE	LESS THAN 25	HIGH GAME	LOW GAME
Christian Laettner, Duke (23)	407	two	twenty-one	31	6
Elvin Hayes, Houston (13)	358	eight	five	49	10
Danny Manning, Kansas (16)	328	five	eleven	42	4
O. Robertson, Cincinnati (10)	324	seven	three	56	18
Glen Rice, Michigan (13)	308	six	seven	39	2
Lew Alcindor, UCLA (12)	304	six	six	38	16
Bill Bradley, Princeton (9)	303	seven	two	58	22
Austin Carr, Notre Dame (7)	289	six	one	61	6
Jerry West, West Virginia (9)	275	eight	one	38	10
Danny Ferry, Duke (19)	269	one	eighteen	34	0
Jerry Lucas, Ohio State (12)	266	six	six	36	9
R. Williams, Georgetown (17)	260	two	fifteen	34	2
Pat Ewing, Georgetown (18)	256	none	eighteen	24	7
Bill Walton, UCLA (12)	254	five	seven	44	4
Stacey King, Oklahoma (12)	246	four	eight	37	2
Stacey Augmon, UNLV (17)	242	one	sixteen	33	3
Todd Day, Arkansas (13)	240	four	nine	31	9
Bobby Hurley, Duke (20)	239	three	seventeen	32	2
Sam Perkins, N. Carolina (15)	237	two	thirteen	26	10
Sean Elliott, Arizona (10)	236	five	five	31	17

Cincinnati's Oscar Robertson led the nation in scoring, but couldn't lead his team to the national title. The Bearcats lost twice in the semifinals with Robertson, but won it two straight years after he left. Kansas' Clyde Lovellette (inset) is the only player to lead the country in scoring and play for a title team.

Shooting Stars

When you look at post play, nobody did it better than Bill Walton. His wondrous field goal shooting for UCLA against Memphis State when he scored a championship game record 44 points in 1973 completely overshadows other outstanding marksmanship from the floor in NCAA Tournament finals. For instance, Jack Givens sank 18 of 27 field goal attempts against Duke and scored Kentucky's last 16 points of the first half en route to a 41-point performance in the 1978 final. Here are the five different sharpshooters to be named Final Four Most Outstanding Player after hitting better than 70 percent of their field-goal attempts in the national title game since statistical crews began regularly charting shots from the floor in the early 1950s (minimum of 10 baskets):

PLAYER, POS., CHAMPIONSHIP TEAM	CHAMPIONSHIP GAME FIELD-GOAL SHOOTING
Bill Walton, C, UCLA '73	21 of 22 against Memphis State (95.5%)
James Worthy, F, N. Carolina '82	13 of 17 against Georgetown (76.5%)
Lew Alcindor, C, UCLA '69	15 of 20 against Purdue (75%)
Anderson Hunt, G, UNLV '90	12 of 16 against Duke (75%)
Lew Alcindor, C, UCLA '68	15 of 21 against North Carolina (71.4%)
Pervis Ellison, F-C, Louisville '86	10 of 14 against Duke (71.4%)

Solo Acts

Four players took out do-it-yourself kits and scored more than 60 percent of their team's points in an NCAA Tournament game. Here is a summary of the four one-man shows:

 Danny Manning supplied 62.7 percent of Kansas' offense by scoring 42 points in the Jayhawks' 67-63 victory against Southwest Missouri State in the second round of the 1987 Southeast Regional.

 Jim (Bad News) Barnes accounted for 61.8 percent of Texas Western's offense by scoring 42 points in the Miners' 68-62 victory against Texas A&M in the first round of the 1964 Midwest Regional.

 Hal Lear manufactured 61.5 percent of Temple's offense by scoring 40 points in the Owls' 65-59 victory against Connecticut in the 1956 East Regional semifinals.

 David Robinson furnished 61 percent of Navy's offense by scoring 50 points in the Middies' 97-82 loss to Michigan in the first round of the 1987 East Regional.

In an abrupt turnaround, it was definitely bad news for Texas Western in its next playoff game in 1964. Barnes was whistled for three quick personal fouls in the opening minutes against Kansas State and spent almost the entire first half on the bench. He was assessed fouls No. 4 and No. 5 early in the second half and fouled out with four points in the Miners' 64-60 defeat.

Unlikely Heroes

There have been times at the Final Four when a player not recognized as an All-America supplies a Herculean performance. One that stands out to me was in 1984 when Georgetown's Michael Jackson, a 6-1 guard averaging 1.4 rebounds per game entering the Final Four, retrieved 10 missed shots against Kentucky's formidable front line.

But nothing compares to the version of Washington coming "out of the valley forge" in 1964 when UCLA's Kenny Washington led the first national championship a John Wooden-coached team won. Washington, the only player with a single-digit season scoring average (6.1) to tally more than 25 points in a championship game, scored 26 points in a 98-83 triumph over Duke in the final.

Although Washington became the only player to score 25 or more points in a final and not be named to the All-Tournament team, he wasn't rebuffed again the next year. Washington, averaging a modest 8.9 points per game entering the 1965 Final Four, scored a total of 27 points in victories over Wichita State and Michigan as the Bruins successfully defended their title en route to 10 crowns in 12 years under Wooden. Washington joined teammates Gail Goodrich and Edgar Lacey on the 1965 All-Tournament team with co-national players of the year Bill Bradley (Princeton) and Cazzie Russell (Michigan).

In 1969, UCLA was without two-time All-Tournament team selection Lucius Allen because of academic problems, but the Bruins got another significant increase in point production at the Final Four from an unlikely source. Guard John Vallely averaged 22 points in victories over Drake and Purdue after arriving at the national semifinals with a 10.2-point average. Only one senior is on the following list of 10 championship team rank-and-file players to average seven points per game or less entering the Final Four before seizing the moment and averaging double digits in scoring in their last two games with an increase of at least 5.8 points per game from their pre-Final Four scoring mark:

Name, Class, Pos., Champion	Season Average	Avg. Before Final Four	Final 4 Average	Average Increase
Kenny Washington, So., F-G, UCLA '64	6.1	5.2	19.5	14.3
Norm Mager, Sr., F, CCNY '50	3.6	3.0	11.5	8.5
John Dick, Jr., F, Oregon '39	6.7	6.3	14.5	8.2
Gene Brown, So., G, USF '56	7.1	6.6	14.0	7.4
Tommy Curtis, Jr., G, UCLA '73	6.4	5.8	13.0	7.2
*Michael Graham, Fr., F, G-town '84	4.9	4.5	11.0	6.5
Frank Oftring, Fr., C-F, Holy Cross '47	4.6	4.2	10.5	6.3
Charles Kraak, Jr., F, Indiana '53	7.2	6.7	13.0	6.3
Tony Yates, So., G, Cincinnati '61	7.4	7.0	13.0	6.0
*Harold Jensen, So., G, Villanova '85	4.5	4.2	10.0	5.8

*Named to NCAA All-Tournament team.

NOTES: Washington State junior guard Kirk Gebert, who scored 21 points in a 39-34 loss to Wisconsin in the 1941 final to finish the year with a 6.6-point average, is the only player other than Washington with a single-digit average to score more than 20 points in a title game.

Star Gazing

The naming of the Final Four Most Outstanding Player can occasionally generate minor controversy. Bobby Hurley, signed to launch a shoe company (Foot Locker spinoff called ITZ), won the award in 1992 although he wasn't able to shoo away dissenters who believed Duke teammate Grant Hill deserved the MOP honor instead. In the two 1992 Final Four games, Hill had more field goals than Hurley (14 to 10), outshot him from the floor (61 percent to 41.7), blocked more shots (5 to 0), outrebounded him (16 to 3) and accumulated just as many assists (11 each).

Moreover, Hurley's 3 of 12 field goal shooting in the final against Michigan was the worst marksmanship from the floor for a Final Four Most Outstanding Player in a championship game since Elgin Baylor of runner-up Seattle went 9 for 32 against Kentucky in 1958. It was the second consecutive year for the Final Four Most Outstanding Player to come from Duke and manage just three baskets and shoot less than 50 percent from the floor in the title game. In 1991, Christian Laettner hit three of eight field goal attempts against Kansas.

Incidentally, Grant Hill scored a total of 21 points on 9 of 14 field goal shooting as a freshman in two 1991 Final Four games after Hurley scored a total of just five points with no field goals and 11 turnovers in two Final Four games as a freshman the previous year. Coach Mike Krzyzewski, assessing Duke's back-to-back titles, told Sports Illustrated that "the guy who played as well as anybody in those four (Final Four) games was Grant." Hurley, after averaging 5.4 points per game in his first eight NCAA Tournament contests, averaged 22.8 in his last five playoff games.

Following are closer looks at many of the great athletes who have been annointed as the Final Four's Most Outstanding Player:

The only individual selected the Final Four's Most Outstanding Player three times was UCLA's **Lew Alcindor**, who averaged 25.7 points and 18.8 rebounds and shot 64.1 percent from the floor in six games from 1967 through 1969. Four other players, all prototype centers like Alcindor, were selected Most Outstanding Player in back-to-back Final Fours — Oklahoma State's **Bob Kurland** (22.3 ppg in four games in 1945 and 1946), Kentucky's **Alex Groza** (22.8 ppg in 1948 and 1949), Ohio State's **Jerry Lucas** (22.8 ppg and 12 rpg in 1960 and 1961) and UCLA's **Bill Walton** (28.8 ppg and 17.8 rpg in 1972 and 1973). Kurland is the only player to score more than half of a championship team's points in a single NCAA Tournament (total of 72 points accounted for 51.8 percent of the Aggies' output in three playoff games in 1946). Groza is the only player to appear at a minimum of two Final Fours and be the game-high scorer in every Final Four contest he played. Alcindor is the only player to couple three unanimous first team All-America seasons with three NCAA titles. Lucas and Walton are the only other three-time consensus first team All-America choices to play in three Final Fours.

These long fellows were poetry in motion when they played in the Final Four. Hakeem Olajuwon led Houston to consecutive runner-up finishes, and was named Most Outstanding Player in 1983. Pervis Ellison won the honor after sparking Louisville to the 1986 championship as a freshman, and UCLA's Bill Walton won the award after leading the Bruins to their 1972 and '73 titles.

UNLV guard **Anderson Hunt**, the 1990 Final Four Most Outstanding Player, was the only one of the 39 Final Four Most Outstanding Players from 1954 through 1992 to never play in the NBA. Two of the 36 different honorees in that span, **Hal Lear** (Temple '56) and **Keith Smart** (Indiana '87), combined for a total of just five games in their NBA careers. Lear, **Art Heyman** (Duke '63) and **Bill Bradley** (Princeton '65) are the only Most Outstanding Players to play for a national third-place team. Smart is the only former junior college player to become Final Four Most Outstanding Player.

Michigan's **Glen Rice**, the 1989 Final Four Most Outstanding Player, is the only player to score more than 25 points in two Final Four games in the last 19 years. He scored 28 points in an 83-81 victory over Illinois in the national semifinals and 31 in an 80-79 overtime win over Seton Hall in the final.

Hakeem Olajuwon, the 1983 Final Four Most Outstanding Player, was the only individual to earn the honor from 1972 through 1993 and not play for the championship team. Olajuwon had a pair of two-point playoff performances the previous year as a freshman and failed to score more than 13 points in any of his first six NCAA Tournament games for Houston. He averaged more than 20 points per game each of his first nine seasons in the NBA with the Houston Rockets and usually notches a higher scoring average in the playoffs than the regular season.

Tom Gola is the only individual to be named both NCAA Final Four Most Outstanding Player and NIT Most Valuable Player in his career. Gola led La Salle to the 1954 NCAA title with a 23-point average. Two years earlier as a freshman when the Explorers won the NIT, he shared the MVP award with teammate **Norm Grekin**. Gola averaged 24.2 points per game in 1955 when La Salle finished national runner-up to San Francisco. Although Gola more than doubled the season scoring average of any of his teammates in 1954 and 1955, he was the Explorers' undisputed game-high scorer in just one of four Final Four outings. His career total (4,663) of points (2,462) and rebounds (2,201) remains the highest in major college history.

Of the 35 Final Four Most Outstanding Players selected from 1946 through 1981 when there was a national third-place game, the only honoree to play for a fourth-place team was Utah forward **Jerry Chambers**. He collected 70 points and 35 rebounds in two Final Four games in 1966.

Guard **Walt Hazzard**, the second-leading scorer over the entire season for UCLA's first championship team in 1964 with an average of 18.6 points per game, was named Most Outstanding Player although he was the Bruins' fourth-leading scorer at the Final Four that year. Hazzard had a two-game total of 30 points, finishing behind the scoring aggregates compiled by teammates **Gail Goodrich** (41), **Kenny Washington** (39) and **Keith Erickson** (36). Hazzard is the only Most Outstanding Player to later coach his alma mater in the NCAA Tournament (1-1 record in 1987).photos of Hazzard, Hakeem, Don Williams, etc.

Howie Dallmar, a sophomore guard for 1942 champion Stanford, is the only Most Outstanding Player to guide a school other than his alma mater to the playoffs. Dallmar posted a 1-1 tourney record with Penn in 1953 before coaching Stanford for 21 years from 1955-75 without directing his alma mater to the NCAA playoffs. The principal culprit in denying Dallmar an NCAA appearance with the Cardinal was UCLA's dynasty under coach **John Wooden**.

The four individuals named Final Four Most Outstanding Player despite scoring fewer than 28 points in two Final Four games are the first three "MOPs" (Indiana guard **Marv Huffman** with 18 points in 1940, Wisconsin forward **John Kotz** with 22 points in 1941 and Stanford guard **Howie Dallmar** with 20 points in 1942) and another honoree more than 40 years later (Georgetown center **Pat Ewing** with 18 points in 1984). Ewing, the only individual to fail to score more than 10 points in either the national semifinal or championship game in the year he was named Most Outstanding Player, tallied eight points in a 53-40 triumph over Kentucky in the semifinals and 10 in an 84-75 decision over Houston in the final. Ewing was the Hoyas' leading scorer during the season with a 16.4-point average, but his two-game scoring total at the Final Four ranked fifth on the team. He is the only Most Outstanding Player to amass as many rebounds as points in two Final Four games since the NCAA started charting rebounds as a Final Four statistic in 1957.

Four Final Four Most Outstanding Players — Kentucky's **Jack Givens** (1978), Marquette's **Butch Lee** (1977), UCLA's **Richard Washington** (1975) and UCLA's **Sidney Wicks** (1970) — were scoreless in their NCAA Tournament debut in a previous season. Incredibly, Givens and Lee were blanked in the same game in their freshman season when Kentucky mauled Marquette (76-54) in the 1975 Mideast Regional. Washington was scoreless as a freshman in the 1974 West Regional when the Bruins outlasted Dayton (111-100 in triple overtime). Wicks, after one season in junior college, was blanked as a sophomore in the 1969 West Regional when UCLA defeated New Mexico State (53-38) and also at the national semifinals when the Bruins defeated Drake (85-82). The only team to win a national title although its season-leading scorer was held more than 10 points below his average in the championship game was UCLA in 1971. Wicks, named national player of the year by the U.S. Basketball Writers Association, managed just seven points in a 68-62 victory over Villanova to finish the campaign with a 21.3-point average.

What a difference a year can make! **Donald Williams**, the Final Four Most Outstanding Player in 1993 as a sophomore, averaged a meager 2.2 points per game for North Carolina the previous year. He finished last season with a 14.3-point average after scoring 25 points in each Final Four game to become the first guard to score at least 25 in the national semifinals and final in the same year since **Rick Mount** for runner-up Purdue in 1969. The last guard for a championship team to score at least 25 points in both the national semifinals and final was UCLA's **Gail Goodrich** in 1965. Goodrich became the only guard to score more than 35 points in a title game when he tallied 42 against Michigan. Williams' Final Four-record 10 three-point baskets (he hit five of seven from long range in each game) represented more successful attempts from beyond the arc than he managed his entire freshman season (9 of 31). One of his treys as a freshman, against Miami of Ohio) in the first round of the tournament, accounted for his only points in Carolina's three playoff games in 1992.

RISING TO THE OCCASION

Five players in the last 42 years were named to an All-NCAA Tournament team despite averaging fewer than seven points per game that season — Tommy Amaker (6.4 ppg/Duke '86), Harold Jensen (4.5 ppg/Villanova '85), Dean Kelley (6.5 ppg/Kansas '52), Jim Ranglos (3.5 ppg/Colorado '55) and Jim Thomas (3.7 ppg/Indiana '81). Thomas' sterling defensive play enabled him to earn a spot on the 1981 All-Tournament team despite his microscopic offensive output (two points in each Final Four game — against LSU in the semifinals and North Carolina in the final). Kelley also was named to the 1953 All-Tournament team after averaging 9.7 points during the regular season.

Ten of the last 13 Final Four Most Outstanding Players had season scoring averages of fewer than 17 points per game after guards Bobby Hurley of Duke '92 and Donald Williams of North Carolina '93 fell into the category. Hurley was just the third of the first 53 Final Four Most Outstanding Players to not rank among the top three scorers on his team.

The lowest team-leading scoring average for an individual in the season he was named Final Four Most Outstanding Player was compiled by George Kaftan, a forward-center with an 11.1-point average for Holy Cross' NCAA champion in 1947. He had become the first player to score 30 points in a Final Four game (30 in a 60-45 victory over CCNY in East Regional final before tossing in a team-high 18 in a 58-47 triumph over Oklahoma in the national final). Following is a chronological look at the season scoring averages of the eight Final Four Most Outstanding Players to not finish among the top two scorers on their squads:

MOST OUTSTANDING PLAYER, TEAM	SEASON AVERAGE (TEAM RANK)	FINAL FOUR POINT TOTAL (RANK)
Marvin Huffman, Indiana '40	4.3 ppg (sixth)	18 points (first)
Howie Dallmar, Stanford '42	6.8 ppg (third)	20 points (third)
Irwin Dambrot, CCNY '50	10.2 ppg (third)	28 points (third)
Hakeem Olajuwon, Houston '83	13.9 ppg (third)	41 points (first)
Pervis Ellison, Louisville '86	13.1 ppg (third)	36 points (first)
Keith Smart, Indiana '87	11.2 ppg (fifth)	35 points (second)
Bobby Hurley, Duke '92	13.2 ppg (fourth)	35 points (first)
Donald Williams, N. Carolina '93	14.3 ppg (third)	50 points (first)

NOTES: No Final Four Most Outstanding Player award was issued for two NCAA tourneys — the inaugural event in 1939 and also in 1951.

Freshmen of Influence

Patience, patience, patience. Many fans expect Diaper Dandies coming out of high school with great reputations to become instant superstars. But the majority of the wet-behind-the-ear freshmen have to experience growing pains.

For example, nine-time All-NBA first team selection Magic Johnson didn't exhibit much wizardry in three tournament games as a freshman for Michigan State in 1978 when he shot a lowly 27.8 percent from the floor (10 of 36). Similarly, the five junior regulars on North Carolina's championship team last season — Eric Montross, Derrick Phelps, Brian Reese, Kevin Salvadori and Pat Sullivan — weathered a generous dose of reality as freshmen in the 1990-91 season when they combined to average a modest 14.6 points per game.

On the other hand, many freshmen had a sudden impact on the NCAA Tournament in the first 20 seasons of the NCAA's freshman-eligibility rule. The only year in that span at least one Final Four team didn't have a vital rookie on its roster was 1988, when the most prominent freshmen were Duke forward Greg Koubek (3.9 points per game) and Oklahoma guard Terrence Mullins (3.7 ppg).

California guard Jason Kidd probably had the most influence of any freshman in last year's tourney, although his team didn't get past the Midwest Regional semifinals. Kidd's patented inside baskets on spontaneous deft moves in the closing seconds helped boost the Bears to victories over two schools making their 10th consecutive NCAA playoff appearance — LSU and Duke.

Perhaps the most frustrated freshman among regal recruits was North Carolina State guard Ernie Myers in 1983, although his team won the ACC Tournament and the national championship. Myers, averaging more than 14 points per game at the end of the regular season, scored a total of just five points in three ACC Tournament games and a total of seven points in five NCAA playoff contests.

Two years ago, Michigan had four freshmen with scoring totals of at least 21 points in two Final Four games — Juwan Howard (21), Jimmy King (24), Jalen Rose (24) and Chris Webber (30).

DePaul's Mark Aguirre and Georgia Tech's Kenny Anderson, the two highest-scoring freshmen for Final Four teams, didn't reach the national championship game. Aguirre notched a tournament scoring average of 23.4 points per game as a freshman after pouring in a Final Four freshman record 34 points in a 96-93 victory over Penn in the 1979 national third-place game. Anderson, the only freshman to score more than 20 points in four playoff games, averaged 27 points per game in his first four tournament outings before he was restricted to 16 in a 90-81 loss to UNLV in the 1990 national semifinals to finish with a 24.8 average.

The only freshmen other than Aguirre to score more than 25 points in a Final Four game did so in 1977 when North Carolina's Mike O'Koren and UNC Charlotte's Chad Kinch achieved the feat. O'Koren became the only freshman to score more than 25 points in a national semifinal or championship game when he tallied 31 in an 84-83 victory over UNLV in the national semifinals. Kinch, limited to four points in a 51-49 setback against Marquette in the national semis, rebounded with 30 in a 106-94 loss to UNLV in the national third-place game.

Here is a chronological list of the 10 first-rate freshmen to score more than 25 points in two Final Four games in the last 20 years (parentheses with Final Four point total shows figures for national semifinal game and championship or third-place game, respectively):

Freshman, School (Team Finish)	Season Average	Final Four Point Total
Mark Aguirre, DePaul '79 (3rd)	24.0 ppg	53 (19/34)
Mike O'Koren, North Carolina '77 (2nd)	13.9 ppg	45 (31/14)
Gene Banks, Duke '78 (2nd)	17.1 ppg	44 (22/22)
Pervis Ellison, Louisville '86 (1st)	13.1 ppg	36 (11/25)
Chad Kinch, UNC Charlotte '77 (4th)	15.4 ppg	34 (4/30)
Michael Jordan, North Carolina '82 (1st)	13.5 ppg	34 (18/16)
Jack Givens, Kentucky '75 (2nd)	9.4 ppg	32 (24/8)
Patrick Ewing, Georgetown '82 (2nd)	12.7 ppg	31 (8/23)
Chris Webber, Michigan '92 (2nd)	15.5 ppg	30 (16/14)
Phil Hubbard, Michigan '76 (2nd)	15.1 ppg	26 (16/10)

NOTES: Freshmen also played varsity basketball in wartime years during the 1940s and early '50s because of manpower shortages, and at earlier times when eligibility requirements were lax. Among the key freshmen for Final Four teams in the mid-1940s were John Mahnken (Georgetown '43), Arnie Ferrin (Utah '44), Herb Wilkinson (Utah '44), George Kok (Arkansas '45) and Irwin Dambrot (CCNY '47).

FINAL FOUR FLUCTUATION

Mike Farmer and Steve Patterson, a pair of pivotmen who had the unenviable task of succeeding stellar players, enjoyed parallel college and professional basketball careers. They had brief stints as major-college coaches after playing in the NBA — Farmer as an assistant at San Francisco and Patterson as head coach at Arizona State. Farmer's college coaching occurred when he capitalized on a second chance at his education. He finished the requirements for a business degree in 1987, a mere 29 years after becoming a consensus second-team All-America.

The similarities between Farmer and Patterson are much greater as players. Farmer, San Francisco's principal big man for two years after two-time consensus first-team All-America Bill Russell sparked the Dons to back-to-back national championships (1955 and 1956), played six seasons in the NBA after becoming a first-round draft choice in 1958. Patterson, UCLA's starting center for two years after three-time consensus first-team All-America Lew Alcindor led the Bruins to three national titles (1967 through 1969), played five seasons in the NBA after becoming the first pick in the second round of the 1971 draft.

Farmer and Patterson are also linked by their significant swings in scoring in Final Four games. In 1956, Farmer, the only player to have a decrease of more than 25 points from his national semifinal game scoring total to his championship game output, had a game-high 26 points in an 86-68 victory over Southern Methodist before going scoreless in an 83-71 triumph over Iowa. In 1971, Patterson, the only player to have a single-digit point total in a national semifinal game and then increase his output by more than 20 points in the championship game, scored six points in a 68-60 victory against Kansas before pouring in a career- and game-high 29 points in a 68-62 victory against Villanova.

In 1992, Duke guard Bobby Hurley had a 17-point swing from his national semifinal point total (26 against Indiana) to the championship game (nine against Michigan). Despite the degression, Hurley isn't among the nine players to have a difference of at least 20 points in their scoring totals from the national semifinals to the title game. Here are the seven players other than Farmer and Patterson to post the most irregular rise and fall or vice-versa in those crucial games:

PLAYER, POS., FINAL FOUR TEAM	---FINAL FOUR SCORING TOTALS---	
	NATIONAL SEMIFINALS	CHAMPIONSHIP GAME
Bill Walton, C, UCLA '73*	14 vs. Indiana	44 vs. Memphis St.
Bill Logan, C, Iowa '56	36 vs. Temple	12 vs. USF
John Morton, G, Seton Hall '89	13 vs. Duke	35 vs. Michigan
Bob Cunningham, G, N.C. '57*	21 vs. Michigan State	0 vs. Kansas
Al Wood, F-G, N. Carolina '81	39 vs. Virginia	18 vs. Indiana
Keith Erickson, F, UCLA '64*	28 vs. Kansas State	8 vs. Duke
Kevin Grevey, F, Kentucky '75	14 vs. Syracuse	34 vs. UCLA

*Won championship game.

YOU WOULD CRY TOO IF IT HAPPENED TO YOU

Indiana was a No. 1 seed entering last year's NCAA Tournament, but many experts didn't pick the Hoosiers to reach the Final Four, let alone win the national title, after star forward Alan Henderson suffered a knee injury. They made a gallant effort behind small forward Calbert Cheaney, the consensus national player of the year, before losing to Kansas in the Midwest Regional final.

It wasn't the first time for Indiana's dream of another NCAA title to be dashed by a disabling injury. In 1975, consensus first-team All-America forward Scott May's broken arm possibly cost the Hoosiers a national championship. That team had gone undefeated during the regular season, and, according to Knight, was better than the 1976 team that won the title. Moreover, although All-America guard Isiah Thomas declared early for the NBA after Indiana won the 1981 national championship, the Hoosiers still had five of their top seven scorers returning for the next year until forward-center Landon Turner, an All-Tournament selection, was paralyzed in a summer auto accident.

But no school's NCAA championship aspirations have been short-circuited more by an assortment of major injuries than the M.A.S.H. unit at North Carolina. Consider this lengthy list of Tar Heel tourney trauma:

1969 — Starting guard Dick Grubar, averaging 13 points per game, injured a knee in the ACC Tournament and was lost for the NCAA playoffs. A standout defensive player, the senior would have drawn the assignment of facing explosive Purdue guard Rick Mount, who went on to score 36 points in a national semifinal victory over Carolina.

1976 — Sophomore playmaker Phil Ford, a second-team consensus All-America, injured a knee in a pickup game after the ACC Tournament and was ineffective (two points, three assists, five turnovers) in the Tar Heels' 79-64 NCAA Tournament first-round defeat against Alabama.

1977 — Senior center Tommy LaGarde was averaging 15.1 points and 7.4 rebounds per game when he injured a knee at midseason and was lost for the remainder of the year. Ford, a first-team consensus All-America and Carolina's leading scorer, hyperextended his shooting elbow (right) in the East Regional semifinals and scored a total of just 20 points in the team's last three playoff games, including six points on 3 of 10 field-goal shooting in a national final defeat against Marquette.

1980 — Standout freshman forward James Worthy was averaging 12.5 points and 7.4 rebounds per game when he sustained a broken ankle at midseason and was lost for the rest of the year. The Tar Heels lost their NCAA playoff opener in double overtime to Texas A&M.

1985 — Junior guard Steve Hale was unable to play the remainder of the tournament after suffering a broken collarbone when thrown to the floor while driving to the basket in Carolina's NCAA playoff opener against Middle Tennessee State. The Tar Heels were eliminated in the Southeast Regional final by eventual champion Villanova (56-44).

A few teams have been able to cope without a key player and go on to win a national championship. Stanford '42 overcame the title game absence of flu-ridden Jim Pollard, who scored 43.4 percent of Stanford's points in its first two tourney games. Kentucky '51 (sans Walt Hirsch) and San Francisco '56 (K.C. Jones) won NCAA titles although key players were ineligible for the tournament. Louisville '80 excelled with a freshman center Rodney McCray, who replaced his brother, Scooter, after Scooter suffered a season-ending knee injury.

Most championship-caliber teams, however, can't afford the loss of such vital components. It's inconceivable to think North Carolina State would have won the 1974 championship if David Thompson didn't recover from a nasty fall to the floor after attempting to block a shot by Pitt in the East Regional final. Thompson, cartwheeling over the shoulders of a teammate, landed with a sickening thud on the back of his head and did not move for four minutes. He regained consciousness, was taken to a hospital and, after getting 15 stitches to mend a head wound, was permitted to return to the arena and watch the end of the game. The mild concussion didn't keep him from being ready for the Final Four, where Thompson was named Most Outstanding Player.

Other potential titlists weren't so fortunate. In 1962, Ohio State All-America center Jerry Lucas wrenched his left knee in the national semifinals against Wake Forest, limiting his effectiveness against Cincinnati counterpart Paul Hogue in the Bearcats' 71-59 triumph in the final. Four years later, Duke guard Bob Verga (mononucleosis) and Kentucky starter Larry Conley (flu) came out of sick bay at the Final Four but weren't 100 percent as Texas Western won the title. Tourney memories are also bittersweet for the following list of teams to deal with a partial deck in their bid for an NCAA championship:

West Virginia '58 — The Mountaineers, ranked No. 1 in the country at the end of the regular season, were upset by Manhattan in the first round of the East Regional at New York after captain Don Vincent broke his left leg in the Southern Conference Tournament. Vincent averaged 12.8 points per game. West Virginia had won by seven points against NCAA champion-to-be Kentucky, handing the Wildcats just their fifth homecourt defeat in 15 years, before ending defending champion North Carolina's 37-game winning streak.

Cincinnati '59 — Oscar Robertson's brilliance wasn't enough to prevent the Bearcats from losing against California (64-58) in the national semifinals. Guard Mike Mendenhall, the team's co-captain and third-leading scorer with a 13.5-point average, was declared ineligible for the playoffs by the NCAA because he played briefly in the 1955-56 season before missing the remainder of the year because of a kidney ailment.

Utah '61 — The Utes, coming off a 26-3 season, and with Twin Towers Billy (The Hill) McGill and Allen Holmes slated to return, were a strong candidate to win it all. They reached the Final Four, although Holmes, the 1959 NJCAA Tournament MVP, didn't play that season after almost losing his right leg in a summer auto accident.

St. Bonaventure '70 — The Bonnies' only regular-season defeat was by two points at Villanova. But their biggest loss against Villanova was in a 23-point victory over the Wildcats in the East Regional final when All-America center Bob Lanier tore a knee ligament in a freak accident. He was clipped accidentally by future Detroit Pistons teammate Chris Ford, the current coach of the Boston Celtics.

Houston '71 — The Cougars, without their third-best scorer and top outside threat Jeff Hickman (declared academically ineligible after the first semester) lost to Final Four-bound Kansas by one point (78-77) in the Midwest Regional semifinals. Houston defeated eventual national runner-up Villanova by 15 points on a neutral court early in the season.

Providence '73 — In the national semifinals, Friars All-America Marvin Barnes suffered a dislocated right kneecap in the first half. PC, entering the Final Four with just two defeats, didn't have enough firepower to keep a nine-point halftime lead and wound up losing against Memphis State (98-85).

Tennessee '76 — With Bernard King idled by a broken right thumb, half of the Bernie-Ernie show was on the sideline and Ernie Grunfeld's 36 points weren't enough to prevent an 81-75 defeat against VMI in the first round of the East Regional. The Volunteers had defeated national runner-up Michigan early in the season.

Louisville '77 — The Cardinals had a 19-3 record when forward Larry Williams broke his foot against Tulsa in mid-February. They went 2-4 to close out the season, erasing memories of an early-season win at Marquette, the eventual national champ.

MAKING THEIR POINTS

Gaudy individual statistics can be very misleading because championship teams have a tendency to exhibit balance. North Carolina boasted four players averaging between 11 and 16 points per game last season, but the Tar Heels aren't the only national champion to have a textbook balanced attack. In a 10-year stretch from 1977 through 1986, Louisville guard Darrell Griffith (22.9 points per game in 1980) was the only player to average more than 20 points per game the season his school captured a national title.

The last player to score the most points in a single game of a tournament and play for a Final Four team was Al Wood. He scored a 1981 playoff-high 39 points for North Carolina in the Tar Heels' 78-65 victory against Virginia in the national semifinals before they lost to Indiana in the championship game.

The last player to score the most points in a single game of a tournament and play for a championship team was David Thompson, who tossed in 40 points for North Carolina State as a junior forward in a 92-78 triumph over Providence in the 1974 East Regional semifinals. Thompson is the only undergraduate non-center to average more than 23 points per game for a national champion. Just three other undergraduates who weren't traditional centers averaged more than 20 points per game for NCAA titlists — junior swingman Tom Gola (23 ppg for La Salle '54), junior guard Gail Goodrich (21.5 ppg for UCLA '64) and junior forward Larry Johnson (20.6 ppg for UNLV '90).

No national championship roster has included a player averaging as many as 30 points per game for the season. Of the 10 different individuals to average more than 23 points per game for a national champion a total of 12 times, Lew Alcindor achieved the feat all three of his seasons at UCLA.

Here is a list of the 10 players to compile the highest season scoring averages for NCAA title teams and their two-game point total at the Final Four that year:

PLAYER, POSITION/CLASS, NCAA CHAMPION	SCORING AVERAGE	FINAL FOUR POINT TOTAL
Lew Alcindor, C/Soph., UCLA '67	29.0 ppg	39 points
Clyde Lovellette, C/Sr., Kansas '52	28.6 ppg	66 points
Lennie Rosenbluth, F/Sr., North Carolina '57	28.0 ppg	49 points
Jerry Lucas, C/Soph., Ohio State '60	26.3 ppg	35 points
Lew Alcindor, C/Jr., UCLA '68	26.2 ppg	53 points
David Thompson, F/Jr., North Carolina State '74	26.0 ppg	49 points
Glen Rice, F/Sr., Michigan '89	25.6 ppg	59 points
*Don Schlundt, C/Soph., Indiana '53	25.4 ppg	59 points
Gail Goodrich, G/Sr., UCLA '65	24.8 ppg	70 points
Danny Manning, F/Sr., Kansas '88	24.8 ppg	56 points
Lew Alcindor, C/Sr., UCLA '69	24.0 ppg	62 points
Scott May, F/Sr., Indiana '76	23.5 ppg	40 points

*Schlundt, a 1955 draft choice of the Syracuse Nationals, is the only player to never appear in the NBA or ABA after averaging more than 20 points per game for a team reaching the NCAA championship game. He became successful in the insurance business after rejecting Syracuse's contract offer of $6,000.

CHANGE OF ADDRESS

Transfer students are a sign of the times. It gets down to one simple thing why so many impatient players choose to switch schools and sit out one season. It's P.T. That's playing time, baby! They need it, they want it, they have got to have it!

Vanderbilt guard Billy McCaffrey, a transfer from Duke, is the only All-Tournament selection to finish his college playing career attending another major university. McCaffrey earned a spot on the 1991 All-Tournament team by scoring 16 points to help Duke defeat Kansas (72-65) in the championship game.

"What I really wanted was consistency; not playing a key factor in some games, very minimal in others," McCaffrey said. "My role probably would have been the same if I had stayed. I felt I could do more. I needed to enjoy the game more. I think a player likes to know that he can be counted on for certain things every night. That's how I get pleasure from the games. Your college career is too short to spend somewhere you're not happy.

"I don't regret leaving. I cherish those memories. I was happy for them (when the Blue Devils repeated in 1972). I knew when I left that they had a good chance to win (again). I took that into consideration when I made my decision to leave. I'd already been a part of a national championship. I have a ring. Maybe that made it easier."

Although there is a stigma attached to transfers, it shouldn't be considered a crime. Each of the last 10 Final Fours featured at least one starter who began his college career at another four-year Division I school.

1993 — Kentucky G Travis Ford (via Missouri) and Kansas G Rex Walters (Northwestern).

1992 — Cincinnati G Anthony Buford (Akron) and F Erik Martin (TCU).

1991 — UNLV G Greg Anthony (Portland) and C Elmore Spencer (Georgia).

1990 — UNLV's Anthony.

1989 — Illinois F Kenny Battle (Northern Illinois).

1988 — Oklahoma F Harvey Grant (Clemson) and Arizona F Tom Tolbert (UC-Irvine).

1987 — Providence G Delray Brooks (Indiana) and UNLV G Mark Wade (Oklahoma).

1986 — Kansas C Greg Dreiling (Wichita State).

1985 — St. John's G Mike Moses (Florida).

1984 — Virginia G Rick Carlisle (Maine).

Success Breeds Success?

As you would expect, the majority of all-time NBA greats performed exceedingly well in the NCAA Tournament if they were fortunate enough to play in the event. Among those to average more than eight points more per game in NBA postseason competition than their NCAA tourney scoring mark (minimum of NCAA playoff five games) are Michael Jordan (34.7-point average in the NBA playoffs), Hakeem Olajuwon (26.4), Dolph Schayes (19.2), John Havlicek (22) and Pat Ewing (23.6).

Incidentally, Schayes is the ultimate Diaper Dandy of Final Four players. He is believed to be the youngest Hall of Famer to appear in an NCAA championship game, joining New York University's varsity lineup in midseason as a 16-year-old freshman and helping the Violets reach the 1945 NCAA final against Oklahoma A&M two months before his 17th birthday. Are you kidding me? Schayes averaged a modest 8.8 points per game in five NCAA playoff outings for NYU in 1945 and 1946 before compiling a 19.8-point average during a 12-year stretch from 1950-61 when he was an All-NBA selection each season with the Syracuse Nationals. He finished his 16-year pro career with an 18.2-point average.

Thirty-two different individuals have been named NBA Most Valuable Player, scored more than 20,000 pro points or were selected to at least five All-NBA teams after participating in the NCAA Division I playoffs. Of the 10 individuals in this category to leave college with eligibility remaining, none of their schools reached the Final Four the year they could have still been in college. Naturally, this historical tidbit doesn't bode well for two of last year's Final Four teams — Michigan (Chris Webber departed as an undergraduate) and Kentucky (Jamal Mashburn).

So many great players made their first imprint on the national conscience in the Final Four. Wilt Chamberlain (above) led Kansas to the 1957 final game, where the Jayhawks lost in three overtimes to undefeated North Carolina. Hardly anybody had ever heard of Jacksonville until Artis Gilmore (above right) led it to the championship game against UCLA in 1970. And Michael Jordan (right) hit a game-winning shot against Georgetown in 1982 that won't ever be forgotten.

Half of the aforementioned 32 NBA standouts played in more than six NCAA playoff games. Adrian Dantley, one of the 10 undergraduates, is the only one of the 16 players with more than six NCAA playoff games to compile a non-winning tourney record. Dantley, a new Towson State assistant coach, was 4-4 in the NCAA playoffs with Notre Dame from 1974 through 1976. He scored from 22 to 34 points in seven of the playoff games, but was limited to just two points in the 1974 Mideast Regional semifinals when the Irish, ranked third by UPI, bowed out against Michigan (77-68).

Here is an alphabetical list of the 32 NBA stars, complete with their NCAA Tournament scoring and rebounding averages and team playoff record (year with school denotes original graduating class):

NBA ALL-TIME GREAT, COLLEGE	------NCAA TOURNAMENT------		
	PPG.	RPG.	W-L (PCT.)
Kareem Abdul-Jabbar, UCLA '69	25.3	16.8	12-0 (1.000)
Nate Archibald, Texas-El Paso '70	36.0	3.0	0-1 (.000)
*Charles Barkley, Auburn '85	23.0	17.0	0-1 (.000)
*Elgin Baylor, Seattle '59	27.0	18.3	4-1 (.800)
Larry Bird, Indiana State '79	27.2	13.4	4-1 (.800)
*Wilt Chamberlain, Kansas '59	30.3	15.5	3-1 (.750)
Bob Cousy, Holy Cross '50	10.6	....	5-3 (.625)
Dave Cowens, Florida State '70	11.0	4.0	0-1 (.000)
*Adrian Dantley, Notre Dame '77	25.4	8.3	4-4 (.500)
Alex English, South Carolina '76	16.8	11.0	2-2 (.500)
Patrick Ewing, Georgetown '85	14.2	8.0	15-3 (.833)
Artis Gilmore, Jacksonville '71	24.0	19.2	4-2 (.667)
Hal Greer, Marshall '58	12.0	....	0-1 (.000)
John Havlicek, Ohio State '62	13.0	8.8	10-2 (.833)
Elvin Hayes, Houston '68	27.5	17.4	9-4 (.692)
Dan Issel, Kentucky '70	29.3	11.3	3-3 (.500)
*Magic Johnson, Mich. St. '81	17.8	8.0	7-1 (.875)
*Michael Jordan, N. Carolina '85	16.5	4.2	8-2 (.800)
Jerry Lucas, Ohio State '62	22.2	16.4	10-2 (.833)
*Karl Malone, Louisiana Tech '86	19.6	12.0	3-2 (.600)
Slater Martin, Texas '49	13.7	....	2-1 (.667)
*Bob McAdoo, N. Carolina '73	20.5	14.0	3-1 (.750)
George Mikan, DePaul '46	15.5	....	1-1 (.500)
Sidney Moncrief, Arkansas '79	17.0	7.1	6-3 (.667)
*Hakeem Olajuwon, Houston '85	15.1	10.2	12-3 (.800)
Bob Pettit, Louisiana State '54	30.5	....	3-3 (.500)
Oscar Robertson, Cincinnati '60	32.4	13.1	7-3 (.700)
Bill Russell, San Francisco '56	23.2	....	9-0 (1.000)
Dolph Schayes, NYU '48	8.8	....	3-2 (.600)
*Isiah Thomas, Indiana '83	19.7	2.4	6-1 (.857)
Bill Walton, UCLA '74	21.2	14.7	11-1 (.917)
Jerry West, West Virginia '60	30.6	13.8	6-3 (.667)

*Left college with eligibility remaining.

Jerry West averaged more than 30 points for West Virginia in nine tournament games. He led his team to the final game in 1959, but the Mountaineers suffered a one-point loss to California. Jerry Lucas (inset) helped Ohio State to the 1960 championship, and was twice named the Final Four's Most Outstanding Player.

Up Close and Personal

A thorough check of an athlete's pedigree is often enlightening. For instance, center Vince Kempton, the only St. Joseph's player to hit more than 50 percent of his field goals in both of the Hawks' Final Four games in 1961, is the father of Tim Kempton, a starting center for Notre Dame's basketball teams that averaged 21 victories per year from 1983-'86.

The relationships are even more intriguing when one of the family members achieves distinction outside the world of basketball. I really believe that these kids learn all about excelling and winning from their participation in athletics. Here are non-basketball facts about the immediate family trees of recognizable Final Four players:

- Starters **Ralph Beard** and **Alex Groza** for Kentucky's NCAA champs in 1948 and 1949 had famous brothers make their mark in other pro sports — **Frank Beard** (pro golfer) and **Lou Groza** (tackle and placekicker selected to nine Pro Bowls before earning induction to the NFL Hall of Fame).

- Backup guard **Ronnie Retton**, the captain of West Virginia's 1959 NCAA runner-up, is the father of Olympic gold-medal winning gymnast **Mary Lou Retton**.

- **Pat Riley**, Kentucky's leading scorer and rebounder in 1966 when "Rupp's Runts" finished national runner-up, is a brother of **Lee Riley**, a defensive back with four different teams in the NFL and AFL from 1955 through 1962. Their father, Leon, was an outfielder-catcher with the Philadelphia Phillies in 1944.

- Forward **Chito Reyes**, who averaged 8.2 points and 4.6 rebounds per game for 1970 national third-place finisher New Mexico State, is a brother of **Gil Reyes**, Andre Agassi's weight/strength coach.

- Center **Bill Walton**, the Final Four Most Outstanding Player in 1972 and 1973 for the last two of UCLA's seven consecutive NCAA champions, is a brother of **Bruce Walton**, an offensive lineman with the Dallas Cowboys from 1973 through 1975.

- Forward-guard **Kelly Tripucka**, a starter as a freshman on Notre Dame's 1978 Final Four team, is the son of **Frank Tripucka**, a quarterback for Notre Dame from 1945 through 1948. The Irish won the national football championship in 1946 and '47 when Tripucka was a backup. He started as a senior when Notre Dame was 9-0-1 and finished second in the AP poll behind Michigan. The elder Tripucka then played professional football through the 1963 season.

- Guard **Gary Garland**, an All-NCAA Tournament selection with a 17-point scoring average for 1979 national third-place finisher DePaul, is a brother of singer/actress **Whitney Houston** and a nephew of singer **Dionne Warwick**.

- Forward **Kiki Vandeweghe**, an All-NCAA Tournament pick as the leading scorer and rebounder for 1980 runner-up UCLA, has a brother, Bruk, who has been on the Pro Beach Volleyball Tour. Their mother, Colleen, is a former Miss America and their sister, Tauna, was a member of the 1976 U.S. Olympic swimming team (100-meter backstroke).

- **Steve Kerr**, a starting guard for Arizona's 1988 Final Four team, is a son of **Malcolm Kerr**, the former president of the American University of Beirut. The elder Kerr was slain by an assassin's bullet during the civil strife in Lebanon during his son's freshman season. Wildcats teammate **Harvey Mason Jr.**, a backup guard, is the son of a renowned jazz drummer who studied at the Berklee New England Conservatory and has played with Grover Washington, George Benson, Bob James and Lee Ritenour.

- Swingman **Grant Hill**, a 1992 All-NCAA Tournament selection who averaged 13.3 points and 7.3 rebounds and shot 62.2 percent from the floor at the Final Four for Duke's back-to-back champs in 1991 and 1992, is a son of **Calvin Hill**, a star running back in the NFL from 1969 through 1981.

- Guard **Thomas Hill**, a starter for Duke's back-to-back champions in 1991 and 1992, is a son of **Thomas Hill Sr.**, a world-class hurdler who earned a bronze medal in the 110-meter event in the 1972 Olympics.

- Guard **Bill McCaffrey**, a transfer to Vanderbilt after finishing as the second-leading scorer for Duke's first national titlist in 1991, is a brother of Stanford graduate **Ed McCaffrey**, a wide receiver with the New York Giants the last three years.

BEHIND THE SCENES

Did you know . . . ?

- CBS analyst **Billy Packer** was the second-leading scorer for Wake Forest's only Final Four squad (1962). After earning a spot on the All-East Regional team, Packer scored a total of 39 points in two Final Four games for the national third-place Demon Deacons to finish the season with a 14.1-point scoring average. The previous year, the All-ACC first-team selection scored a total of just 16 points in three NCAA Tournament games by shooting 6 of 24 from the floor. He hit just 1 of 10 field-goal attempts in a 97-74 victory over St. John's in the first round of the East Regional, but Wake Forest still became the only team to ever trail by as many as 10 points at halftime of a tournament game (46-36) and then win the contest by more than 20. Packer had been averaging 18.5 points per game after earning a spot on the All-ACC Tournament first team.

- The only freshman to lead a national champion in scoring was forward **Arnie Ferrin** of Utah in 1944. Of the seven sophomores to lead a national titlist in scoring average, the only guard in the group was **Isiah Thomas** of Indiana with 16 points per game in 1981.

Hey, some of those who talk a good game used to be able to play one too! Billy Packer (above, with his arm around teammate Dave Budd) played for Wake Forest in the 1962 Final Four. Curt Gowdy (left) played for Wyoming's 1941 tournament team. And that's me in the photo below, back when I played for East Rutherford (N.J.) High. I know it's hard to believe, but I used to have hair.

Longtime network broadcaster **Curt Gowdy** played in the 1941 NCAA Tournament for Wyoming. He was scoreless in two West Regional defeats (to Arkansas in regional semifinal and Creighton in regional third-place game).

 Dave DeBusschere is the only player to post the highest-scoring game in a single tournament and also play major league baseball the same year. DeBusschere scored 38 points for Detroit in a 90-81 loss to Western Kentucky in the first round of the 1962 Mideast Regional. He compiled a 3-4 pitching record for the Chicago White Sox in 1962 and 1963.

UNC Charlotte coach **Jeff Mullins** is the leading scorer and rebounder among the first 78 individuals to both play and coach in the NCAA Tournament. Mullins garnered a total of 200 points and 63 rebounds in eight playoff games to help Duke reach the Final Four in 1963 and 1964.

The only players to crack the 30-point plateau in losing efforts in NCAA Tournament finals were Seton Hall guard **John Morton** and Kentucky forward **Kevin Grevey**. In 1989, Morton's game-high 35 points, including 17 in the last eight minutes of regulation, weren't enough to prevent an 80-79 defeat in overtime against Michigan as he missed two field-goal attempts with the Pirates ahead in the last 1 1/2 minutes of the extra session. In 1975, Grevey's game-high 34 points were wasted in a 92-85 setback against UCLA after he squandered a chance to put the Wildcats ahead with 6 1/2 minutes remaining by missing the front end of a one-and-one free-throw opportunity and then a technical foul shot.

Three men have been the leading scorers for their team in an NCAA Tournament championship game and later played for and coached NBA titlists — **Bill Russell** (leading scorer with 26 points for San Francisco's second championship team in 1956/member of 11 NBA titlists with the Boston Celtics from 1957 through 1969/coach of NBA champions in 1968 and 1969); **K.C. Jones** (leading scorer with 24 points for NCAA champion San Francisco in 1955 final/member of eight NBA titlists with the Celtics from 1959 through 1966/coach of Celtics when they captured NBA championships in 1984 and 1986); **Pat Riley** (All-Tournament team selection tied **Louie Dampier** for team-high point total with 19 for NCAA runner-up Kentucky in 1966 final/member of the Lakers' championship team in 1972/Lakers' coach when they won NBA titles in 1982, 1985, 1987 and 1988).

The tournament scoring leader (minimum of three games) has averaged more than 20 points each of the last 45 years. The highest mark was 52.7 by Notre Dame guard **Austin Carr** in 1970 and the lowest figure for a tourney leader in that span was 20.3 by Iowa center **Greg Stokes** in 1983.

Dick's Top 5

Dynamic Dazzlers at Tourney Time

1. **ACC** — Compiled a total of at least 12 tourney triumphs each of the last five seasons while no other league has ever had back-to-back years with more than 10. The ACC is the only league to have all of its current members compile winning tourney records and each of them appear in at least 10 NCAA playoff games.

2. **Big Ten** — More Final Four teams than any conference.

3. **Big East** — Who can ever forget when it had three Final Four teams in 1985?

4. **Big Eight** — Kansas has been an incredible leader over the decades.

5. **Pacific-10** — Can't leave them out only because of UCLA's success.

ROLLS ROYCERS
From The Big Leagues

I scream and scream and scream on ESPN and ABC that I firmly believe the power conferences get too many teams invited to the Big Dance. They're like sororities with reputations for having pretty girls, so they get the call when the invitations go out.

I believe that if a team can't finish in the first division or finish with at least a .500 record in league play, it should not get to play in the tourney.

Don't take away the dreams of kids from mid-major conference teams that win 20 to 25 games but don't have any clout in terms of strength of schedule. Well, the big boys won't give them a chance to play them, and if they do, it's only at their home facility. How do we really know how good some of these teams are? I think there is so much parity now that a lot of these teams can play with the big guys if given a shot.

But a team with a losing conference records can get an at-large bid to the NCAA Tournament. No such squad was invited last year for the first time since the tournament expanded to at least 52 teams. A minimum of one at-large team not to win at least half of its league games was chosen from 1983 through 1992, with a high of three in 1991.

Virginia '84, one of eight ACC teams to compile a losing league record and still receive an at-large invitation, is the only club with a sub-.500 conference mark to reach the Final Four. The Cavaliers, after finishing in a tie for fifth place in the regular-season standings, became the only squad to reach the national semi-finals after losing in the opening round of their conference tournament (63-51 against Wake Forest). Two years later, LSU reached the Final Four after finishing in a tie for fifth place in the SEC with a .500 record (9-9).

Four other teams reached the Final Four after finishing fourth or lower in regular-season conference competition — Providence '87 (fourth in Big East), Georgia '83 (tied for fourth in SEC), Iowa '80 (fourth in Big Ten) and UCLA '80 (fourth in Pacific-10). Of the six schools in this category, the only one to advance to the NCAA final was UCLA. The Bruins notched a 12-6 Pac-10 record in 1980, but finished behind Oregon State, Arizona State and Washington State in the standings after going 2-4 against the threesome.

No team with a losing league record got past the second round in the last six NCAA tourneys. Iowa State compiled the worst league mark (5-9 in the Big Eight in 1992) among the following 17 at-large teams with losing conference records:

Year	Team (Conference)	Won-Loss Records		NCAA Playoff Performance
		League	Overall	
1983	Alabama (SEC)	8-10	20-12	#6 seed lost in first round
1984	Virginia (ACC)	6-8	21-12	#7 seed lost in national semis
1985	Auburn (SEC)	8-10	22-12	#11 seed lost in regional semis
	Boston College (Big East)	7-9	20-11	#11 seed lost in regional semis
1986	Maryland (ACC)	6-8	19-14	#5 seed lost in second round
1987	LSU (SEC)	8-10	24-15	#10 seed lost in regional final
	N.C. State (ACC)	6-8	20-15	#11 seed lost in first round
1988	Iowa State (Big Eight)	6-8	20-12	#12 seed lost in first round
	Maryland (ACC)	6-8	18-13	#7 seed lost in second round
1989	Providence (Big East)	7-9	18-11	#12 seed lost in first round
1990	Indiana (Big Ten)	8-10	18-11	#8 seed lost in first round
	Virginia (ACC)	6-8	20-12	#7 seed lost in second round
1991	Georgia Tech (ACC)	6-8	17-13	#8 seed lost in second round
	Villanova (Big East)	7-9	17-15	#9 seed lost in second round
	Virginia (ACC)	6-8	21-12	#7 seed lost in first round
1992	Iowa State (Big Eight)	5-9	21-13	#10 seed lost in second round
	Wake Forest (ACC)	7-9	17-12	#9 seed lost in first round

Finalists from a League of their Own

Teams from the same league have met in the national championship game on three occasions — 1976 (champion Indiana and runner-up Michigan from the Big Ten), 1985 (Villanova and Georgetown from Big East) and 1988 (Kansas and Oklahoma from Big Eight).

The ACC and Big Ten both lost regional finals last year to prevent them from having two representatives reach the national semifinals. Two teams from the same conference had advanced to the Final Four each of six consecutive years from 1987 through 1992. At least one of the two members from the same league participated in the national championship game in the following six-year span:

YEAR	FINAL FOUR RESULTS OF TWO TEAMS FROM THE SAME CONFERENCE
1987	Syracuse was runner-up to Indiana after defeating fellow Big East member Providence in the national semifinals.
1988	Kansas defeated fellow Big Eight member Oklahoma in the final game.
1989	Michigan won the championship game against Seton Hall after the Wolverines defeated fellow Big Ten member Illinois in the national semifinals.
1990	UNLV defeated two ACC members — Georgia Tech in the national semifinals and Duke in the championship game.
1991	Kansas split two games with ACC members. The Jayhawks defeated North Carolina in the national semifinals before losing to Duke in the championship game.
1992	Duke defeated two Big Ten members — Indiana in the national semifinals and Michigan in the championship game.

WELL REPRESENTED

Recognition for a conference seems to be predicated on how a league fares in postseason play. The Big Eight Conference has become much more than just a football conference although it squandered a chance to gain widespread acceptance as being on a par with the ACC and Big Ten because of a lukewarm showing in NCAA action the last two years.

The Big Eight, doubling its representation from the previous year, sent more teams (six) to the 1992 NCAA Tournament than any league and tied the ACC for the most playoff delegates in 1993 with six. But the Big Eight, without a team winning a Final Four game for 30 years until Kansas and Oklahoma both won in 1988, trails four conferences for the most entrants since the field was expanded to 64 teams in 1985. The Big Ten, ACC and Big East are running neck and neck for most representation in the last nine years.

The Big Eight is also behind those three conferences in tournament winning percentage for three major reasons. First, Big Eight powers Kansas and Oklahoma each had two teams ranked among the top five in final wire-service polls from 1989 through 1992 fail to reach regional finals: Oklahoma '89 (lost to Virginia in Southeast Regional semifinals), Oklahoma '90 (lost to North Carolina in Midwest second round), Kansas '90 (lost to UCLA in East second round), Kansas '92 (lost to Texas-El Paso in Midwest second round).

The Big Eight also had losing playoff records each of the last two years (5-6) and has just a .500 record in the past five years (23-23). And, the Big Eight is the only one of the premier leagues to have two members at least three games below .500 in the playoffs since 1985 (Missouri is 3-6 and Nebraska 0-3). The only other school from a consensus top five conference to be three games below .500 in that span is Georgia from the SEC with a 1-4 tourney record.

Of the five most prestigious leagues, the Big Ten is the only one with more than one member not appearing in the tournament since 1985, but it had seven different schools participate at least five times. Sizing up the NCAA playoff performances of the top five conferences in the last nine years:

League	Entrants	Tournament W-L Record	Only Member(s) Not Participating
ACC	50	104-47 (.689)	All nine schools appeared in playoffs
Big Ten	50	80-48 (.625)	Northwestern, Wisconsin
Big East	47	79-46 (.632)	Miami (Fla.)
SEC	41	52-41 (.559)	Mississippi
Big Eight	40	53-39 (.576)	Colorado

Conference (ACC)olades

No league has as much excitement and enthusiasm for college hoops as the ACC, which dazzles you with success after success in the Big Dance. The ACC sent eight teams to the Final Four in a six-year period from 1988-93; Duke alone went five consecutive years. The Big Ten and Big Eight were the only other conferences to even come close to matching that success.

The Big East is the only league to have three representatives at a single Final Four (Georgetown, St. John's and Villanova in 1985 after they all defeated an ACC member in regional finals). But the Big East, losing its last five playoff games against Duke, didn't have a member advance to the Final Four in the past five seasons despite generating a whopping total of 24 entrants in that span. Just six of the 24 Big East teams reached the regional semifinals (round of 16).

Reflecting actual membership, here is a league rundown of the Final 16, Final Eight and Final Four teams in the last six years since Duke's run:

Conference	F16	F8	F4	Final Four Teams (Year)
Atlantic Coast	20	11	8	Duke (1988-89-90-91-92), North Carolina (1991 and 1993), Georgia Tech (1990)
Atlantic 10	6	3	0	did not participate
Big East	10	7	1	Seton Hall (1989)
Big Eight	9	5	4	Kansas (1988-91-93), Oklahoma (1988)
Big Ten	16	8	5	Illinois (1989), Indiana (1992), Michigan (1989-92-93)
Big West	4	3	2	UNLV (1990 and 1991)
Colonial	1	0	0	did not participate
Great Midwest	3	3	1	Cincinnati (1992)
Metro	3	0	0	did not participate
Mid-American	2	0	0	did not participate
Midwestern Coll.	1	0	0	did not participate
Pacific-10	6	2	1	Arizona (1988)
Southeastern	8	2	1	Kentucky (1993)
Southwest*	3	3	1	Arkansas (1990)
Sun Belt	1	0	0	did not participate
West Coast	1	1	0	did not participate
Western Athletic	2	0	0	did not participate

*Arkansas subsequently joined the Southeastern Conference.

BLOOD, SWEAT AND CHEERS

Five consecutive victories for Duke over Big Ten teams through 1992 — after the Big Ten's eight-year drought from 1981-88 when Indiana was the only league member to reach the Final Four — enabled the ACC to bypass the Big Ten as the conference with the highest winning percentage in the 55-year history of the NCAA Tournament. The ACC is the only league to have all of its members play at least 10 games in the NCAA playoffs. Incredibly, all nine ACC members have compiled winning NCAA Tournament records.

Reflecting membership entering the 1994 NCAA Tournament, here is an alphabetical list of the all-time records of the 33 Division I conferences (ranking in parentheses is by winning percentage):

CONFERENCE (RANK)	PLAYOFF TEAMS	TOURNAMENT ENTRANTS	W-L RECORD	PCT.	FINAL FOUR	NCAA TITLES
Atlantic Coast (1)	9	117	216-114	.655	29	7
Atlantic 10 (12)	9	74	67-81	.453	6	0
Big East (7)	10	135	167-141	.542	15	2
Big Eight (4)	8	101	135-106	.560	24	4
Big Sky (21)	6	33	14-37	.275	0	0
Big South (T29)	3	5	0-5	.000	0	0
Big Ten (2)	10	120	206-117	.638	34	9
Big West (9)	9	54	57-59	.491	5	1
Colonial (20)	5	16	9-16	.360	0	0
East Coast (T29)	1	2	0-2	.000	0	0
Great Midwest (5)	7	84	108-90	.545	13	3
Ivy League (19)	8	50	35-60	.368	4	0
Metro (8)	7	43	54-46	.540	8	2
Metro Atlantic (18)	7	15	10-17	.370	0	0
Mid-American (22)	9	42	17-46	.270	0	0
Mid-Continent (T24)	5	6	2-6	.250	0	0
Mid-Eastern Athletic (T29)	4	12	0-12	.000	0	0
Midwestern Collegiate (10)	6	33	29-31	.483	3	2
Missouri Valley (13)	10	44	37-46	.446	5	0
North Atlantic (23)	4	14	5-14	.263	0	0
Northeast (28)	6	14	1-14	.067	0	0
Ohio Valley (27)	7	28	9-30	.231	0	0
Pacific-10 (3)	10	101	140-100	.583	26	13
Patriot (16)	6	25	17-27	.386	2	1
Southeastern (6)	12	118	145-121	.545	18	5
Southern (T24)	8	33	12-36	.250	0	0
Southland (T29)	4	9	0-9	.000	0	0
Southwest (15)	8	69	63-84	.429	10	0
Southwestern Athletic (26)	4	13	4-13	.235	0	0
Sun Belt (14)	8	43	34-45	.430	2	0
Trans America (T29)	2	3	0-3	.000	0	0
West Coast (11)	7	43	41-45	.477	4	2
Western Athletic (17)	10	81	58-93	.384	5	3

The Super Seven

The argument rages each season: Which conference plays the best basketball? The debate has attained new heights since the Big East Conference's initial campaign, 1980, the year the NCAA Tournament also expanded its field to 48 teams.

How do the seven leagues to have more than one current member reach the Final Four from 1980-93 stack up against each other in NCAA playoff competition? The Atlantic Coast Conference shows a clear superiority among the "Super Seven," while the Pacific-10 has the worst mark. The ACC is the only league with a non-losing record against each of the other six conferences — Big East, Big Eight, Big Ten, Great Midwest, Pac-10 and Southeastern. Incidentally, these leagues have the seven best conference records in the history of the NCAA Tournament (reflecting actual or current league membership).

The six league matchups where there is at least five games difference between current members: ACC over Big Eight (9-4 edge), ACC over SEC (16-10), ACC over Big East (17-12), Big Ten over Big East (12-6), Big East over Great Midwest (8-3) and SEC over Pac-10 (6-1). Reflecting present membership, here is a look at head-to-head NCAA playoff competition in 14 years from 1980-'93 between teams from these seven conferences (intraleague playoff games not included):

League	ACC	Big E.	Big 8	Big 10	GMC	Pac-10	SEC	Overall
ACC	...	17-12	9-4	16-14	5-5	5-5	16-10	68-50 (.576)
Big East	12-17	...	5-3	6-12	8-3	3-1	11-7	45-43 (.511)
Big Eight	4-9	3-5	...	6-6	4-4	4-3	7-3	28-30 (.483)
Big Ten	14-16	12-6	6-6	...	3-5	5-4	8-9	48-46 (.511)
Great Midwest	5-5	3-8	4-4	5-3	...	1-2	3-4	21-26 (.447)
Pacific-10	5-5	1-3	3-4	4-5	2-1	...	1-6	16-24 (.400)
SEC	10-16	7-11	3-7	9-8	4-3	6-1	...	39-46 (.459)

Where the Winners Are

I believe the Pacific-10 Conference has been hurt in the recruiting wars because of the importance of television and the three-hour time difference from the East Coast to the West Coast.

The Pac-10 hasn't prospered in the NCAA Tournament of late, losing an opening-round game to an opponent seeded 12th or worse each of the last five years. Since UCLA's appearance in the championship game in 1980, 30 of the league's 38 playoff representatives have lost in the first or second round. But the Pac-10, with nine of its 10 schools advancing to the national semifinals at least once, boasts the highest percentage of present league members to reach the Final Four in the first 55 years of the NCAA Tournament.

Arizona State is the only current Pac-10 member never to participate in the Final Four. The Sun Devils came close several times, but they lost three West Regional finals under coach Ned Wulk (1961, 1963 and 1975).

Of 46 different schools to reach the NCAA Tournament championship game, six conferences have had a minimum of four current members advance to the final — Big Ten (seven), Big East (five), Pacific-10 (five), ACC (four), Big Eight (four) and Great Midwest (four). Reflecting current membership, here are the 18 conferences to have at least one Final Four team through 1993 (ratio of members advancing to the national semifinals is in parentheses):

RANK	LEAGUE (FINAL FOUR RATIO)	FINAL FOUR PARTICIPANTS
1.	Pacific-10 (9 of 10, 90%)	Arizona, California*, Oregon*, Oregon State, Stanford*, UCLA*, USC, Washington, Washington State*
2.	Big Ten (9 of 11, 81.8%)	Illinois, Indiana*, Iowa*, Michigan*, Michigan State*, Ohio State*, Penn State, Purdue*, Wisconsin*
3.	Atlantic Coast (7 of 9, 77.8%)	Duke*, Florida State*, Georgia Tech, North Carolina*, N.C. State*, Virginia, Wake Forest
4.	Big Eight (6 of 8, 75%)	Colorado, Iowa State, Kansas State*, Kansas*, Oklahoma*, Oklahoma State*
5.	Great Midwest (5 of 7, 71.4%)	Cincinnati*, Dayton*, DePaul, Marquette*, Memphis State*
6.	Big East (7 of 10, 70%)	Georgetown*, Pittsburgh, Providence, St. John's*, Seton Hall*, Syracuse*, Villanova*
7.	Atlantic 10 (6 of 9, 66.7%)	Duquesne, Rutgers, St. Bonaventure, St. Joseph's, Temple, West Virginia*
8.	Southwest (4 of 8, 50%)	Baylor*, Houston*, SMU, Texas
9.	Missouri Valley (4 of 9, 44.4%)	Bradley*, Drake, Indiana State*, Wichita State
10.	Ivy League (3 of 8, 37.5%)	Dartmouth*, Penn, Princeton
T11.	Midwestern Collegiate (2 of 6, 33.3%)	La Salle*, Loyola of Chicago*
T11.	Southeastern (4 of 12, 33.3%)	Arkansas, Georgia, Kentucky*, Louisiana State
13.	Western Athletic (3 of 10, 30%)	Texas-El Paso*, Utah*, Wyoming*
14.	Metro (2 of 7, 28.6%)	Louisville*, UNC Charlotte
15.	West Coast (2 of 8, 25%)	San Francisco*, Santa Clara
T16.	Big West (2 of 10, 20%)	New Mexico State, UNLV*
T16.	Sun Belt (2 of 10, 20%)	Jacksonville*, Western Kentucky
18.	Patriot (1 of 8, 12.5%)	Holy Cross*

*Reached championship game.

NOTES: The only current independent to play in a Final Four was Notre Dame in 1978.

ANNUAL REPORT

Perhaps the greatest testimony to the ACC's consistent brilliance is the league's average of 11 tournament victories annually since the field expanded to 52 teams in 1983. The ACC has won at least 12 tourney games each of the last five years. No other conference has ever combined for more than 10 playoff wins in back-to-back seasons. The ACC had at least one Final Four team in the last six years and 11 of the last 13 (denied in 1985 and 1987). Reflecting actual membership, here is a look at the year-by-year records of the seven premier conferences since the tournament field expanded to 64 teams:

YEAR	ACC	BIG EAST	BIG EIGHT	BIG TEN	GMC	PAC-10	SEC
1985	12-5	18-5	4-3	4-6	dnp	0-4	7-5
1986	13-6	4-4	7-5	4-6	dnp	0-2	12-4
1987	5-6	14-5	5-4	12-5	dnp	1-2	8-6
1988	9-5	7-6	14-4	7-5	dnp	4-2	6-5
1989	12-6	11-5	4-4	15-4	dnp	3-4	0-5
1990	14-5	7-6	2-4	8-7	dnp	4-4	3-3
1991	13-5	11-7	7-3	6-5	dnp	3-4	2-5
1992	12-4	5-5	5-6	14-5	7-3	4-4	6-4
1993	14-5	2-3	5-6	10-5	3-3	3-3	8-4
Overall	104-47	79-44	53-39	80-48	10-6	22-29	52-41
Pct.	.689	(.642)	(.576)	(.625)	(.625)	(.431)	(.559)

WHAT ACTUALLY HAPPENED?

Only 10 of the 33 Division I conferences have compiled winning records in the history of the NCAA Tournament. The fledgling Great Midwest Conference got off to a great start in its inaugural season (1991-92), vaulting to the top of the all-time league rankings as league members Cincinnati and Memphis State met in the Midwest Regional final.

Although it slipped to fourth after last season, the seven-member Great Midwest exhibits impeccable credentials. Reflecting present membership, the Great Midwest has non-losing tournament records against the ACC (5-5), Big Eight (4-4) and Big Ten (5-3) since the Big East's inception in 1980. Furthermore, the Great Midwest is the only one of the premier conferences not to have one of its present members get upset in the first round of the playoffs by a team seeded 13th or worse since the tournament field was expanded to 64 teams.

Despite these achievements, the Great Midwest will continue to face an uphill battle because playoff exposure is basically a numbers game, and half of 10 (the average number of members for the other top six conferences) is two more than half of the six members the Great Midwest started with. And the more playoff teams a conference produces, the better visibility it gets and the better the players it can successfully recruit. Consequently, whatever move the Great Midwest makes in regard to expansion after adding Dayton as its seventh member will likely determine whether the alliance will enjoy long-term success like the ACC.

The ACC had a minimum of two teams reach a regional semifinal and at least one member advance to a regional final each of the first 14 years since the tournament field was expanded to at least 48 teams in 1980. The ACC's playoff record has been at least three games above .500 in 12 of the last 13 tournaments (faltered in 1987 with a 5-6 mark).

Reflecting actual conference membership for each season, here is a breakdown of how the 33 existing leagues had fared in the NCAA Tournament through 1992. (regional third-place games were played through 1975 and national third-place games were conducted from 1946 through 1981):

(Key: F8 — reached regional finals; F4 — reached Final Four; C — NCAA championship)

RANK	LEAGUE (TOTAL OF ENTRANTS)	RECORD	PCT.	F8	F4	C
1.	Atlantic Coast (103)	202-99	.671	44	26	7
2.	Big Ten (114)	199-109	.646	51	33	9
3.	Big East (66)	108-64	.628	19	8	2
4.	Great Midwest (6)	10-6	.625	3	1	0
5.	Pacific-10 (86)	124-83	.599	38	25	13
6.	Big Eight (91)	119-96	.553	36	19	2
7.	Southeastern (96)	121-98	.553	33	14	5
8.	Metro (40)	45-38	.542	5	5	2
9.	Big West (34)	37-34	.521	7	3	1
10.	Missouri Valley (57)	65-61	.516	24	16	4
11.	Atlantic 10 (32)	32-32	.500	4	0	0
12.	West Coast (45)	43-45	.489	14	3	2
13.	Southwest (75)	70-87	.446	22	12	0
14.	Sun Belt (29)	20-30	.400	2	1	0
15.	Western Athletic (52)	37-58	.389	5	1	0
16.	Southland (18)	12-19	.387	0	0	0
17.	Ivy League (48)	35-57	.380	11	4	0
18.	Midwestern Collegiate (15)	9-15	.375	0	0	0
19.	Colonial Athletic Assn. (19)	11-19	.367	1	0	0
20.	Southern (47)	26-51	.338	9	3	0
21.	Ohio Valley (40)	20-44	.313	1	1	0
22.	Mid-Continent (10)	4-10	.286	0	0	0
23.	Mid-American (43)	17-47	.266	1	0	0
24.	East Coast (33)	12-37	.245	3	1	0
25.	Southwestern Athletic (13)	4-13	.235	0	0	0
26.	North Atlantic (19)	6-20	.231	0	0	0
27.	Big Sky (26)	8-28	.222	1	0	0
28.	Northeast (19)	5-20	.200	1	1	0
29.	Metro Atlantic Athletic (10)	1-10	.091	0	0	0
30.	Trans America Athletic (12)	1-12	.077	0	0	0
T31.	Patriot League (2)	0-2	.000	0	0	0
T31.	Big South (3)	0-3	.000	0	0	0
T31.	Mid-Eastern Athletic (12)	0-12	.000	0	0	0

MOMENTUM ISN'T MOMENTOUS

Does winning a regular-season league championship give a team a boost in its bid to the reach the Final Four? Probably not. A total of 27 Final Four teams in the last 14 years — almost half of the entrants since the field expanded to 48 in 1980 — did not win outright or share a regular-season league title.

How about winning a prestige postseason conference tournament? Is that a launching pad for winning the national championship? Absolutely not! Of the top seven conferences (ACC, Atlantic 10, Big East, Big Eight, Great Midwest, Metro and SEC) conducting postseason tournaments, four times as many of their tourney champions have lost in the first round of the NCAA playoffs since the field expanded to 64 in 1985 as have gone on to win the national title.

In fact, getting beat in a postseason conference tournament can often better prepare a team for the NCAA Tournament than winning. Three national champions from 1985 through 1991 received at-large invitations to the NCAA playoffs after losing in their postseason conference tournament by at least 15 points — Duke (lost to North Carolina by 22 points in the 1991 ACC final), Kansas (lost to Kansas State by 15 in the 1988 Big Eight semifinals) and Villanova (lost to St. John's by 15 in the 1985 Big East semifinals).

Two other squads have reached the Final Four after losing by more than 15 points in their conference tournament — Virginia (lost to Maryland by 23 in the 1984 ACC quarterfinals) and Providence (lost to Georgetown by 18 in the 1987 Big East semifinals).

Louisville '86 and Duke '92 are the only two of the last 54 eligible teams from these seven conferences to win an NCAA championship after gaining an automatic berth by winning a league tournament. The eight league tourney champions from this group eliminated in the opening round in that span were North Carolina State (ACC in 1987), Missouri (Big Eight in 1987), Alabama (SEC in 1989), Rutgers (Atlantic 10 in 1989), Temple (Atlantic 10 in 1990), UNC Charlotte (Metro in 1992), Georgia Tech (ACC in 1993) and Missouri (Big Eight in 1993).

Memphis State (Metro Tournament champ in 1987) and Missouri (Big Eight in 1991) were banned from the NCAA playoffs because they were on probation.

Here is a look at how far the conference tournament winners from these seven prominent leagues progressed in the NCAA playoffs in the last nine years:

	1ST/2ND ROUND		REGIONALS		----FINAL FOUR----		
CONFERENCE	F64	F32	F16	F8	F4	F2	CH
Atlantic Coast	2	0	1	1	3	1	1
Atlantic 10	2	5	1	1	0	0	0
Big East	0	4	0	4	0	1	0
Big Eight	2	2	1	1	1	1	0
Great Midwest	0	0	0	1	1	0	0
Metro	1	2	3	0	1	0	1
Southeastern	1	0	5	2	1	0	0

NCAA Tournament Conference Leaders through 1993

(Reflecting actual conference membership for each season)

Most Final Fours
1. Big Ten	33
2. ACC	26
2. Pacific-10	25
4. Big Eight	19
5. Missouri Valley	16

Most Title Games
1. Big Ten	18
2. Pacific-10	16
3. ACC	14
4. Big Eight	9
4. Missouri Valley	9

Most Championships
1. Pacific-10	13
2. Big Ten	9
3. ACC	7
4. SEC	5
5. Missouri Valley	4

Most Victories
1. Big Ten	202
2. ACC	199
3. Pacific-10	124
4. Big Eight	121
5. SEC	119

Best Winning Percentage
1. Great Midwest	.671
2. ACC	.646
3. Big Ten	.628
4. Big East	.635
5. Pacific-10	.599

Most Appearances
1. Big Ten	114
2. ACC	103
3. SEC	96
4. Big Eight	91
5. Pacific-10	86

(Reflecting current conference membership)

Most Final Fours
1. Big Ten	34
2. ACC	29
3. Pacific-10	26
4. Big Eight	24
5. SEC	18

Most Title Games
1. Big Ten	18
2. Pacific-10	16
3. ACC	16
4. Big Eight	12
5. Big East	9

Most Championships
1. Pacific-10	13
2. Big Ten	9
3. ACC	7
4. SEC	5
5. Big Eight	4

Most Victories
1. ACC	216
2. Big Ten	206
3. Big East	167
4. Pacific-10	145
4. SEC	140

Best Winning Percentage
1. ACC	.655
2. Big Ten	.638
3. Pacific-10	.583
4. Big Eight	.560
5. Great Midwest	.545

Most Appearances
1. Big East	135
2. Big Ten	120
3. SEC	118
4. ACC	117
5. Pacific-10	101

Dick's Top 5

"SHOCK CITY" CHAMPIONSHIP COACHES

1. **Jim Valvano** — Amazing accomplishment in 1983 when N.C. State became the only school to have as many as four playoff games decided by one or two points on its way to a championship.

2. **Rollie Massimino** — Unbelievable run in 1985 when Villanova shot a championship game-record 78.6 percent from the floor to defeat mighty Georgetown and become the only national champion in the last 34 years to enter the tournament with fewer than 20 victories.

3. **Larry Brown** — Who can ever forget Danny (Manning) and the Miracles in 1988 when Kansas rebounded from a 12-8 midseason record?

4. **Bob Knight** — He had some solid players in 1987, but certainly not reminiscent of his 1976 Indiana squad that in my humble opinion is the greatest team ever assembled. The '87 Hoosiers are the only one of the last 30 NCAA champions to not have a player become an NBA first-round draft choice.

5. **Mike Krzyzewski** — Defeated UNLV's sensational team in 1991 national semifinals after getting blitzed by the Runnin' Rebels by 30 points in the championship game the previous year.

Nobody FLAT OUT DID IT BETTER

I'm still surprised by the number of fans who tell me they didn't know I was a coach. They would really be stunned to learn that if I had remained in college coaching another six years and maintained the winning percentage I compiled in my four seasons at the University of Detroit (.772 with 78-30 record at what is now Detroit Mercy), I would rank sixth among the winningest coaches percentage-wise in NCAA Division I history.

That's right, baby! I would be up there right behind the legends — Jerry Tarkanian, Clair Bee, Adolph Rupp, John Wooden and Dean Smith — although I don't think they scheduled cupcake games against Hillsdale, St. John's (Minn.), Oakland, Wisconsin-Parkside, Illinois Wesleyan, Wayne State, Grand Valley, Kalamazoo and Iowa Wesleyan like I did. But hey, give me some credit! I could have also scheduled Adrian, Albion, Alma, Aquinas, Calvin, Hope and Olivet. Still, it took four grueling years until I took the Titans to the NCAA Tournament.

Only 14 of the 91 coaches to direct at least two schools to the NCAA playoffs were at the helm when those universities appeared in the tournament for the first time. Amazingly, Joe Williams was in charge in back-to-back years when two institutions — Jacksonville (national runner-up in 1970) and Furman (first-round loser in 1971) — made their initial playoff appearance. The only coach in the last 15 years to take two universities to the playoffs for the first time was Matt Furjanic. An alphabetical list of the 14 coaches in this category through 1993:

COACH	SCHOOLS (YEAR FOR FIRST TOURNEY GAME/RESULT)
Forddy Anderson	Bradley (1950/W) and Michigan State (1957/W)
Buster Brannon	Rice (1940/L) and Texas Christian (1952/L)
Ozzie Cowles	Dartmouth (1941/L) and Michigan (1948/L)
*Hugh Durham	Florida State (1968/L) and Georgia (1983/W)
Matt Furjanic	Robert Morris (1982/L) and Marist (1986/L)
Eddie Hickey	Creighton (1941/W) and St. Louis (1952/W)
Howard Hobson	Oregon (1939/W) and Yale (1949/L)
Eugene Lambert	Arkansas (1945/W) and Memphis State (1955/L)
Jim McCafferty	Loyola, La. (1954/L) and Xavier (1961/L)
Frank McGuire	St. John's (1951/W) and South Carolina (1971/L)
*Eldon Miller	Western Mich. (1976/W) and N. Iowa (1990/W)
Jerry Tarkanian	Long Beach State (1970/W) and UNLV (1975/W)
Joe Williams	Jacksonville (1970/W) and Furman (1971/L)
Matt Zunic	Boston Univ. (1959/W) and Mass. (1962/L)

*Active college coaches.

NOTES: Anderson and Durham eventually took both schools to the Final Four.

BACK FOR MORE

It seems as if the same names are banging on the championship door year in and year out. It's not a matter of luck that some coaches know how to blend teams together at the right time. They have a special talent to unite teams and define roles and have people win.

Just six active coaches guided teams to the Final Four more than twice through 1993 — North Carolina's Dean Smith (nine Final Four appearances), Louisville's Denny Crum (six), Duke's Mike Krzyzewski (six), Indiana's Bob Knight (five), Michigan's Steve Fisher (three) and Georgetown's John Thompson (three). The departures of Lou Carnesecca and Jerry Tarkanian from the collegiate ranks after the 1991-92 season left just nine active coaches who had participated in more than 13 NCAA Tournaments in their careers. Following are the active tournament-tested coaches to have the most playoff appearances through 1993:

23 — Dean Smith (all with North Carolina)

17 — Denny Crum (Louisville), Bob Knight (Indiana)

16 — Lou Henson (six with New Mexico State and nine with Illinois), Eddie Sutton (one with Creighton, nine with Arkansas, three with Kentucky and two with Oklahoma State), John Thompson (Georgetown)

14 — Jim Boeheim (Syracuse), Don Haskins (Texas-El Paso), Lute Olson (five with Iowa and eight with Arizona)

NOTES: Joining Carnesecca (18 with St. John's) and Tarkanian (16 with Long Beach State and UNLV) among coaches no longer in the collegiate ranks who had at least 14 NCAA playoff appearances are Adolph Rupp (20 with Kentucky), John Wooden (16 with UCLA), Digger Phelps (15 with Fordham and Notre Dame) and Guy Lewis (14 with Houston).

SUCCESS ON A SILVER PLATTER?

A lot of people have a tendency to forget that some prominent coaches inherited programs that weren't in despair. Seven active coaches hit the jackpot, reaching their first Final Four, at least partially by inheriting distinctive players recruited by their predecessor.

From 1972 through 1991, a total of 10 coaches directed teams assembled for the most part by other men to the Final Four. Two of the 10 did it twice each — Larry Brown (UCLA '80 after succeeding Gary Cunningham and Kansas '86 after Ted Owens) and Lee Rose (UNC Charlotte '77 after Bill Foster and Purdue '80 after Fred Schaus). The third inactive coach in this category is Jim Valvano (North Carolina State '83 after Norman Sloan).

At one end of the spectrum among the active coaches to inherit quality teams before reaching the Final Four for the first time are Louisville's Denny Crum and Indiana's Bob Knight. They combined for 11 Final Four appearances through 1993 and are two of just four active coaches to win more than one national title. At the opposite end of the spectrum is Mercer's Bill Hodges, who hasn't coached an NCAA playoff team since Larry Bird's eligibility expired at Indiana State.

A closer look at the coaches to profit from someone else's recruits reveals they are basically men who go on to establish themselves as premier coaches — Alabama-Birmingham's Gene Bartow (succeeded John Wooden at UCLA), Michigan's Steve Fisher (Bill Frieder), Kentucky's Rick Pitino (Joe Mullaney at Providence) and Kansas' Roy Williams (Larry Brown).

The predecessors in this group weren't exactly rejects, however. Among those who left Final Four teams behind, Sloan captured a national title at N.C. State in 1974, Brown won a championship at Kansas in 1988 and Owens twice coached Kansas squads to the Final Four. Mullaney steered Providence to prominence in the 1960s. Foster was successful at Clemson after leaving UNCC. Wooden is a legend. And Frieder compiled six straight 20-win seasons at Michigan, including the Wolverines' first back-to-back Big Ten titles (1985 and 1986) in 20 years, before he left, allowing Fisher's fairy tale story to unfold in 1989.

Here is a chronological list of the active coaches to benefit from someone else's signees in reaching the Final Four:

COACH, CURRENT SCHOOL	FIRST FINAL FOUR	RECORD	PREDECESSOR
Denny Crum, Louisville	Louisville '72	26-5	**John Dromo**

Comment: The Cardinals' top five scorers, including eventual seven-year NBA guard Jim Price, were recruited by Dromo. Louisville compiled a 38-18 record in the previous two seasons.

Bob Knight, Indiana	Indiana '73	22-6	**Lou Watson**

Comment: Steve Downing and John Ritter, the Hoosiers' top two scorers, were recruited by Watson, who compiled a 17-7 mark in his final season (1970-71) when George McGinnis played his only year in college before turning pro.

COACH, CURRENT SCHOOL	FIRST FINAL FOUR	RECORD	PREDECESSOR
Gene Bartow, UAB	UCLA '76	27-5	John Wooden

Comment: Richard Washington, the Final Four Most Outstanding Player in 1975, and Marques Johnson, the national player of the year in 1977, were among the Bruins' top six scorers all recruited by Wooden. UCLA registered a 54-7 record in the previous two seasons.

Bill Hodges, Mercer	Indiana State '79	33-1	**Bob King**

Comment: The Sycamores' top seven scorers, including unanimous first-team All-America Larry Bird, were signed when King was head coach. Indiana State compiled a 48-12 record in the previous two seasons.

Rick Pitino, Kentucky	Providence '87	25-9	**Joe Mullaney**

Comment: Four of the Friars' top five scorers, including All-Big East first-team selection Billy Donovan, were recruited by Mullaney. Providence compiled an 11-20 record in Mullaney's final season (1984-85).

Steve Fisher, Michigan	Michigan '89	30-7	**Bill Frieder**

Comment: The Michigan roster Fisher inherited at the start of the playoffs included future NBA first-round draft choices Terry Mills, Glen Rice, Rumeal Robinson and Loy Vaught. The Wolverines compiled a 24-7 record entering the tournament after going 26-8 the previous season.

Roy Williams, Kansas	Kansas '91	27-8	**Larry Brown**

Comment: Starting forwards Mark Randall and Mike Maddox were recruited by Brown, but weren't factors on the 27-11 title team in 1988.

KRZYZEWSKI AND FISHER CHALLENGE WOODEN ATOP ILLUSTRIOUS LIST

The four coaches to converge at the 1993 Final Four rank among the seven winningest active coaches by percentage — Michigan's Steve Fisher (1st), Kentucky's Rick Pitino and Kansas' Roy Williams (tied for 3rd) and North Carolina's Dean Smith (7th).

Acclaimed active coaches Gene Bartow, Dale Brown, Denny Crum, Hugh Durham, Lou Henson and John Thompson each guided at least two teams to the Final Four during their careers. But these six coaches combined for four fewer NCAA playoff victories (22) from 1988 through 1993 than Mike Krzyzewski, who had 26 wins while directing Duke to five straight Final Four berths before it was eliminated in the second round by Cal last year. Even if another coach to reach the Final Four twice, Lute Olson, is added to the list, Krzyzewski managed an 18-13 edge in NCAA playoff wins from 1990 through 1993 over this group of seven standout coaches. Smith compiled 14 wins the last four years, Williams had 10 the last three years and Pitino had seven the last two years.

Krzyzewski, helping Duke become the first school since UCLA (1967 through 1973) to repeat as national champion, did the unthinkable and passed legendary Bruins coach John Wooden (47-10, .8246) for the top spot in all-time NCAA playoff winning percentage (minimum of 20 games). Krzyzewski needed to reach the championship game of the NCAA Tournament for the fourth consecutive year to stay ahead of Wooden, but the Blue Devils were eliminated in the second round in 1993. Fisher moved ahead of Wooden and Krzyzewski by reaching the national final for the third time in five years. Michigan must win its first two games in its next tournament appearance to keep Fisher atop the list.

Consistent season-long excellence is what all coaches should strive for, but like it or not, a key criteria employed in evaluating coaches is how their teams perform in postseason competition. The career NCAA playoff records of the 47 active coaches with at least 10 games in the Division I Tournament through 1993 and their highlights or lowlights (FF denotes Final Four appearances):

RANK	COACH, CURRENT SCHOOL	YRS.	W-L	PCT.	FF.
1.	Steve Fisher, Michigan	4	17-3	.850	3

Comment: Briefly moved ahead of former Cincinnati coach Ed Jucker for all-time best record (minimum of 10 games). Jucker was 11-1 (.917).

| 2. | Mike Krzyzewski, Duke | 10 | 34-8 | .810 | 6 |

Comment: Won all nine NCAA playoff games against Big East and Big Ten teams in a three-year span from 1990 through 1992.

| T3. | *Rick Pitino, Kentucky | 4 | 11-4 | .733 | 2 |

Comment: Three of his wins came against former Final Four coaches — UAB's Gene Bartow (with Memphis State and UCLA), Georgetown's John Thompson and Iowa State's Johnny Orr (with Michigan).

| T3. | Roy Williams, Kansas | 4 | 11-4 | .733 | 2 |

Comment: All four of his defeats were against schools that won a national title at one point in their histories — UCLA, Duke, Texas-El Paso and North Carolina.

| 5. | Bob Knight, Indiana | 17 | 38-14 | .731 | 5 |

Comment: Compiled sterling 7-2 Final Four career mark, including three victories in as many championship games. Absorbed three first-round defeats from 1986 through 1990.

| 6. | P.J. Carlesimo, Seton Hall | 5 | 12-5 | .706 | 1 |

Comment: First four defeats were against three No. 1 seeds (Arizona '88, UNLV '91, Duke '92) and a No. 3 seed that became champion (Michigan '89).

Maybe Mike Krzyzewski and Bob Knight (below) would have smiled more often when they were at West Point together if they could have known of the success they would have in the NCAA Tournament. Rick Pitino (right) has taken firm control of Kentucky's program, and Roy Williams (above) has a head start on continuing Kansas' great tradition.

Rank	Coach, Current School	Yrs.	W-L	Pct.	FF.
7.	Dean Smith, North Carolina	23	55-23	.705	9

Comment: Only coach to be eliminated from tournament by champion on at least six occasions (1968, 1977, 1981, 1985, 1986 and 1989). Won 10 of 12 NCAA Tournament games decided by three points or less. Four of six playoff defeats from 1985 through 1990 were by at least 12 points.

8.	Bob Huggins, Cincinnati	3	7-3	.700	1

Comment: First two defeats were against Michigan (70-64 with Akron in 1986 and 76-72 with the Bearcats in 1992) before overtime loss against North Carolina last year.

9.	Denny Crum, Louisville	17	35-17	.673	6

Comment: Reached regional final just once (1986 titlist) in 10 years from 1984 through 1993 after compiling an 11-4 playoff mark from 1980 through 1983.

10.	Rollie Massimino, UNLV	11	20-10	.667	1

Comment: Won 11 of 12 NCAA Tournament games decided by four points or less while coaching Villanova.

11.	John Thompson, Georgetown	16	28-15	.651	3

Comment: Lost his first three NCAA Tournament games from 1975-79 before winning all 11 first-round games from 1982-92. Reached the regional semifinals (round of 16) seven times in 10 years from 1980-89.

T12.	*Tom Davis, Iowa	8	14-8	.636	0

Comment: Never lost a first-round playoff game, but met eventual champion Duke in the second round of both the 1991 and 1992 tourneys.

T12.	Jud Heathcote, Michigan State	8	14-8	.636	1

Comment: Three of four NCAA playoff defeats from 1986-'91 were in overtime (Kansas '86, Georgia Tech '90, Utah '91).

14.	Billy Tubbs, Oklahoma	11	18-11	.621	1

Comment: Last eight NCAA playoff defeats through 1992 were by six points or less, including three losses by two points.

15.	Clem Haskins, Minnesota	4	6-4	.600	0

Comment: Advanced to at least the regional semifinals in his first two playoff appearances with the Golden Gophers (1989 and 1990) before they were eliminated by ACC opponents.

RANK	COACH, CURRENT SCHOOL	YRS.	W-L	PCT.	FF.
16.	John Chaney, Temple	9	13-9	.591	0

Comment: First nine defeats were against teams combining to average almost 29 victories in those seasons. Eliminated in opening round just twice (1990 vs. St. John's and 1992 vs. Michigan).

T17.	Tom Penders, Texas	5	7-5	.583	0

Comment: NCAA playoff defeats from 1988 through 1992 were against five teams combining to average almost 26 victories.

T17.	Sonny Smith, Va. Commonwealth	5	7-5	.583	0

Comment: Three of his victories while coaching Auburn were by one or two points.

T17.	Butch van Breda Kolff, Hofstra	4	7-5	.583	1

Comment: Hasn't participated in the NCAA playoffs since 1967, when he was coach at Princeton.

20.	*Eddie Sutton, Oklahoma State	16	22-16	.579	1

Comment: The only coach to guide four different colleges to the playoffs has a winning tourney record with each school (Creighton, Arkansas, Kentucky and Oklahoma State).

21.	Jim Boeheim, Syracuse	14	19-14	.576	1

Comment: No more than one playoff victory any year in his first eight appearances although those teams all finished the season with more than 20 triumphs. His last six defeats from 1987 through 1992 were by an average of just four points.

22.	Bobby Cremins, Georgia Tech	10	13-10	.565	1

Comment: Won seven of nine playoff games in one stretch. Only coach to be eliminated five times by opponents with double-digit seeds, including four consecutive years from 1986 through 1989.

23.	Gene Bartow, Ala.-Birmingham	11	14-11	.560	2

Comment: Hasn't won since 1986, but could become the first coach to guide three different colleges to the Final Four.

24.	Lefty Driesell, James Madison	11	15-12	.556	0

Comment: Split his last six NCAA playoff games while coaching Maryland, with all of the contests decided by six points or less.

Rank	Coach, Current School	Yrs.	W-L	Pct.	FF.
25.	Nolan Richardson, Arkansas	9	11-9	.550	1

Comment: Would have reached the regional semifinals each of the last four years if not for an 82-80 upset loss to Memphis State in 1992. Won just one of his first six NCAA Tournament contests before 1990, when the Razorbacks reached the Final Four.

Rank	Coach, Current School	Yrs.	W-L	Pct.	FF.
26.	Bill Frieder, Arizona State	5	6-5	.545	0

Comment: Struggled at Michigan as a top three seed to defeat Fairleigh Dickinson (1985), Akron (1986) and Boise State (1988).

Rank	Coach, Current School	Yrs.	W-L	Pct.	FF.
27.	Jim Calhoun, Connecticut	8	9-8	.529	0

Comment: Winningest Big East coach in playoff competition from 1990 through 1992 with a total of six victories.

Rank	Coach, Current School	Yrs.	W-L	Pct.	FF.
28.	Lou Henson, Illinois	16	19-17	.528	2

Comment: Nine NCAA playoff defeats with the Illini from 1981 through 1990 were by an average of 3.2 points.

Rank	Coach, Current School	Yrs.	W-L	Pct.	FF.
29.	Don Haskins, Texas-El Paso	14	14-13	.519	1

Comment: Compiled a ragged 3-9 record from 1970 through 1991, with six of the defeats by at least 13 points, before beating two better-seeded teams in 1992. He is in danger of becoming the only championship team coach other than Wyoming's Everett Shelton to finish his career with a non-winning Division I playoff record.

Rank	Coach, Current School	Yrs.	W-L	Pct.	FF.
30.	Dale Brown, Louisiana State	13	15-14	.517	2

Comment: His 1986 team and Rick Pitino's 1987 Providence squad are probably the two biggest overachievers to reach the Final Four since the field expanded to 64. LSU didn't get beyond the second round in six tournaments from 1988-93 and lost seven of its last nine playoff games. Suffered six first-round defeats from 1984 through 1993. Eliminated five times from 1979 through 1987 by teams that eventually won national title.

Rank	Coach, Current School	Yrs.	W-L	Pct.	FF.
31.	Lute Olson, Arizona	14	16-15	.516	2

Comment: Sluggish 9-9 mark with Arizona, including five first-round defeats, despite playing in natural region (West) eight of nine years.

Rank	Coach, Current School	Yrs.	W-L	Pct.	FF.
T32.	Johnny Orr, Iowa State	10	10-10	.500	1

Comment: Reached regional final while coaching Michigan three times in his four appearances from 1974 through 1977. First-round exits were by double-digit margins in four of his first six trips with the Cyclones.

RANK	COACH, CURRENT SCHOOL	YRS.	W-L	PCT.	FF.
T32.	Hugh Durham, Georgia	8	8-8	.500	2

Comment: Lost last four NCAA playoff games from 1985 through 1991 although two of them were in overtime.

T32.	Paul Evans, Pittsburgh	7	7-7	.500	0

Comment: Amazing victory at Syracuse while coaching Navy . But he didn't win more than one game in any year in his first five NCAA playoff appearances with the Panthers.

35.	Jim Harrick, UCLA	9	8-9	.471	0

Comment: Five NCAA Tournament defeats from 1983 through 1990 were against ACC schools (three while coaching Pepperdine).

T36.	Joey Meyer, DePaul	7	6-7	.462	0

Comment: Lost three consecutive NCAA Tournament games through 1992 by an eye-popping average of 13.3 points.

T36.	Jerry Pimm, UC Santa Barbara	7	6-7	.462	0

Comment: Four of his five NCAA Tournament defeats from 1977 through 1983 while coaching Utah were against Final Four teams.

38.	Eldon Miller, Northern Iowa	6	5-6	.455	0

Comment: Won his first NCAA playoff game with Western Michigan (1976), Ohio State (1980) and Northern Iowa (1990).

T39.	Don DeVoe, Navy	7	5-7	.417	0

Comment: Lost to a No. 1 seed three straight years from 1981 through 1983 while coaching Tennessee, losing twice to Virginia.

T39.	Pete Gillen, Xavier	7	5-7	.417	0

Comment: Incurred first-round defeats against eventual national champions in back-to-back years (Kansas '88 and Michigan '89).

T39.	Pat Kennedy, Florida State	7	5-7	.417	0

Comment: Lost his first two NCAA playoff games with Iona by one point each (1984 against Virginia and 1985 against Loyola of Chicago).

42.	Dave Bliss, New Mexico	6	4-6	.400	0

Comment: At SMU, lost by one point to eventual champion Georgetown (39-38 in 1984), but his other five defeats have all been by at least 13 points.

RANK	COACH, CURRENT SCHOOL	YRS.	W-L	PCT.	FF.
43.	Norm Stewart, Missouri	13	8-13	.381	0

Comment: Worst record in NCAA playoff history for any of the 40 coaches with at least 20 decisions. Notched just one tourney victory over a team with a better seed (87-84 in overtime against #4 Notre Dame in the 1980 Midwest Regional when the Tigers were #5).

T44.	Gale Catlett, West Virginia	10	5-10	.333	0

Comment: Registered just one NCAA Tournament victory from 1985 through 1993. Eight of his teams entered the tourney with more than 20 victories but none reached a regional final.

T44.	Gene Keady, Purdue	10	5-10	.333	0

Comment: Two tourney opening-round games on opponent's home court in three years — at Memphis State in 1984 and LSU in 1986 — didn't help matters as he became the only current Big Ten Conference coach to compile a losing NCAA Tournament career record. None of his five victories were against a team with a better seed.

T44.	Neil McCarthy, New Mexico State	8	4-8	.333	0

Comment: Only NCAA playoff victory while coaching Weber State was against his current school, New Mexico State, in overtime in 1979.

47.	Pete Carril, Princeton	10	3-10	.231	0

Comment: Lost eight first-round games although his last four playoff defeats were by a total of just 15 points.

*Pitino (7-2 at Kentucky), Davis (9-6 at Iowa) and Sutton (5-3 at Oklahoma State) are the only active coaches to compile NCAA playoff records at least two games above .500 at two different schools.

Records at previous schools: Bartow (3-2 at Memphis State and 5-2 at UCLA), Bliss (1-1 at Oklahoma and 3-3 at SMU), Calhoun (3-5 at Northeastern), Catlett (2-3 at Cincinnati), Cremins (0-1 at Appalachian State), Davis (5-2 at Boston College), DeVoe (0-1 at Virginia Tech and 5-6 at Tennessee), Driesell (5-4 at Davidson and 10-8 at Maryland), Durham (4-3 at Florida State), Evans (4-2 at Navy), Frieder (5-4 at Michigan), Harrick (1-4 at Pepperdine), Clem Haskins (1-2 at Western Kentucky), Heathcote (1-2 at Montana), Henson (7-7 at New Mexico State), Huggins (0-1 at Akron), Keady (0-1 at Western Kentucky), Kennedy (0-2 at Iona), Massimino's games were when he was coaching at Villanova, McCarthy (1-4 at Weber State), Miller (1-1 at Western Michigan and 3-4 at Ohio State), Olson (7-6 at Iowa), Orr (7-4 at Michigan), Penders (2-1 at Rhode Island), Pimm (5-5 at Utah), Pitino (0-1 at Boston University and 4-1 at Providence), Richardson (0-3 at Tulsa), Sonny Smith's games were when he was at Auburn, Sutton (2-1 at Creighton, 10-9 at Arkansas and 5-3 at Kentucky), Tubbs (3-2 at Lamar) and van Breda Kolff's games were when he was at Princeton.

That's big John Thompson (previous page) slammin' and jammin' for Providence in 1962. But what's that dalmation doing on the end of the floor? Apparently he wasn't too impressed with your hang time, John! That's Ohio State's Randy Ayers (left) when he was a standout player for Miami of Ohio. Like a lot of us, Randy used to have more hair than he does now. Jim Boeheim (above) beat me in a one-on-one game for charity once, but I wasn't ashamed. He was a good player at Syracuse in the 1960s. It's hard to imagine Seton Hall Coach P.J. Carlesimo (below, right) not having a beard, but he was clean-shaven as a player at Fordham. Recognize No. 34? That's Eddie Sutton, as a player at Oklahoma State.

DO AS I SAY AND AS I DID?

When you think about the first taste of tourney time for coaches, what about the guys that laced 'em up and shot the J as players? Many of them weren't superstars, but John Thompson certainly was special at Providence.

Big John is the only person to play for a National Basketball Association championship team (Boston Celtics '65) and subsequently coach an NCAA titlist (Georgetown '84). He averaged 3.6 points and 3.6 rebounds per game as a rookie backup to Hall of Famer Bill Russell after leading Providence in scoring and rebounding each of the previous two seasons. The Friars won the 1963 NIT in Thompson's junior season.

While not casting as large a shadow as Thompson, it was a familiar script for six coaches currently toiling at their alma maters — Jim Boeheim (Syracuse), Gale Catlett (West Virginia), Larry Finch (Memphis State), Jeff Jones (Virginia), Jack Rohan (Columbia) and Eddie Sutton (Oklahoma State) — because they played in the NCAA playoffs and later coached their alma mater to the national tournament. First-year Vanderbilt coach Jan van Breda Kolff, the 1974 SEC Player of the Year, hopes to join the list this season. Clem Haskins achieved the feat at Western Kentucky and Lon Kruger did likewise at Kansas State before accepting coaching jobs at Minnesota and Florida, respectively.

Washington coach Bob Bender deserves special recognition because he is the only player in NCAA history to play for two different teams in the NCAA championship game. As a freshman, Bender played in the closing seconds for Indiana's 1976 undefeated titlist. After transferring to Duke, the backup guard scored seven points in 16 minutes of the 1978 national final for the Blue Devils' team that lost to Kentucky (94-88).

"I certainly wasn't a major factor, but to be part of the Final Four was incredible," Bender said. "Sunday (the day before the final) is when you realize it when you know there are only two teams still left practicing. You're totally overwhelmed by it whether you're on a team expected to be there (averaged 2.1 points per game for Indiana in 1976) or a team not expected to be there (5.1 ppg for Duke's young happy-go-lucky upstarts in 1978)."

Bender and four other active coaches were backup players on the rosters of national championship teams — Evansville's Jim Crews (3.3 ppg for Indiana '76), Indiana's Bob Knight (3.7 ppg for Ohio State '60), San Jose State's Stan Morrison (1 ppg for California '59) and North Carolina 's Dean Smith (1.5 ppg for Kansas '52).

Following is a look at the NCAA Tournament playing statistics and won-loss records as players of the 33 active coaches to both play and coach in the playoffs (year with college denotes graduating class):

| | | -----NCAA STATS----- | | | |
COACH, CURRENT SCHOOL	COLLEGE	G.	(W-L)	PTS.	REB.
Tom Apke, Appalachian State	Creighton '65	3	(1-2)	0	9
Tom Asbury, Pepperdine	Wyoming '67	2	(0-2)	26	16
Randy Ayers, Ohio State	Miami of Ohio '78	2	(1-1)	38	18
Tony Barone, Texas A&M	Duke '68	2	(3-1)	2	1
Butch Beard, Howard	Louisville '69	4	(2-2)	73	27
Bob Bender, Washington	Duke '80	10	(11-3)	35	12
Jim Boeheim, Syracuse	Syracuse '66	2	(1-1)	29	4
Jim Brovelli, San Francisco	San Francisco '64	4	(2-2)	39	9
P.J. Carlesimo, Seton Hall	Fordham '71	3	(2-1)	0	0
Gale Catlett, West Virginia	West Virginia '63	4	(2-2)	26	11
Jim Crews, Evansville	Indiana '76	10	(10-2)	34	16
Fran Dunphy, Penn	La Salle '70	1	(0-1)	2	2
*Jarrett Durham, Robert Morris	Duquesne '71	4	(2-2)	74	22
Hank Egan, San Diego	Navy '60	3	(1-2)	10	3
*Larry Finch, Memphis State	Memphis State '73	4	(3-1)	107	10
Ed Fogler, South Carolina	North Carolina '70	8	(5-3)	37	9
*Clem Haskins, Minnesota	Western Kentucky '67	4	(2-2)	68	45
Don Haskins, Texas-El Paso	Oklahoma State '53	2	(1-1)	0	..
Jeff Jones, Virginia	Virginia '82	7	(5-2)	69	16
Bob Knight, Indiana	Ohio State '62	11	(10-2)	30	14
Lon Kruger, Florida	Kansas State '74	4	(2-2)	56	21
Stan Morrison, San Jose State	California '61	4	(8-1)	5	..
*Jeff Mullins, UNC Charlotte	Duke '64	8	(6-2)	200	63
Jim O'Brien, Dayton	St. Joseph's '74	2	(0-2)	12	3
Tom Penders, Texas	Connecticut '67	2	(0-2)	11	4
Jerry Pimm, UC Santa Barbara	Southern Cal '60	1	(0-1)	16	7
Roger Reid, Brigham Young	Weber State '68	1	(0-1)	4	1
Nolan Richardson, Arkansas	Texas-El Paso '63	1	(0-1)	4	2
Jack Rohan, Columbia	Columbia '53	1	(0-1)	0	0
Dean Smith, North Carolina	Kansas '53	8	(7-1)	4	..
Eddie Sutton, Oklahoma State	Oklahoma State '59	3	(2-1)	20	11
*John Thompson, Georgetown	Providence '64	1	(0-1)	18	3
Paul Westhead, George Mason	St. Joseph's '61	5	(3-3)	10	11

*Played in the NBA or ABA after leaving college.

NOTES: Apke (Creighton), Barone (Creighton), Brovelli (San Diego), Kruger (Kansas State), Morrison (Pacific and Southern Cal) and Westhead (La Salle and Loyola Marymount) have not guided their current schools to the NCAA playoffs, but they did direct teams to the national tournament at previous jobs. . . . Barone, Bender, Crews, Knight, Morrison and Westhead did not appear in all of the NCAA playoff games their college teams played.

DOUBLE DUTY

Only five men both played for and coached teams in the Final Four — Vic Bubas, Dick Harp, Bob Knight, Bones McKinney and Dean Smith. McKinney, who averaged 9.8 points per game as a junior center for 1946 NCAA runner-up

North Carolina, is the only one of the quintet to average more than 5.5 points per game as a player in the season his alma mater reached the Final Four.

Knight and Smith, the only men to have played for and coached national champions, compiled modest career scoring averages of 3.8 and 1.6 points per game, respectively. Knight, hitting 14 of 36 field goal attempts, scored 30 points in 11 NCAA Tournament games for Ohio State and Smith scored four points in seven playoff games for Kansas. Knight and Smith combined for fewer points as players in 10 Final Four games (eight) than their total of Final Four appearances as coaches (14).

Harp averaged 4.9 points per game for 1940 runner-up Kansas and Bubas averaged 5.5 points per game for 1950 third-place finisher North Carolina State. Here is a capsule look at the five individuals to experience the glory of the Final Four as both a player and as a head coach:

---FINAL FOUR EXPERIENCE---

NAME	PLAYER	HEAD COACH
Vic Bubas	N.C. State (1950)	Duke (1963-64-66)
Dick Harp	Kansas (1940)	Kansas (1957)
Bob Knight	Ohio St. (1960-61-62)	Indiana (1973-76-81-87-92)
Bones McKinney *	North Carolina (1946)	Wake Forest (1962)
Dean Smith	Kansas (1952-53)	N.C. (1967-68-69-72-77-81-82-91-93)

*McKinney played two seasons for North Carolina State prior to World War II military duty.

U-TURNS

A four- or five-year contract isn't necessary to reverse the fortunes of a struggling program. In five seasons from 1989 through 1993, seven coaches engineered turnarounds including an NCAA Tournament appearance in their first year at a new job although the school compiled a losing record the previous season.

Last year's rags-to-riches story involved 29-year-old Todd Bozeman, who was promoted at California following a controversial midseason firing of Lou Campanelli. For the first time in its 66-year history, the National Association of Basketball Coaches publicly condemned the dismissal of one of its member coaches. The NABC's principal concern was the absence of due process after Campanelli was accused of verbally abusing the Cal players. Campanelli, who I think did an outstanding job rejuvenating Cal basketball, subsequently filed a $5 million lawsuit against the school, charging the administration violated due process by not properly warning him that it disapproved of his treatment of players.

Nothing against Todd because he got the Cal players to play as a unit, but there's no way Campanelli should have been let go in the middle of the season because someone didn't like some of the verbiage coming out of the locker room.

At any rate, Bozeman hopes to reverse a trend. The other seven active coaches in this category have non-winning NCAA playoff records. A look at some impressive about-faces:

Hey, The General was once a foot soldier! Bob Knight was a reserve player on the great Ohio State teams of the early 1960s with Jerry Lucas and John Havlicek. Believe me, Knight could flat-out shoot the rock.

COACH, SCHOOL	W-L RECORD FIRST YEAR	W-L RECORD PREVIOUS YR.	GAMES IMPROVED
Todd Bozeman, California *	21-9 in '93	10-18 in '92	+10
Bob Wenzel, Rutgers	18-13 in '89	7-22 in '88	+10
Jim O'Brien, Dayton	22-10 in '90	12-17 in '89	+8½
Don DeVoe, Tennessee	21-12 in '79	11-16 in '78	+7
Rick Barnes, Providence	18-11 in '89	11-17 in '88	+6½
Roger Reid, Brigham Young	21-9 in '90	14-15 in '89	+6½
Bob Bender, Illinois State	18-13 in '90	13-17 in '89	+4½
Oliver Purnell, Old Dominion	15-15 in '92	14-18 in '91	+2

*Cal was 11-2 under Bozeman.

NOTES: DeVoe is currently coaching at Navy and Bender is at Washington.

CLOSE CALLS

Uh huh! Uh huh! I like to be young and have fun, as a prominently-displayed photo at my home testifies. You should have seen me trying to keep up with the Uh Huh Girls. Even Ray Charles can see close counts in more than just horse-shoes, hand grenades and what remains of drive-in movies.

Everyone knows the NCAA Tournament has a steady diet of peppy cliff-hangers, including an eight-year span from 1982-89 when five champions won at least two playoff games by one or two points. Among those titlists was North Carolina State, a winner in four games decided by one or two points in 1983 on its improbable journey as the first school requiring six victories to capture the crown.

Equally inexplicable is three-year Michigan coach Steve Fisher winning his first 10 NCAA playoff games decided by five points or less, giving him more tournament victories in "close" games through 1993 than venerable Bob Knight, who notched an ordinary 7-8 mark in the category in his first 17 playoff appearances with Big Ten rival Indiana. "It takes good players and luck," said the self-effacing Fisher. "Maybe we should have won some of the games by more than we did. Knight's record probably proves this (close game) category doesn't mean too much."

North Carolina's Dean Smith, compiling a rousing 10-2 record in his first 12 playoff games decided by three points or less, reiterated the "sometimes it's just luck" theme. But there has got to be more to winning the gut-wrenching contests than good fortune.

A real crisis facing many coaches is what they do at tournament time. The emphasis on the tourney has created a nightmare for some of them, especially if they have a penchant for losing close games. Think about all the success Lute Olson has had at Arizona, yet nearly everybody out there is screaming about the Wildcats' losing in the first round the last two years. When that happens, many fans forget about the 25 or more victories during the regular season.

Getting to the heart of what makes for a regal bench coach, here are the NCAA playoff records of active coaches (minimum of 10 games overall through 1993) to have more than five down-to-the-wire tournament contests decided in regulation by fewer than six points or in overtime:

COACH, CURRENT SCHOOL	1	2	3	4	5	OT	-OVERALL- W-L	PCT.
Steve Fisher, Michigan	0-0	1-0	1-0	1-0	3-0	4-0	10-0	1.000
Rollie Massimino, UNLV	2-0	4-0	2-0	2-1	0-1	1-0	11-2	.846
Tom Davis, Iowa	0-1	1-0	3-1	3-0	0-0	1-1	8-3	.727
John Chaney, Temple	0-0	1-0	1-1	0-0	0-1	2-0	4-2	.667
Bobby Cremins, Georgia Tech	1-0	1-0	1-0	0-2	2-0	1-1	6-3	.667
Mike Krzyzewski, Duke	2-1	1-1	1-1	2-0	1-1	1-0	8-4	.667
Joey Meyer, DePaul	0-0	0-0	1-0	1-0	1-2	1-0	4-2	.667
Johnny Orr, Iowa State	1-0	1-1	1-0	1-1	1-0	1-1	6-3	.667
Dean Smith, North Carolina	3-1	5-1	2-0	1-4	4-2	1-1	17-9	.654
Hugh Durham, Georgia	0-0	2-0	1-0	1-0	1-1	0-2	5-3	.625
Denny Crum, Louisville	0-1	2-1	2-1	1-1	2-1	4-2	11-7	.611
Lefty Driesell, James Madison	1-0	0-2	0-1	1-1	2-0	2-0	6-4	.600
Don Haskins, Texas-El Paso	0-0	1-2	0-0	1-1	1-0	3-1	6-4	.600
John Thompson, Georgetown	2-2	0-2	3-1	1-0	1-0	0-0	7-5	.583
Jim Calhoun, Connecticut	2-1	1-0	1-0	0-0	0-0	0-2	4-3	.571
Dale Brown, Louisiana State	0-1	2-1	0-2	0-1	2-0	1-0	5-5	.500
Pete Gillen, Xavier	1-0	0-0	1-1	0-0	1-2	0-0	3-3	.500
Eldon Miller, Northern Iowa	0-0	0-0	1-1	0-1	1-1	1-0	3-3	.500
Jerry Pimm, UC Santa Barbara	0-0	0-0	1-0	2-1	0-2	1-1	4-4	.500
Bob Knight, Indiana	3-1	0-3	1-2	2-1	1-1	0-0	7-8	.467
Billy Tubbs, Oklahoma	2-0	0-2	1-0	1-3	1-1	1-1	6-7	.462
Nolan Richardson, Arkansas	0-0	1-2	1-0	1-2	0-0	0-0	3-4	.429
Jim Boeheim, Syracuse	0-1	1-0	1-2	1-1	1-1	1-2	5-7	.417
Jud Heathcote, Michigan State	0-0	2-1	0-2	1-0	0-0	1-3	4-6	.400
Lou Henson, Illinois	0-2	2-4	2-4	2-0	0-1	0-0	6-11	.353
Paul Evans, Pittsburgh	1-0	0-0	0-1	0-1	0-1	1-1	2-4	.333
Eddie Sutton, Oklahoma State	1-2	1-3	1-2	1-0	1-1	0-2	5-10	.333
Norm Stewart, Missouri	0-2	1-1	0-2	1-1	0-1	1-1	3-8	.273
Lute Olson, Arizona	1-2	0-1	0-1	0-2	1-0	0-2	2-8	.200
Gene Keady, Purdue	0-2	1-0	0-1	0-0	0-0	0-2	1-5	.167

Coaches with at least 10 NCAA playoff games overall through 1993 but five or fewer close contests: .800 (4-1 record) — Virginia Commonwealth's Sonny Smith; .667 (2-1) — Minnesota's Clem Haskins; .600 (3-2) — UAB's Gene Bartow, Navy's Don DeVoe and Arizona State's Bill Frieder; .500 (2-2) — Seton Hall's P.J. Carlesimo and Texas' Tom Penders; .500 (1-1) — New Mexico State's Neil McCarthy; .400 (2-3) — Florida State's Pat Kennedy; .333 (1-2) — Cincinnati's Bob Huggins and Kentucky's Rick Pitino; .250 (1-3) — West Virginia's Gale Catlett and Hofstra's Butch van Breda Kolff; .200 (1-4) — Princeton's Pete Carril and UCLA's Jim Harrick, and .000 (0-1) — New Mexico's Dave Bliss and Kansas' Roy Williams.

Touching all the Bases

Most people don't know this, but my first coaching job was in baseball, just before and right after I earned by B.A. from Seton Hall-Paterson's School of Business Management in June, 1962. A local tire company sponsored a baseball team in Garfield, N.J., for 16-to-19-year-olds in the All-American Amateur Baseball Association. We were good enough to represent the state in the national tournament at Johnstown, Pa.

Many fans have heard the old saying that the catcher is the brains behind a baseball club. Hey, that's right! After all, North Carolina coach Dean Smith, a backup guard on Kansas' Final Four teams in 1952 and 1953, was a letterman for the Jayhawks' baseball squad in 1951 and 1952 as a catcher. That's probably where he learned how to take charge.

I really am a fanatic for the diamond sport. Whenever I'm home in Sarasota in February and March, I'm constantly at spring training reliving those days when I was a heck of a Little League pitcher. I'm like a kid running around getting autographs, meeting with all the players and taking photographs. The players drive me nuts, though, because all they want to talk about is March Madness.

A striking number of NCAA basketball championship coaches have had strong ties to baseball, such as Hank Iba, Phog Allen, Fred Taylor, Pete Newell, Frank McGuire, Everett Dean and Ed Jucker.

Iba, third on the all-time list of winningest major-college basketball coaches with 767 victories, also coached Oklahoma A&M's baseball team and didn't compile a losing record in any of his eight seasons from 1934 through 1941. Iba, an outfielder with Danville in the St. Louis Cardinals' farm chain in 1931, had a 90-41 record as the Aggies baseball coach. His most acclaimed baseball protege was Allie Reynolds, a pitcher who compiled a 182-107 record for Cleveland and the New York Yankees, and was 7-2 in the World Series with the Yankees.

Allen, fifth on the all-time list of winningest major-college coaches with 746 triumphs, had only two losing seasons in 37 years as Kansas' basketball coach but suffered losing records in both of his seasons coaching the Jayhawks' baseball squad (1941 and 1942).

Taylor, a first baseman who played sparingly for the Washington Senators in parts of three seasons from 1950 through 1952, is the only coach of an NCAA championship team (Ohio State '60) to previously play major league baseball.

Newell played minor league baseball as a center fielder with Pine Bluff in the Cotton States League, hitting .217 in 21 games in 1939. Twenty years later, he guided California to the 1959 basketball title.

McGuire guided St. John's baseball team (21-6 record) to its first College World Series in 1949 three years before he directed the school's basketball squad to the NCAA Tournament championship game in his last season with the Redmen before going to North Carolina. Current St. John's Athletic Director Jack Kaiser captained the '49 baseball team and the third baseman-center fielder was named college player of the year by Varsity Magazine. One of Kaiser's teammates was utility infielder Lou Carnesecca, who later became head basketball coach for the Redmen when Kaiser was an assistant.

Dean is another Naismith Memorial Basketball Hall of Fame coach to direct the same school to the NCAA basketball championship game and College World Series in baseball. He was coach of the 1942 titlist in basketball before leading Stanford to its first College World Series appearance in 1953 in one of his six seasons as baseball coach. McGuire lost both of his College World Series contests with St. John's, enabling Dean to become the only NCAA basketball championship coach to also win a CWS baseball game.

A total of 133 different men have taken teams to the College World Series. The only NCAA baseball championship coach to direct a basketball team to the Final Four was Sam Barry of Southern California. Barry, USC 's all-time winningest basketball coach with 260 victories in 17 seasons from 1930 through 1941 and from 1946 through 1950, was in charge when the Trojans participated in the 1940 Final Four. In 1948, he was coach when USC's baseball squad won the second College World Series (at Kalamazoo, Mich.). The next year at Wichita, Kan., the last year before the CWS moved permanently to Omaha in 1950, Barry guided the Trojans' baseball team to a national third-place finish.

Jucker was Cincinnati's baseball coach for seven years before he was promoted to head basketball coach and directed the Bearcats to three consecutive championship game appearances from 1961 through 1963. His most famous baseball pupil was wild lefthanded pitcher Sandy Koufax, a basketball scholarship athlete who played one year of freshman basketball under Jucker before signing with the Dodgers in 1954 and eventually conquering his control problems to become a baseball Hall of Famer.

The links to baseball continue today. Texas coach Tom Penders played in the NCAA Tournament and College World Series in the same year (1965) while attending Connecticut. Following are Penders and the five other active Division I coaches to play minor league baseball before entering the basketball coaching profession and having at least one NCAA playoff team:

COACH, CURRENT SCHOOL	ORGANIZED BASEBALL CAREER
Dick Davey, Santa Clara	C in San Francisco Giants farm system in 1964 and 1965
Ted Fiore, St. Peter's	3B in Cincinnati Reds farm system in 1962
*Lon Kruger, Florida	P in St. Louis Cardinals farm system in 1974
Tom Penders, Texas	INF-OF in Cleveland Indians farm system in 1968
Roger Reid, Brigham Young	INF in Atlanta Braves and Chicago White Sox farm systems from 1968-70
Norm Stewart, Missouri	P in Baltimore Orioles farm system in 1957

* Kruger directed Kansas State to the NCAA Tournament four straight years from 1987-90.

NOTES: Fiore is the only coach in this group to not win an NCAA playoff game.

Shoe Wars

It's noxious to many observers when they hear an announcer profusely identify a school by a coach's name. But you can't deny college basketball fosters larger-than-life coaches. The players come and go, but the personable coaches remain, and their names become synonymous with the universities. The coaches virtually have perpetual cult followings in their propitious kingdoms. In other words, a successful coach like Rick Pitino is the Julius Caesar of Kentucky.

A potential conflict-of-interest exists, however, when high profile coaches receive perks of six figures to endorse certain brands of sneakers. Where is a coach's allegiance at times after he sold his sole and receives more money from an outside interest than he earns in base salary?

Converse was king of the shoe industry before Nike aggressively started signing prominent coaches to endorsement deals in the late 1970s. In the 1980s, other companies such as Reebok, Puma, Pony, L.A. Gear and adidas entered the "shoe wars." When the perks seemingly turned obscene (more than $200,000 annually for several coaches), some of the companies chose to invest their promotional dollars elsewhere. Although detractors suggest Odor-Eaters should be in vogue because the arrangement stinks when coaches and not players are paid by sneaker companies, the bidding war for celebrated coaches remains as intense as ever.

The grand payoff for shoe companies arrives each March when the NCAA playoffs provide untold millions of dollars in free advertising.

"The NCAA Tournament might be the biggest sporting event in the U.S., if not the world," said Ed Janka, Nike's manager of basketball marketing.

At the 1985 Final Four in Lexington, Ky., Nike crowed when all four teams wore their "swoosh" sneakers. While Nike appeared to be overdosing on signing as many coaches as possible (85 to 90 have been on its advisory board in the last few years), a firm such as adidas was more selective and had just two coaches under contract the previous three seasons — Indiana's Bob Knight and Duke's Mike Krzyzewski. It's difficult to dispute the argument that adidas, with five championship game appearances in seven years from 1986-92, might have received the best return on its investment in that period. But that was before Nike, with at least one team wearing its shoes at the Final Four the last seven years, lured Krzyzewski away from adidas and North Carolina's Dean Smith away from Converse before the start of this season. Reportedly, the 15-year contract cooked up with "Shoe-chefski" included a $1 million signing bonus, $375,000 annually plus stock options. Talk about coaches who want to "Be Like Mike!"

Coaches should get down on their hands and knees and thank the Lord for Sonny Vaccaro for starting the shoe endorsement situation. It was Sonny who came up with the idea for Nike and started signing coaches to multi-year promotional deals. Sonny has left Nike and is now heading adidas' fortunes and once again this means gold for the coaches because it raises the stakes, baby, and competition means more dollars for the guys working the sideline.

At the National Association of Basketball Coaches (NABC) convention each year during the Final Four, sneaker companies play footsy with the coaching community via elaborate booths and hospitality rooms to make a forcible presence. Here is a sneaker scorecard assessing the companies benefiting the most from Final Four exposure since the playoff field expanded to 64 teams in 1985:

1985 — Nike 4 (Georgetown, Memphis State, St. John's, Villanova).

1986 — Converse 2 (Louisville, LSU), adidas 1 (Duke), Puma 1 (Kansas).

1987 — Nike 2 (Syracuse, UNLV), adidas 1 (Indiana), Converse 1 (Providence).

1988 — Nike 2 (Arizona, Kansas), Converse 1 (Oklahoma), adidas 1 (Duke).

1989 — Nike 2 (Michigan, Seton Hall), adidas 1 (Duke), Converse 1 (Illinois).

1990 — Nike 2 (Georgia Tech, UNLV), adidas 1 (Duke), Converse 1 (Arkansas).

1991 — Converse 2 (Kansas, North Carolina), adidas 1 (Duke), Nike 1 (UNLV).

1992 — adidas 2 (Duke, Indiana), Nike 2 (Cincinnati, Michigan).

1993 — Converse 3 (Kansas, Kentucky, North Carolina), Nike 1 (Michigan).

Final Four Totals (since 1985): Nike 16, Converse 11, adidas 8, Puma 1.

A DEAN'S LIST VIEW FROM THE TOP

When you think about North Carolina and coach Dean Smith, you never hear the word investigation or hear any rumors of anything illegal. And when you check out Dean's numbers, they are absolutely amazing.

Smith became the first coach in NCAA Tournament history to reach the 50-win plateau in playoff competition last year when he raised his record of playoff appearances to 23 and North Carolina won its opening game for the 13th consecutive year. The defending champion Tar Heels are poised to tie UCLA this year for the longest string of Final 16 trips in tourney history (14 from 1967 through 1980).

Smith, on a pace to surpass former Kentucky coach Adolph Rupp (875 victories) late in the 1996-97 season or early in the 1997-98 campaign for most triumphs in major-college history, truly is the "Dean" of coaches. He is the only coach to direct teams to Final Fours in four different decades. Nothing could be finer in Carolina, unless, of course, you're a Duke or N.C. State fan. Smith has two more NCAA playoff victories (55) than the total compiled by the following

That's Dean Smith in the white jersey chasing after a loose ball. Smith played on the Kansas team that won the title in 1952 and was runner-up to Indiana in 1953. He has won two championships as a coach at North Carolina (1982 and '93), and don't be surprised if he adds a third one this season.

11 active coaches with at least 10 tournament decisions (85 appearances overall): New Mexico's Dave Bliss, Princeton's Pete Carril, West Virginia's Gale Catlett, Navy's Don DeVoe, Xavier's Pete Gillen, Purdue's Gene Keady, Florida State's Pat Kennedy, New Mexico State's Neil McCarthy, DePaul's Joey Meyer, Northern Iowa's Eldon Miller and UC Santa Barbara's Jerry Pimm.

Smith doesn't believe his greatest achievement is the NCAA victory total, 19 consecutive playoff appearances or 13 consecutive trips to the regional semifinals. "I'm most proud of reaching the Final Four four times in six years from 1967-72," Smith said. "Back in the old days (before 1975), we had to win the ACC Tournament just to go to the playoffs. That's real pressure!"

Carolina's four ACC Tournament defeats from 1966 through 1973 were by a total of just six points. Sixteen of the 21 times the Tar Heels were eliminated in the playoffs under Smith came against Final Four teams, including 11 NCAA finalists and six champions. The principal infirmity in Smith's playoff portfolio is an 8-9 record in Final Four games with the nine defeats by an average of 15.2 points. He is the only coach to lose more than 20 NCAA Tournament games.

The only coach to win a total of more than 25 NCAA Tournament games with more than one school is Jerry Tarkanian (seven tourney victories with Long Beach State and 30 with UNLV). The most impressive thing about Tarkanian's coaching was that he won big at Long Beach emphasizing more of a ball-control pattern offense and zone defense before winning big at UNLV with a high octane fastbreak offense and man-to-man pressure defense. That is the ultimate in coaching, my friends, when you remain successful making those kinds of tactical adjustments.

Five of the nine mentors to compile more than 25 NCAA playoff victories are still active. Following are the coaches with the most NCAA Tournament triumphs through 1993 (FF signifies Final Four appearances):

Coach, School(s)	NCAA Wins	Tourney Titles	Final Fours	Final Four W-L Record	
*Dean Smith, North Carolina	55	two	9	8-9	(.471)
John Wooden, UCLA	47	ten	12	21-3	(.875)
*Bob Knight, Indiana	38	three	5	7-2	(.778)
Jerry Tarkanian, Long Beach State /UNLV	37	one	4	3-3	(.500)
*Denny Crum, Louisville	35	two	6	5-5	(.500)
*Mike Krzyzewski, Duke	34	two	6	6-4	(.600)
Adolph Rupp, Kentucky	30	four	6	9-2	(.818)
*John Thompson, Georgetown	28	one	3	4-2	(.667)
Guy Lewis, Houston	26	none	5	3-6	(.333)

* Denotes active status.

COACHES' CLASS: THE IBA INFLUENCE

During the National Association of Basketball Coaches convention conducted annually during the Final Four, no coach commanded as much widespread respect as Henry (Hank) Iba. Believe me, no NABC assembly will be the same again after Mr. Iba died January 15, 1993 at the age of 88.

He was the "father of defense," and I'll never forget the affection and emotion that Indiana coach Bob Knight poured out about Mr. Iba in a private conversation with yours truly in the General's office.

Iba was the only coach with six or more NCAA Tournament appearances to reach the regional finals every time. His Oklahoma A&M Aggies won two national championships, were national runner-up once, finished fourth once, and were regional runners-up on four occasions in eight playoff appearances from 1945 through 1965. The school is now pegged Oklahoma State Cowboys.

The engaging Iba, hailed as the patriarch of basketball's first family of coaches, had seven of his former Oklahoma State players eventually coach teams into the NCAA playoffs: John Floyd (Texas A&M), Jack Hartman (Kansas State), Don Haskins (Texas-El Paso), Moe Iba (Nebraska), Bud Millikan (Maryland), Doyle Parrack (Oklahoma City) and Eddie Sutton (Creighton, Arkansas, Kentucky, Oklahoma State). "Mr. Iba's system was so sound and he inspired such confidence that there was never any question in my mind that his philosophy offered the best opportunity to be successful," Sutton said. "The things he gave us are as valid today as they were 30 years ago."

Five generations of major college coaches emanate from Hank Iba, encompassing those coaches who were either players or assistant coaches for Iba or later generations of coaches with ties to the sage. More than 40 active Division I coaches are branches of Iba's coaching tree. At last count, it is believed a total of 37 coaches who can trace their coaching lineage to Iba have made a total of 171 NCAA Tournament appearances with 42 different colleges.

Among the prominent second-, third- and fourth-generation active coaches linked to Iba are Ricky Byrdsong (Northwestern), Tom Davis (Iowa), Tommy Joe Eagles (Auburn), Steve Fisher (Michigan), Tim Floyd (New Orleans), Pat Foster (Nevada), Leonard Hamilton (Miami), Clem Haskins (Minnesota), Lou Henson (Illinois), Gene Keady (Purdue), Lon Kruger (Florida), Nolan Richardson (Arkansas), Charlie Spoonhour (St. Louis) and Norm Stewart (Missouri). Mike Boyd, a former Michigan assistant under Fisher, became the first fifth-generation coach on the Iba family tree when Cleveland State hired him prior to the start of the 1990-91 season.

Hank Iba is one of just six former college coaches with at least 20 NCAA playoff decisions to win more than two-thirds of his tournament games. Hank Iba, former Tulsa coach Clarence Iba (Hank's brother) and longtime DePaul mentor Ray Meyer are the only coaches to direct teams to the NCAA playoffs and also have a son achieve the same feat. Moe Iba (Hank's son/Nebraska '86), Gene Iba (Clarence's son/Houston Baptist '84 and Baylor '88) and DePaul's Joey Meyer are members of the "Like Father, Like Son" club.

The only coaches to register as many or more regional final appearances as Mr. Iba are Adolph Rupp (15 with Kentucky), Dean Smith (13 with North Carolina), John Wooden (13 with UCLA) and Bob Knight (8 with Indiana).

Here are the NCAA playoff records of Iba, Wooden and Rupp and the other 14 former college coaches to amass at least 20 decisions (FF denotes Final Four appearances):

		NCAA Appearances		
Coach, School(s)	Yrs.	(Seasons)	W-L	Pct.	FF
John Wooden, UCLA	16	(1950-'75)	47-10	.825	12
Larry Brown, UCLA and Kansas	7	(1980-'88)	19-6	.760	3
Jerry Tarkanian, Long Beach State and UNLV	16	(1970-'91)	37-16	.698	4
Joe B. Hall, Kentucky	10	(1973-'85)	20-9	.690	3
Al McGuire, Marquette	9	(1968-'77)	20-9	.690	2
Henry (Hank) Iba, Oklahoma State	8	(1945-'65)	15-7	.682	4
Jim Valvano, Iona and North Carolina State	9	(1979-'89)	15-8	.652	1
Frank McGuire, St. John's, North Carolina and South Carolina	8	(1951-'74)	14-8	.636	2
Adolph Rupp, Kentucky	20	(1942-'72)	30-18	.625	6
Terry Holland, Davidson and Virginia	10	(1970-'90)	15-10	.600	2
Guy Lewis, Houston	14	(1961-'84)	26-18	.591	5
Wimp Sanderson, Alabama	10	(1982-'92)	12-10	.545	0
Don Donoher, Dayton	8	(1965-'85)	11-10	.524	1
Jack Gardner, Kansas State and Utah	8	(1948-'66)	12-12	.500	4
Digger Phelps, Fordham and Notre Dame	15	(1971-'90)	17-17	.500	1
Ray Meyer, DePaul	13	(1943-'84)	14-16	.467	2
Lou Carnesecca, St. John's	18	(1967-'92)	17-20	.459	1

Experience not Necessary

Last summer, I had the thrill of sitting up front with my family and watching a Tina Turner concert. She had the Sun Coast Dome in St. Petersburg rockin' and rollin'. If South Florida coach Bobby Paschal could have the Sun Coast Dome jumping with jubilation like she did, he'd be in great shape.

If Tina Turner sang about a coaching phenomenon, the title of the pithy tune probably would be "What's Experience Got to Do With It?" She would be referring to almost half of the 117 coaches to take at least one team to the Final Four through 1993 who reached the national semifinals in their initial tournament appearance.

Of course, it wasn't just beginner's luck. Many of the first 56 coaches to achieve the feat did so in the formative years of the event since it began in 1939. One of them, Stanford 's Everett Dean, is the only unbeaten coach in the history of the NCAA playoffs. Dean was 3-0 in 1942 in his only appearance in the national tournament in 28 seasons as a head coach, including 14 years at Indiana.

Rutgers has been a breeding ground for coaches. Three of them merged there in the 1960s. Head coach Bill Foster, left, later coached Duke into the final game, and coached at South Carolina and Northwestern. Bob Wenzel, now the head coach at Rutgers, is kneeling. And the guy on the right is Jim Valvano, who was a wet-behind-the-ears assistant there before becoming the head coach at Iona and North Carolina State. I broke into the collegiate ranks at Rutgers myself.

Just four coaches advanced to the Final Four in their first tournament appearance since the field expanded to at least 32 teams in 1975. Following is a capsule look at those four coaches (years of major-college coaching experience at the time is in parentheses):

YEAR	COACH, SCHOOL (YEARS OF EXPERIENCE)	FINAL FOUR RESULT
1977	Lee Rose, UNC Charlotte (2 seasons)	Finished in fourth place
1978	Bill Foster, Duke (15)	Runner-up to Kentucky
1980	Larry Brown, UCLA (1)	Runner-up to Louisville
1989	Steve Fisher, Michigan (1)	Won national championship

KANSAS IS CRADLE OF COACHES

One of my favorite places to visit is Lawrence, Kan. I get such a charge out of the Kansas crowd chanting "Rock . . . Chalk . . . Jayhawk!" It might be the cheer I most adore in all of sports. The adrenaline and the excitement at a KU game combined with the school's tradition and history make it the epitome of what college hoop hysteria is all about.

The last five coaches for Kansas took the Jayhawks to the Final Four during their tenures and four of them reached the national semifinals at least twice — Phog Allen (Final Four trips in 1940, 1952 and 1953), Dick Harp (1957), Ted Owens (1971 and 1974), Larry Brown (1986 and 1988) and Roy Williams (1991 and 1993). Of the 117 Final Four coaches through 1993, the only other school to have as many as four different mentors advance that far is Arkansas — Glen Rose (1941), Eugene Lambert (1945), Eddie Sutton (1978) and Nolan Richardson (1990).

Of the 507 coaches to guide teams to the NCAA Tournament through 1993, Notre Dame, Oklahoma State and St. Joseph's have had the most graduates coach in the playoffs with seven each. Kansas and Ohio State are next on the list with six apiece.

Allen and Harp are among the six KU grads to compile 106 playoff victories, with 20 Final Fours, 14 in championship games and seven titlists, all NCAA highs. The only one of the six to take more than one college to the NCAA playoffs was Ralph Miller. There has been at least one Kansas graduate coaching a team in 34 of the last 38 NCAA tournaments. Here is a capsule look at the playoff achievements of the six Jayhawk alumni:

COACH (YR. GRADUATED)	TOURNAMENT APPEARANCES	PLAYOFF RECORD	FINAL SEASON
Phog Allen ('06)	4 (Kansas)	10-3	1956
Frosty Cox ('30)	3 (Colorado)	2-4	1960
Dick Harp ('40)	2 (Kansas)	4-2	1964
Ralph Miller ('42)	10 (Wichita State, Iowa, Oregon State)	5-11	1989
Adolph Rupp ('23)	20 (Kentucky)	30-18	1972
Dean Smith ('53)	23 (North Carolina)	55-23	Active

Thanks a Lot

The well-groomed NCAA playoffs present college basketball at its best. It's all a nice, neat package. Behind the scenes, however, the sport isn't always quite so pristine when the TV cameras aren't rolling. Much too often, it's a preoccupation with dollars and cents.

The importance placed on not only participating in the NCAA Tournament but also making an imprint on the playoffs by winning a game or two has reached the stage where many athletic directors, boosters and college presidents will settle for little else. Engulfed by a win-at-all-costs mentality, it's no wonder an abundance of coaches are paranoid.

It is very unfortunate that coaches are losing their jobs because of not being successful at tournament time or because the W's don't exceed the L's. What bothers me most are the statements by a lot of school presidents and chancellors about all the different things that need to take place to rectify the problems in college athletics. I salute any emphasis on graduating players, but the bottom line in far too many cases is coach X walks in and says, "But Mr. President, all my players have graduated. My new recruits are all honor roll students. We've done a super job off the court and worked hard on it. Our players are never in trouble with the law." And then the president looks at him and says, "Well, the boosters are grousing because 7-20 doesn't make it baby. So it's time to move on." Well, as long as that big business outlook exists and that kind of pressure is applied, you are going to have guys bending the rules to try to avoid the ziggy and get to that next contract. Some sanity needs to be brought into the coaching situation because what you did yesterday doesn't matter and that's one of the real crimes facing college athletics.

In the what-have-you-done-for-me-lately world of coaching, the following men were ushered out the door right after a season they directed a team to the NCAA playoffs: Don DeVoe (19-11 at Tennessee in 1988-89), Moe Iba (19-11 at Nebraska in 1985-86), Norman Sloan (21-13 at Florida in 1988-89). Elsewhere, Eldon Miller was forced out at Ohio State before guiding the Buckeyes to the 1986 NIT title.

Incidentally, none of the four schools have set the NCAA Tournament ablaze since discarding these coaches. Tennessee and Florida didn't appear in the tourney the last four years, Nebraska is still winless in playoff competition and Ohio State compiled a 7-4 record in four NCAA appearances in the last seven years.

Perhaps the biggest atrocity was Iba getting fired in the aftermath of guiding Nebraska to its first NCAA playoff bid. He still has difficulty discussing the topic at length. "Everyone wants a winner," said the late Hank Iba, Moe's father and a Naismith Memorial Hall of Famer. "That's fine. Everyone should want to excel in life. You should never take the desire to excel away from the human race.

"But the thing I wonder about is just what stand some of these universities seem to be taking. I wonder, what are they looking for? I'm not so sure they know what they want. But it looks like, in some cases, that it's more important that the athlete won the game than if he went to school and graduated."

Triple Crown Winners

The record of the General, Robert Montgomery Knight, is absolutely astounding. Think about his achievements in terms of preparation, ability to motivate for the big game and getting the maximum out of his personnel. Yes, he's the trifecta man, baby, in big-time style.

Knight is the only one of the seven coaches to reach the NCAA Final Four a minimum of five times to also advance to the national semifinals of the NIT on at least five occasions. He is one of three coaches to win basketball championships at every major level — the NCAA, NIT and Summer Olympics. Following is a capsule look at the triumvirate and the years the elegant craftsmen captured the three titles:

Coach	NCAA	NIT	Olympics (Site)
Bob Knight	1976, 1981, 1987	1979	1984 (Los Angeles)
Pete Newell	1959	1949	1960 (Rome)
Dean Smith	1982	1971	1976 (Montreal)

NOTES: Knight and Smith won their NCAA and NIT titles with Indiana and North Carolina, respectively. Newell won the NCAA championship with California after capturing the NIT with San Francisco.

A Winner Either Way

Roy Williams was an assistant under North Carolina's Dean Smith for 10 years before Smith helped persuade his alma mater, Kansas, to hire Williams because Smith knew that Roy was a diamond ready to make his mark. The only Final Four games to have both coaches opposing their alma mater involved Williams meeting his mentor in the national semifinals in 1991 and 1993. "I remember not seeing the end of the (1991) game," said Smith, who was ejected after a questionable technical foul in the Tar Heels' defeat in 1991. "I just want them (his alma mater and former assistant coach) to do well. That's why we don't schedule each other (during the regular season). It was like playing an intrasquad game in terms of execution."

Here is a chronological list of the seven Final Four games when a coach went up against his alma mater:

Coach (Alma Mater)	FF Game	Final Four Result
Ken Loeffler (Penn State '24)	'54 semis	La Salle 69, Penn State 54
John Wooden (Purdue '32)	'69 final	UCLA 92, Purdue 72
Denny Crum (UCLA '59)	'72 semis	UCLA 96, Louisville 77
Denny Crum (UCLA '59)	'75 semis	UCLA 75, Louisville 74 (OT)
Denny Crum (UCLA '59)	'80 final	Louisville 59, UCLA 54
Dean Smith (Kansas '53)	'91 semis	Kansas 79, North Carolina 73
Roy Williams (N. Carolina '72)	'91 semis	Kansas 79, North Carolina 73
Dean Smith (Kansas '53)	'93 semis	North Carolina 78, Kansas 68
Roy Williams (N. Carolina '72)	'93 semis	North Carolina 78, Kansas 68

Johnny Wooden's accomplishments at UCLA are unbelievable. He won 10 national championships, and seven in a row. And if there had been an NCAA Tournament when Wooden played for Purdue from 1930-32, he probably would have won more as a player. He was a three-time consensus All-America guard for the Boilermakers, who were widely considered the best team in the country.

GREENER PASTURES CAN TURN BROWN

I think Rollie Massimino is the guy who can break a jinx for NCAA championship coaches. But if last season was an indication, Massimino, who coached Villanova to that unforgettable championship in 1985, won't be an exception to a pragmatic rule after moving to UNLV. The Rebels' streak of consecutive Big West Conference championships ended at 10 when they compiled a 4-5 league road record, notched a 2-5 mark in games decided by five points or less, endured an academic fiasco involving star player J.R. Rider and lost their NIT opener at home before just 5,000 fans in 19,000-seat Thomas & Mack Center after failing to receive an at-large bid to the NCAA Tournament. It probably didn't enter Massimino's decision-making process while mulling over whether to leave Philadelphia and head West, but NCAA championship coaches who changed jobs and wound up coaching other colleges have never repeated their success of capturing a national title.

Perhaps that accounted for some of the gut-level thinking when Don Haskins maneuvered to get out of a deal to coach Detroit after winning the 1966 national title with Texas Western (now Texas-El Paso) and why Bob Knight chose to stay at Indiana rather than accept a lucrative offer from New Mexico. Of the first five coaches to win a Division I title and eventually coach another university, none of them rediscovered what they formerly possessed. The experiences of championship coaches who sampled the wine on the mountaintop and then moved to other major schools is chilling. Consider the following track records stacking the odds against Massimino compiling a winning tourney mark at UNLV much less capturing another title:

COACH, CHAMPIONSHIP TEAM	LAST COLLEGE JOB (NCAA PLAYOFF MARK)
Howard Hobson, Oregon '39	Yale, 1949-56 (0-2)
Alvin Julian, Holy Cross '47	Dartmouth, 1951-67 (4-3)
Ken Loeffler, La Salle '54	Texas A&M, 1956-57 (did not appear)
Frank McGuire, North Carolina '57	South Carolina, 1965-1980 (4-5)
*Norman Sloan, N.C. State '74	Florida, 1981-1989 (3-3)

*Sloan also coached Florida from 1961 through 1966.

NOTES: Three individuals to coach a total of five Division I championship teams — Everett Shelton (Wyoming '43), Phil Woolpert (San Francisco '55 and '56) and Ed Jucker (Cincinnati '61 and '62) — ended their college coaching careers at small schools. Shelton, who had just one losing record at Wyoming from 1941 through 1955, incurred five losing marks in nine seasons at Sacramento State although he became the only coach to reach the championship game in both the Division I and Division II Tournaments (Sacramento State was runner-up to Mt. St. Mary's in 1962). Woolpert, who didn't sustain more than seven losses with San Francisco in five consecutive years from 1954 through 1958, had at least 10 defeats in all seven of his seasons at San Diego. Jucker, who averaged 22.6 victories annually in his five seasons with Cincinnati, never reached the 20-win plateau in all five of his years at Rollins.

SHORT AND SWEET

I wonder what Bill Frieder was thinking when his Michigan team won the 1989 championship game? Oh yes, I did see him walking around the lobby of the hotel in Seattle, saying, "Why did I ever leave (for Arizona State)?"

Steve Fisher, Frieder's successor, needs to remain at Michigan through the 1994-95 campaign to avoid joining the list of championship coaches to not stay at the school more than six seasons as head coach. Here is a look at the short stints of the first five coaches to fit in this category:

COACH, CHAMPIONSHIP TEAM	SCHOOL TENURE (LAST YEAR/REASON)
*Alvin Julian, Holy Cross '47	three seasons (1948/went to NBA)
Larry Brown, Kansas '88	five seasons (1988/went to NBA)
*Ed Jucker, Cincinnati '61 and '62	five seasons (1965/went to NBA)
Ken Loeffler, La Salle '54	six seasons (1955/hired by Texas A&M)
Pete Newell, California '59	six seasons (1960/retired)

*Julian and Jucker subsequently returned to the collegiate ranks at Dartmouth and Rollins (Fla.), respectively.

STAR-CROSSED CROSSING OVER FROM COLLEGE TO THE NBA

Yours truly got a cup of coffee as an NBA coach after leaving the University of Detroit. But early in my second season, I got the ax in November, 1979, the same month that ESPN came into existence. I've been with the cable network ever since. ESPN stuck with me through the early days ... or weeks ... well, maybe months ... I mean years ... when I really rambled and when many folks in the NCAA establishment didn't appreciate my candor.

The biggest adjustment I faced in the pros was a whole different time frame. Although I should have, I wouldn't listen to All-Pro Bob Lanier when he told me the NBA is a four-game-a-week league and that my three-hour practices and pregame drills wouldn't cut it.

But I did last longer in the pros than Jerry Tarkanian, one of the great college coaches of all time. His tepid 20-game stint with the San Antonio Spurs at the start of the 1992-93 season before getting fired was typical of the nondescript NBA coaching careers of the five men to be hired by an NBA team after winning an NCAA championship. Tarkanian, who captured the 1990 title with UNLV, joined Larry Brown (Kansas '88), Ed Jucker (Cincinnati '61 and '62), Frank McGuire (North Carolina '57) and Doggie Julian (Holy Cross '47) in this category. The only one of the five to compile a non-losing NBA playoff record is Frank McGuire, who was 6-6 with the Philadelphia Warriors in the 1962 playoffs.

Three coaches directed teams to the NCAA Final Four and the NBA championship series. They are Jack Ramsay (St. Joseph's 1961 and Portland Trail Blazers 1977), Fred Schaus (West Virginia 1959 and the Los Angeles Lakers 1962, 1963, 1965, 1966) and Butch van Breda Kolff (Princeton 1965 and the Lakers 1968, 1969). Neither Ramsay (8-11) nor Schaus (6-7) finished their collegiate coaching careers with winning NCAA playoff records, however.

I've been fortunate to coach in the NCAA Tournament and in the NBA. My University of Detroit team won its first-round game over Middle Tennessee State in 1977 before losing to Michigan. I later coached the Detroit Pistons in the NBA. Other coaches have done even better, taking teams to the Final Four and coaching in the NBA playoffs. Larry Brown (below left) coached UCLA to the final game in 1980, won a championship at Kansas in 1988, and has coached five NBA teams. West Virginia reached the Final Four in 1959 under Fred Schaus (below right), who later coached the Los Angeles Lakers.

Following is an alphabetical list summarizing the NBA careers of the 12 individuals to take over NBA teams after coaching a college team to the Final Four:

COACH, NCAA FINAL FOUR TEAM(S)	NBA YRS.	NBA WON-LOSS RECORD REG. SEA.	PLAYOFFS
*Larry Brown, UCLA '80/Kansas '86 & '88	10	434-342	19-26
**Bob Feerick, Santa Clara '52	2	63-74	0-2
Ed Jucker, Cincinnati '61 & '62 & '63	2	80-84	0-0
Alvin Julian, Holy Cross '47 & '48	2	47-81	0-0
Frank McGuire, St. John's '52/N. Carolina '57	1	49-31	6-6
Harold Olsen, Ohio St. '39 & '44 & '45 & '46	3	95-63	7-11
Rick Pitino, Providence '87	2	90-74	6-7
Jack Ramsay, St. Joseph's '61	21	864-783	44-58
Fred Schaus, West Virginia '59	7	315-245	23-38
Jerry Tarkanian, UNLV '77 & '87 & '90 & '91	1	9-11	0-0
Butch van Breda Kolff, Princeton '65	9	266-253	21-12
Tex Winter, Kansas State '58 & '64	2	51-78	0-0

*Brown's NBA record is at the conclusion of the 1992-93 season.

**Feerick's NBA record includes one season with the Washington Capitols (1949-50) before he was named coach at Santa Clara.

NOTES: Jucker (Rollins), Julian (Dartmouth), McGuire (South Carolina), Olsen (Northwestern), Pitino (Kentucky), Schaus (Purdue), van Breda Kolff (Lafayette and Hofstra) and Winter (Northwestern and Long Beach State) returned to college as head coaches after their stints in the NBA. . . . Ken Loeffler was coach of the St. Louis Bombers and Providence Steamrollers for three seasons (1946-47 through 1948-49) before directing La Salle to back-to-back Final Fours (1954 champion and 1955 runner-up). . . . Phil Woolpert, coach of San Francisco's back-to-back NCAA champions (1955 and 1956), coached the San Francisco Saints for one season in the old American Basketball League.

BACK TO THE FUTURE

There's something special about watching your alma mater play in an NCAA championship game. I enjoyed it in 1989, although Seton Hall lost a heartbreaker in overtime to Michigan . It has got to be even more gratifying to coach your alma mater to an NCAA title. In fact, I'm waiting for the folks in South Orange, N.J., to give me a call. Come on guys, my record's been impeccable and I'm undefeated the last 15 years at ESPN! P.J. (Carlesimo), if you don't get the Pirates to the Promised Land, they have got to call me and try to lure me out of retirement!

Eight coaches have returned to their alma mater and led it to the national championship. None of them participated as players in the NCAA Tournament, however. The last 19 champions, directed by 14 different men, were not coached by a graduate of the university. That's distressing news for the 30 to 40 coaches who annually coach their alma mater. The first three NCAA championship coaches are among the eight men to guide their alma maters to a total of 10 national titles:

COACH, GRADUATING CLASS	NCAA TOURNAMENT WON-LOSS RECORD	TITLE TEAM(S)
*Howard Hobson, Oregon '26	3-2 (1939-49)	1939
Branch McCracken, Indiana '30	9-2 (1940-58)	1940 and 1953
Bud Foster, Wisconsin '30	4-1 (1941-47)	1941
Vadal Peterson, Utah '20	3-2 (1944-45)	1944
Phog Allen, Kansas '06	10-3 (1940-53)	1952
Fred Taylor, Ohio State '50	14-4 (1960-71)	1960
Ed Jucker, Cincinnati '40	11-1 (1961-63)	1961 and 1962
*Norman Sloan, N.C. State '51	8-5 (1970-89)	1974

*The playoff records for Hobson (also coached Yale) and Sloan (Florida) include appearances with other schools.

NOTES: The only coach to have played for the school he coached to an NCAA title was Joe B. Hall. He played in just two games as a sophomore for Kentucky's 1949 kingpin before transferring to and graduating from the University of the South in Sewanee, Tenn. Hall directed Kentucky to the 1978 national title.

WE CAME A LONG WAY, BABY!

I'm testimony to the fact that circumstances can change dramatically in just a few years. In the early 1970s, I was a sixth grade teacher in Jersey earning peanuts, picking up a little extra change coaching a local high school basketball team, yet before the end of the decade I was coaching in the NBA.

So I know firsthand that timing is everything, and sometimes it takes awhile for a coach to install his program and get things rockin' and rollin'. Rollie Massimino, hired to coach UNLV prior to the 1992-93 season after 19 years as coach at Villanova, is the only individual to be more than 10 games below .500 in his initial season as a major-college head coach and subsequently guide a team to a national championship.

Elsewhere, Mike Krzyzewski compiled a winning record in his maiden season at Duke. But the Blue Devils were nine games below .500 after his first three seasons (38-47 from 1981 through 1983), including a school-record 43-point loss against Virginia in the first round of the ACC Tournament to end his third season. "I don't think there ever was a time I was afraid for my job," Krzyzewski said in retrospect. "But I was concerned that we'd never achieve what we wanted to achieve at Duke."

Krzyzewski withstood the firestorm and eventually created what some observers call the "Dynasty in Durham." Eight of the 15 different coaches to win an NCAA title since 1967 suffered a losing record in their first major-college season or their first season at the school where they eventually won it all. Coach Dean Smith of defending champion North Carolina is among the following alphabetical list of 12 coaches enduring losing records in their first season as a major-college head coach before capturing an NCAA title (records of teams are in parentheses):

COACH	CHAMPIONSHIP TEAM(S)	FIRST MAJOR-COLLEGE SEASON
Mike Krzyzewski	Duke '91 & '92 (66-9)	Army '76 (11-14)
Ken Loeffler	La Salle '54 (26-4)	Yale '36 (8-16)
Rollie Massimino	Villanova '85 (25-10)	Villanova '74 (7-19)
Al McGuire	Marquette '77 (26-6)	Marquette '65 (8-18)
Pete Newell	California '59 (25-4)	San Francisco '47 (13-14)
Vadal Peterson	Utah '44 (21-4)	Utah '28 (6-11)
Everett Shelton	Wyoming '43 (31-2)	Wyoming '40 (7-10)
Norman Sloan	N.C. State '74 (30-1)	The Citadel '57 (11-14)
Dean Smith	N.C. '82 & '93 (66-6)	North Carolina '62 (8-9)
John Thompson	Georgetown '84 (34-3)	Georgetown '73 (12-14)
Jim Valvano	N.C. State '83 (26-10)	Bucknell '73 (11-14)
Phil Woolpert	USF '55 & '56 (57-1)	San Francisco '51 (9-17)

NOTES: Newell (9-16 record with Cal in 1954-55) and Sloan (7-19 with N.C. State in 1966-67) also had losing records in their initial season at the school they later directed to a national crown. . . . Jud Heathcote never compiled a losing mark in his first five seasons as a head coach with Montana before he was hired by Michigan State, where he went 12-15 in his initial campaign with the Spartans in 1976-77 before Magic Johnson helped him win the NCAA championship two years later with a 26-6 record.

TWICE IS NICE

Only two coaches took two different schools to the NCAA championship game — Frank McGuire, St. John's (runner-up in 1952) and North Carolina (champion in 1957), and Larry Brown, UCLA (runner-up in 1980) and Kansas (champion in 1988). Last year, Rick Pitino became the 10th coach to direct two different schools to the Final Four.

My feeling is Pitino can take my jump shot and any four other guys that can't play and inspire us to win. Here is an alphabetical list of the 10 successful job-hopping coaches:

COACH	FIRST FINAL FOUR SCHOOL	SECOND FINAL FOUR SCHOOL
Forddy Anderson	Bradley '54 (2nd place)	Michigan State '57 (4th)
Gene Bartow	Memphis State '73 (2nd)	UCLA '76 (3rd)
Larry Brown	UCLA '80 (2nd)	Kansas '88 (1st)
Hugh Durham	Florida State '72 (2nd)	Georgia '83 (3rd*)
Jack Gardner	Kansas St. '48 (4th) & '51 (2nd)	Utah '61 (4th) & '66 (4th)
Lou Henson	New Mexico State '70 (3rd)	Illinois '89 (3rd*)
Frank McGuire	St. John's '52 (2nd)	North Carolina '57 (1st)
Lute Olson	Iowa '80 (4th)	Arizona '88 (3rd*)
Rick Pitino	Providence '87 (3rd)	Kentucky '93 (3rd*)
Lee Rose	UNC Charlotte '77 (4th)	Purdue '80 (3rd)

*Tied for third place.

TAKE THIS JOB AND LOVE IT

Who knows? Maybe I would still be back in my home state of New Jersey coaching Rutgers if the Scarlet Knights had promoted me from assistant to head coach in 1973 when Dick Lloyd stepped down. But Rutgers' new athletic director at the time didn't give me much consideration, although I offered to work one year for the assistant's salary I already was making.

Eleven of the 34 different coaches to win a national title through 1993, including five active coaches, have spent their entire college head coaching careers at the same university. Bud Foster, who had 13 non-winning seasons at Wisconsin, is the only championship coach to finish his college career with a losing record (265-267). Here is an alphabetical list of the 11 championship coaches to stay put at one college:

COACH, SCHOOL	TENURE	NCAA TITLE(S)
*Denny Crum, Louisville	22 years	1980 and 1986
*Steve Fisher, Michigan	5 years	1989
Bud Foster, Wisconsin	25 years	1941
*Don Haskins, Texas-El Paso	32 years	1966
Nat Holman, City College of New York	37 years	1950
George Ireland, Loyola of Chicago	24 years	1963
Vadal Peterson, Utah	26 years	1944
Adolph Rupp, Kentucky	41 years	1948, 1949, 1951, 1958
*Dean Smith, North Carolina	32 years	1982, 1993
Fred Taylor, Ohio State	18 years	1960
*John Thompson, Georgetown	21 years	1984

*Active coaches.

FIRST-YEAR FLASHES

I had mixed emotions about my first year as a college head coach in 1973-74. I was on Cloud Nine when my Detroit team defeated in-state rivals Michigan and Michigan State on our way to a 17-9 record, but we missed getting a shot at the NIT after losing four of our last five games. I don't even want to remember a 43-point defeat at Southern Illinois (95-52) after beating the Salukis five games earlier to improve our record to 15-5 at the time.

But a few head coaches have gone all the way to the Final Four in their first college season. Amazing! Perhaps the rookie coach overcoming the biggest obstacle to reach the national semifinals was Gary Thompson of Wichita State, the 1965 Missouri Valley Conference champion. The Shockers' roster was depleted in the second half of Thompson's first season after the departures of both of their high NBA draft picks — All-America forward Dave (The Rave) Stallworth and first-round draft choice center Nate Bowman. Stallworth completed his eligibility after the first 16 games and Bowman was declared ineligible for the second semester. Nonetheless, Wichita State emerged victorious out of a relatively feeble Midwest Regional field.

Here is a glimpse of Thompson and the five other rookie college coaches to be in charge of the right team at the right place at the right time:

FIRST-YEAR COACH	RECORD	FINAL FOUR TEAM (FINISH)	PREDECESSOR
Ray Meyer	19-5	DePaul '43 (T3rd)	Bill Wendt
Gary Thompson	21-9	Wichita State '65 (4th)	Ralph Miller
Denny Crum	26-5	Louisville '72 (4th)	John Dromo
Bill Hodges	33-1	Indiana State '79 (2nd)	Bob King
Larry Brown	22-10	UCLA '80 (2nd)	Gary Cunningham
Steve Fisher	*6-0	Michigan '89 (1st)	Bill Frieder

*Michigan finished with an overall record of 30-7 after Fisher succeeded Frieder just before the start of the NCAA Tournament.

RETURN ENGAGEMENTS

Nothing remotely compares to John Wooden's coaching achievements at UCLA.

I don't mean to take anything away from Red Auerbach, the father of the NBA, and his nine NBA titles with the Boston Celtics. They won two-thirds of their playoff games in capturing an amazing eight consecutive championships from 1959 through 1966. But in the NBA, you can lose as many as 11 games in four series and still become champion. Not in the NCAA Tournament! You've got to go undefeated in postseason play to win that dance. One off-night in the NCAA tourney for your team or one great game by an opponent and it's all over, baby.

UCLA won 47 of its last 52 NCAA playoff games under Wooden, with four of the five losses by a total of just eight points. The Bruins prevailed in all of their 10 championship games under Wooden, winning seven of the 10 finals by more than 10 points for an incandescent 13.4-point average margin of victory.

To try to give an idea of the magnitude of Wooden's 21 Final Four triumphs, consider that he has two more Final Four victories than the total compiled by the following 26 coaches with more than 500 career wins (minimum of 10 years at Division I since NCAA Tournament started in 1939):

Phog Allen (four Final Four wins/Kansas), Frank McGuire (three/St. John's and North Carolina), Jerry Tarkanian (three/UNLV), Gene Bartow (two/Memphis State and UCLA), Don Haskins (two/Texas-El Paso), Norman Sloan (two/North Carolina State), Lou Henson (one/New Mexico State), Ray Meyer (one/DePaul), Eddie Sutton (one/Arkansas), Harold Anderson (Bowling Green State), Lou Carnesecca (none/St. John's), Gary Colson (none/Pepperdine, New Mexico and Fresno State), Ed Diddle (none/Western Kentucky), Lefty Driesell (none/ Davidson, Maryland and James Madison), Fred Enke (none/Arizona), Slats Gill (none/Oregon State), Marv Harshman (none/Washington State and Washington), Tony Hinkle (none/Butler), Abe Lemons (none/Oklahoma City, Pan American and Texas), Eldon Miller (none/Western Michigan, Ohio State and Northern Iowa), Harry Miller (none/North Texas, Wichita State and Stephen F. Austin State), Ralph Miller (none/Wichita State, Iowa and Oregon State), C.M. Newton (none/Alabama and Vanderbilt), Norm Stewart (none/Missouri), Glenn Wilkes (none/Stetson) and Tom Young (none/American, Rutgers and Old Dominion).

The only year as many as three Final Four teams returned to the national semifinals for a second consecutive season was 1968 with UCLA (champion both years under Wooden), Houston (third in '67 and fourth in '68 under Guy Lewis) and North Carolina (fourth in '67 and runner-up in '68 under Dean Smith). Dayton was the fourth Final Four team in 1967 when four junior starters with double-figure scoring averages (Don May, Bobby Joe Hooper, Rudy Waterman and Glinder Torain) led the Don Donoher -coached Flyers to a second-place finish behind UCLA, but didn't participate in the 1968 NCAA Tournament. They did win the 1968 NIT to become the only school other than Kentucky to participate in the NCAA championship game one year and the NIT final the next season, or vice versa. Kentucky was NIT runner-up in 1947 and NCAA champion in 1948 before finishing NCAA runner-up in 1975 and NIT champion in 1976.

Last season marked the fourth occasion all four coaches converged at the national semifinals with previous Final Four experience. Here is a look at the four years when coaches got back to business at the Final Four:

1951 — Kentucky (Adolph Rupp), Kansas State (Jack Gardner), Illinois (Harry Combes), Oklahoma A&M (Hank Iba).

1968 — UCLA (John Wooden), North Carolina (Dean Smith), Ohio State (Fred Taylor), Houston (Guy Lewis).

1984 — Georgetown (John Thompson), Houston (Guy Lewis), Kentucky (Joe B. Hall), Virginia (Terry Holland).

1993 — North Carolina (Dean Smith), Michigan (Steve Fisher), Kansas (Roy Williams), Kentucky (Rick Pitino).

BEHIND THE SCENES

Did you know . . . ?

Fred Schaus (West Virginia from 1955-'60) and **Pete Gillen** (Xavier from 1986-'91) participated in the NCAA playoffs in their first six years as a head coach. Schaus lost his first four tournament games and Gillen lost four of his first five. "The average fan has no idea how difficult it is to get into the tournament, let alone advance a couple of rounds," Gillen says. "People sometimes take things for granted —that's why I don't think your goal should be pleasing people. The focus should be primarily doing the best you can with the talent available. It's not the end of the world if you don't make it to the Final Four."

All four coaches to guide Kentucky to the NCAA Tournament have winning playoff records with the Wildcats — **Adolph Rupp** (30-18 mark from 1942-72), **Joe B. Hall** (20-9 from 1973-85), **Eddie Sutton** (5-3 from 1986-88) and **Rick Pitino** (7-2 in 1992 and 1993). The only other school to have as many as three coaches direct teams to the tournament and post winning playoff records with that institution is Dartmouth — **Ozzie Cowles** (4-3 from 1941-43), **Earl Brown** (2-1 in 1944) and **Doggie Julian** (4-3 from 1956-59).

The only school to go to the NCAA Tournament under three of its former coaches who remain active in Division I is Creighton. The ex-Bluejays coaches are Appalachian State's **Tom Apke** (guided Creighton to 0-3 NCAA playoff record in 1975, 1978 and 1981), Texas A&M's **Tony Barone** (1-2 in 1989 and 1991) and Oklahoma State's **Eddie Sutton** (2-1 in 1974).

Naismith Memorial Basketball Hall of Famers **Lou Carnesecca** (17-20 with St. John's) and **Ray Meyer** (14-16 with DePaul) are the only coaches to compile losing records among the 26 individuals with at least 25 decisions in the NCAA playoffs. Carnesecca made the most appearances in the tournament before reaching the Final Four of any coach (12th in 1985). Meyer had the longest time between a coach's first and last appearance in the playoffs (41 years from 1943 until 1984).

Larry Brown is the only coach to leave an NCAA champion before the next season for another coaching job. The peripatetic Brown left the Jayhawks to coach the NBA's San Antonio Spurs for 3 1/2 seasons before moving over to the Los Angeles Clippers for 1 1/2 years. Then, he joined the Indiana Pacers before the start of the current campaign. Two other NCAA champion coaches, **John Wooden** (UCLA '75) and **Al McGuire** (Marquette '77), retired after winning titles.

Of the 47 coaches to reach the national semifinals at least twice, the only one to go undefeated in Final Four games is **Branch McCracken**. He was 4-0 after directing Indiana to national titles in 1940 and 1953.

Big Ten Conference Commissioner **Jim Delany**, former chairman of the NCAA Division I Basketball Committee, was a roommate of first-year South Carolina coach **Eddie Fogler** at North Carolina. They were 5-11 guards for the Tar Heels' 1968 and 1969 Final Four squads in their sophomore and junior seasons. The highest-scoring game either of them managed at the Final Four was by Fogler against Drake in the 1969 national third-place game, but he had more turnovers (11) than points (seven) in the Tar Heels' 104-84 setback.

Elmer Gross was the first coach in NCAA playoff history to reach the Final Four after he played in the tournament. Gross played in two playoff games as Penn State 's co-captain in 1942 before directing his alma mater to the 1952 tournament. In 1954, he guided the Nittany Lions to their only Final Four appearance. **Doyle Parrack**, an essential member of Oklahoma State's 1945 championship team, was the first Final Four player to coach a team in the playoffs. Parrack also participated in the 1952 tournament as coach of Oklahoma City, which was 1-5 in the playoffs under him in four appearances from 1952 through 1955.

Of the 10 coaches to take at least three different schools to the tournament, the only one to win his first two playoff games with each school is **Gene Bartow** (Memphis State '73, UCLA '76 and Alabama-Birmingham '81). Bartow's leading scorer for Memphis State when the Tigers finished NCAA runner-up to UCLA was guard **Larry Finch**, the current Memphis State coach who averaged 24 points per game and was an All-Tournament team selection. Bartow began his coaching career at Central Missouri State, a Division II school that also lists Division I championship coaches **Phog Allen** of Kansas and **Joe B. Hall** of Kentucky among its former head coaches. Allen posted an 84-31 record in seven seasons at Central Missouri from 1913-19, Bartow was 47-21 in three seasons from 1962-64 and Hall was 19-6 in one season (1964-65). Central Missouri, winner of the first two NAIA Tournaments in 1937 and 1938, captured the NCAA Division II crown in 1984 under **Lynn Nance**, the coach at St. Mary's (Calif.) in 1989 when the Gaels made their first NCAA Tournament appearance in 30 years.

George Edwards, the first coach to take a Missouri team to the NCAA Tournament (1944), was the school's sports information director at the same time. Edwards, a former president of the National Association of Basketball Coaches, wrote the NABC creed the organization still embraces.

Dick Tarrant, who compiled a 5-5 playoff record with Richmond, gained a reputation as an East Regional giant-killer when three of his teams with the Spiders were seeded 12th or worse but still pulled off first-round upsets against Auburn '84 (star players were **Charles Barkley** and **Chuck Person**), Indiana '88 (**Jay Edwards**, **Dean Garrett** and **Keith Smart**) and Syracuse '91 (**LeRon Ellis**, **Dave Johnson** and **Billy Owens**). Tarrant was 4-1 in tournament games decided by fewer than five points. The tenacity displayed by Tarrant's teams might have stemmed at least in part because he played basketball at Fordham when NFL Hall of Fame coach **Vince Lombardi** was the Rams' freshman basketball coach. Tarrant served four years at his alma mater as an assistant under **John Bach**, an assistant coach specializing in defense for the three-time NBA champion Chicago Bulls.

Dick's Top 5

Streaks that May Never be Broken

1. **30** — UCLA's winning streak in tournament play. The Bruins were unbeaten from 1967 through 1974, when they lost to North Carolina State in the national semifinals in double overtime.

2. **13** — North Carolina's current streak of Sweet Sixteen appearances. Probably the only team that can break it is the Tar Heels, who will try to continue it this season.

3. **7**— Consecutive years that UCLA won the national championship. What more can you say? These days, two in a row is considered astounding.

4. **4** — Number of games in which Austin Carr scored 45 or more points in the tournament. Carr had games of 61, 52 and 45 for Notre Dame in 1970 and opened the 1971 tournament with a 52-point performance. He followed that with a mere 26 points, but came back with 47 in his final tournament game.

5. **3** — Number of years in which Lew Alcindor (Kareem Abdul-Jabbar) won the Most Outstanding Player award at the Final Four. He was named a unanimous All-America and played for the championship team each of those years as well.

It would have been far-fetched to predict a guard wearing uniform No. 23 would hit a last-second game-winning basket from the left side of the Louisiana Superdome court in the championship game last year for the third consecutive time the Final Four was in New Orleans. Still, some trivia nuts were keeping an eye out for Kansas' Rex Walters to do exactly that after North Carolina's Michael Jordan and Indiana's Keith Smart achieved the feat in 1982 and 1987, respectively.

It didn't happen, but other more likely coincidences should be considered before filling out the NCAA Tournament bracket. For those who want the edge before jumping into the office pool, here are trends to keep in mind before the 64-team field begins marching along the treacherous Road to the Final Four:

 Ten different schools won the last 11 titles from 1983 through 1993.

 The Big East failed to have a team win the national title in eight consecutive years from 1986-93 and had just one school (Seton Hall '89) reach the Final Four in the last six years.

 At least two Final Four teams annually from 1988 through 1993 reached a regional semifinal (round of 16) the previous season.

171

- Teams with fewer victories than their opponents won 14 of 27 Final Four games from 1985-93 after the field was expanded to 64.

- Excluding three times North Carolina State was on NCAA probation (1955, 1959 and 1973), the other 13 ACC undisputed regular-season champions to also win the league's postseason tournament all reached the Final Four through 1993.

- Just three of the total of 21 postseason tournament champions from the ACC, Big East and Big Eight from 1987 through 1993 — Duke '92, Connecticut '91 and Duke '88 — advanced deeper into the national playoffs than all of the representatives from their conferences.

- Villanova, entering the 1985 playoffs with 19 victories, is the only national champion in 35 years from 1959-93 to enter the tournament with fewer than 20 wins. The average number of triumphs entering the playoffs for the 36 Final Four teams since the field was expanded to 64 is 25.9.

MARGIN FOR ERROR

If the tiebreaker for the office pool is to guess the combined point total in the championship game, keep in mind that the average is 150.1 in the last seven years since the inception nationwide of both the shot clock and three-point field goal.

The average margin of victory in an NCAA Tournament game is 11.5 points over the last nine years, which is higher than the average margin of a normal NBA game (seven points). Figures for college regular-season games are unavailable.

The average margin is at least eight points for each of the six rounds of the NCAA tourney. Of the first four rounds leading up to the Final Four, the only round with a single-digit average margin is the regional semifinals (third round differential of 9.5).

The pressure of nearing the Final Four has caused a striking number of teams to become unnerved in the regional finals, which has the largest margin of victory over the last six years: 13.2 points. The opening-round margin in that span is 12.9.

Here's a glance at the average margins of victory from round to round since the tournament expanded to 64 teams:

Year	First Round	Second Round	Regional Semifinals	Regional Finals	National Semifinals	Title Game
1985	10.0	7.4	6.9	7.3	12.5	2
1986	12.2	10.8	6.9	9.8	7.5	3
1987	12.3	10.0	9.1	5.8	9.0	1
1988	11.3	14.8	10.5	15.0	7.5	4
1989	11.1	15.1	8.4	17.8	9.5	1
1990	11.4	7.4	7.3	9.0	11.5	30
1991	12.7	10.4	16.0	11.0	4.0	7
1992	14.5	10.6	7.0	15.8	3.5	20
1993	16.5	15.1	13.3	10.8	6.5	6
Overall	12.4	11.3	9.5	11.3	7.9	8.2

Business As Usual

The Final Fours in recent years have been exclusively for the powerbrokers. The rich are getting richer because success in college starts with recruiting, and with the new recruiting rules and regulations limiting the number of visits and phone calls to prospects, the superstar player is more likely to go to the school that has that presence and visibility.

If the current rules existed when I was an assistant at Rutgers, we probably would not have been able to successfully recruit Phil Sellers and Mike Dabney, the key players for the squad that was undefeated entering the 1976 Final Four. I made an unbelievable number of visits to Brooklyn chasing Sellers, who was the No. 1 high school player in the nation. That doesn't happen any longer under the current recruiting guidelines, and it denies coaches who want to work and climb that ladder of opportunity.

Thus, the recent Final Fours haven't included stirring Cinderella stories. The last three Final Fours have been a Who's Who of College Basketball, as eight of the nine schools with the highest NCAA Tournament winning percentage (minimum of 25 games) graced Indianapolis (1991), Minneapolis (1992) and New Orleans (1993) with their presence.

Ten-time champion UCLA, supplanted by Duke in 1992 as the all-time leader in school winning percentage, hasn't reached the national semifinal round since 1980. But at least UCLA participated in the playoffs eight times in the last 13 seasons. Cincinnati, ranking sixth in winning percentage, did not appear in the tournament for 14 consecutive years until highlighting the Great Midwest Conference's inaugural season by reaching the 1992 Final Four. It was the first time for a first-year league member to advance that far since UNC Charlotte represented the Sun Belt Conference in 1977.

Kentucky, North Carolina or UCLA have won at least two playoff games in each of the last 30 tournaments. The 1994 tournament in Charlotte probably will include more familiar faces, because at least two of the following 11 schools to win more than 65 percent of their playoff games played in each of the eight Final Fours from 1986 through 1993, and at least one appeared at the last 14 Final Fours:

Rank	School (Final Fours)	Record	Pct.	Titles	Championship Coach(es)
1.	Duke (10)	51-16	.761	2	Mike Krzyzewski
2.	UCLA (14)	68-23	.747	10	John Wooden
3.	Indiana (7)	48-17	.738	5	Branch McCracken, Bob Knight
4.	UNLV (4)	30-11	.732	1	Jerry Tarkanian
5.	Michigan (6)	37-15	.712	1	Steve Fisher
6.	Cincinnati (6)	27-11	.711	2	Ed Jucker
7.	North Carolina (11)	62-27	.697	3	Frank McGuire, Dean Smith
8.	Kansas (10)	47-22	.681	2	Phog Allen, Larry Brown
9.	Kentucky (10)	62-32	.660	5	Adolph Rupp, Joe B. Hall
10.	N.C. State (3)	27-14	.659	2	Norman Sloan, Jim Valvano
11.	Georgetown (4)	30-16	.652	1	John Thompson

I Can Seed Clearly Now

NCAA Tournament teams were issued seeds when placed in the bracket starting with the 1979 playoffs. In the first 15 years of the process, the better-seeded team won more than 70 percent of the games in the four regionals. Final Four games, however, have virtually broken even in regard to the original seedings.

Better-seeded teams won at least 23 of the 32 first-round games every year except one (20 in 1989) since the tournament expanded to a 64-team field in 1985. But as can be expected, better-seeded teams win fewer games as the playoffs progress — from the first round (.745 winning percentage) to second round (.696) to regional semifinals (.650) to regional finals (.633).

In 1981, the committee adopted a computer ranking system (Rating Percentage Index) to provide objective data to use in selecting at-large teams. The bracket doesn't raise a racket like it previously did as the Division I Tournament Committee appears to have refined the process over the years. For example, better-seeded teams combined to win a total of just 29 of 56 games (.518) in the second round, regional semifinals and regional finals in 1980 and 1981. During the same three rounds in the last three years, however, better-seeded teams won 67 of 84 games (.798). Moreover, for seven years from 1982 through 1988, at least one team seeded sixth or worse reached the Final Four. But of the total of 20 Final Four teams in the last five years, just one (#6 Michigan in 1992 Southeast Regional) was seeded so unfavorably.

Here is a round-by-round breakdown of how seeding has influenced the playoffs (B denotes games won by better-seeded teams and W denotes games won by worse-seeded teams):

Year	First Round B W	Second Round B W	Regional Semifinals B W	Regional Finals B W	Final Four B W
1979	4 4	11 5	6 2	2 2	3 1
1980	14 2	9 7	3 5	0 4	2 2
1981	11 5	8 8	5 3	4 0	1 3
1982*	11 5	13 3	3 5	4 0	2 0
1983*	10 6	13 3	6 2	2 2	0 2
1984*	11 5	10 6	4 4	3 1	2 0
1985*	25 7	10 6	7 1	2 2	0 2
1986*	26 6	8 8	6 2	3 1	1 1
1987*	23 9	11 5	6 2	2 2	2 0
1988*	27 5	10 6	6 2	2 2	0 2
1989*	20 12	15 1	4 4	3 1	0 2
1990	25 7	8 8	4 4	3 1	3 0
1991	23 9	16 0	4 4	3 1	1 2
1992	24 8	13 3	7 1	2 2	2 1
1993*	26 6	12 4	7 1	3 1	1 0
Totals	280 96	167 73	78 42	38 22	20 18

*Years at least one Final Four game matched teams with the same seeding.

OPENING-GAME JITTERS

An easy formula for success simply doesn't exist for the NCAA Tournament, especially for coaches entering the playoff pressure cooker for the first time. You can believe I was a nervous wreck in my only tourney with Detroit in 1977.

Hey, even legendary coach John Wooden had a shaky start coaching in the Final Four, and we all know what he accomplished. The Wizard of Westwood took UCLA teams to 12 Final Fours and won 10 of them, but can you believe he lost his first five NCAA playoff games from 1950-'56 by an average of 11.4 points? Wooden didn't participate in a Final Four until his 14th season with the Bruins; he finished fourth that year, 1962. Hey, you *know* it ain't easy if Wooden struggled. But he figured it out. Oh, man, did he ever!

"When I look back at the early years when we got in the tournament and lost early, I realize I didn't handle it well," Wooden said. "We should have done better. When we got in tournament play in my early years, I overworked them mentally and emotionally. I forgot what got us there. I always wanted to add something else, and I tried to teach something new in a hurry. I think subconsciously I wanted to win so much that I hurt ourselves in doing that. I think I learned a lot as I got more tournament experience."

Of the 15 coaches to make their NCAA Division I Tournament debuts in 1993, five of them won their openers — California's Todd Bozeman, Santa Clara's Dick Davey, St. John's Brian Mahoney, Rhode Island's Al Skinner and Western Kentucky's Ralph Willard. Bozeman and Willard each won two of three games to enable them to join a minority group of just 22.7 percent (115) of the 507 individuals to coach in the NCAA playoffs and have a winning tournament record. Bozeman, Davey, Mahoney, Skinner and Willard joined a group of 56 active coaches to win their tournament debuts through 1993. More than 60 percent of the active coaches to appear in the playoffs lost their first game.

Among the active luminaries to get off on the wrong foot before eventually reaching the Final Four were Georgia Tech's Bobby Cremins (lost opener while coaching Appalachian State), Georgia's Hugh Durham (Florida State), Texas-El Paso's Don Haskins, Illinois' Lou Henson (New Mexico State), Duke's Mike Krzyzewski, Arizona's Lute Olson (Iowa), Arkansas' Nolan Richardson (Tulsa), Georgetown's John Thompson and Hofstra's Butch van Breda Kolff (Princeton). Krzyzewski (lost to Washington in 1984), Olson (Toledo in 1979) and Richardson (Houston in 1982) dropped their debuts by four points or less despite having better-seeded teams than their initial opponents.

SEEDING THINGS FROM A DIFFERENT VIEW

It is difficult for most fans — hey, for that matter, anyone else — to understand the seeding process for the tournament.

What you have to keep in mind is that the entire 64-team field is seeded in four brackets of 16. Then, the committee matches the four regions as closely as possible. Committee members have to perform some pretty nifty juggling acts to maintain competitive balance because of the multiple entrants from prestige conferences. They also cannot allow teams from the same league to play each other prior to a regional final, which means they might have to raise or lower some teams a spot in the seedings.

Following is an appraisal of the impact of the seeding process in its first 15 years:

- A No. 1 seed has won the title six times (North Carolina '82, Georgetown '84, Indiana '87, UNLV '90, Duke '92 and North Carolina '93). The Final Four did not have more than two No. 1 seeds in any year until 1993 when Kentucky, Michigan and North Carolina advanced that far. It wasn't easy for Michigan and North Carolina, however, as the finalists each had to overcome double-digit deficits in two regional games to reach the Final Four.

- The only championship game to not have at least one No. 1 or No. 2 seed was 1989, when a pair of No. 3 seeds clashed (Michigan from the Southeast Regional and Seton Hall from the West).

- The worst seed to capture the national title was Villanova (No. 8 in 1985). Villanova '85 and North Carolina State '83 (No. 6 seed) are the only teams to defeat two No. 1 regional seeds in a single tournament. Villanova defeated #1 seed Michigan (59-55) in the second round of the Southeast Regional before edging East Regional champion Georgetown (66-64) in the national final. N.C. State nipped #1 seed Virginia (63-62) in the West Regional final before frustrating Midwest Regional champion Houston (54-52) in the national title game.

- The worst-seeded team to reach the Final Four and defeat a top seed was No. 11 LSU. The Tigers edged No. 1 seed Kentucky (59-57) in the 1986 Southeast Regional final despite starting guard Derrick Taylor misfiring on all nine of his shots from the floor. They had lost to the Wildcats a total of three times during the regular season and SEC Tournament. Three other teams seeded worse than sixth have reached the Final Four — Penn (#9 in East in 1979), UCLA (#8 in West in 1980) and Virginia (#7 in East in 1984).

- Better-seeded teams win more than 70 percent of their games in the tournament.

- No. 1 seeds did not lose any of the first 36 opening-round games against No. 16 seeds since the field was expanded to 64 teams in 1985. No. 1 seeds coming closest to getting upset were Oklahoma, which edged East Tennessee State (72-71), and Georgetown, which nipped Princeton (50-49). Both games were in 1989.

- It seems as if at least one No. 2 seed annually fails to advance past the second round. Duke '79 was the first of a total of 18 No. 2 seeds to fail to reach the regional semifinals. There were only two years (1982 and 1989) when all four No. 2 seeds progressed that far.

There has been a jinx of sorts on No. 3 seeds. At least one No. 3 seed lost in the opening round each of the last eight years from 1986-93 — Indiana (lost to Cleveland State in 1986), Notre Dame (Arkansas-Little Rock in 1986), Illinois (Austin Peay State in 1987), North Carolina State (Murray State in 1988), Stanford (Siena in 1989), Missouri (Northern Iowa in 1990), Nebraska (Xavier in 1991), Arizona (East Tennessee State in 1992) and Georgia Tech (Southern in 1993).

Defending national champion North Carolina has been seeded worse than fourth only once. The Tar Heels were the No. 8 seed in the 1990 Midwest Regional, but they advanced to the regional semifinals (round of 16) by upsetting top-ranked Oklahoma in the second round.

A No. 12 seed reached the round of 16 (regional semifinals) the last four years — Ball State '90, Eastern Michigan '91, New Mexico State '92 and George Washington '93.

Teams seeded 13th or worse defeated teams seeded among the top four in a regional a total of 18 times in nine years from 1985-93. Since the seeding process started in 1979, never have all of the top four seeds in each regional survived their opening round.

Winners All the Way

It was a privilege for me to coach two state championship teams in my seven years as a high school coach in Group I, the smallest of the divisions in New Jersey. I'll always be indebted to the sacrifices the players made and to my assistant, Bob Stolarz, who was technically as sharp as any coach I've been with.

I wonder what the odds are for a player or coach to be involved with championship teams at every level — high school, college and the NBA? Three Louisville alums are among the eight players in a prestigious class to be members of teams that won a state high school championship, NCAA title and NBA crown. Here is an alphabetical list of the ultimate triple crown champions:

Player	High School	College	NBA Team
Lucius Allen	Wyandotte (MO) '65)	UCLA '67-'68	Bucks '71
Quinn Buckner	Thornridge (IL) '71-'72	Indiana '76	Celtics '84
Magic Johnson	Lansing (MI) '77	Mich. State '79	Lakers '80-82-85-87-88
Jerry Lucas	Middletown (OH) '58	Ohio State '60	Knicks '73
Rodney McCray	Mt. Vernon (NY) '78-'79	Louisville '80	Bulls '93
Rick Robey	Brother Martin (LA) '74	Kentucky '78	Celtics '81
Billy Thompson	Camden (NJ) '82	Louisville '86	Lakers '87-'88
Milt Wagner	Camden (NJ) '79	Louisville '86	Lakers '88

NOTES: Buckner (1976), Johnson (1992) and Lucas (1960) constitute the unique group that also won an Olympic gold medal. McCray was a member of the 1980 U.S. team that boycotted the Moscow Olympics after the Soviet Union's invasion of Afghanistan.

Dick's Top 5

Best Teams Not to Go to the Big Dance

1. **Kentucky '54 (25-0)** — Declined bid after being put on probation the previous season.

2. **Maryland '74 (23-5)** — Len Elmore, John Lucas and Tom McMillen certainly could have cut the nets down if more than one team from a conference was allowed to participate in the tourney.

3. **N.C. State '73 (27-0)** — The Wolfpack, led by David Thompson, defeated league NCAA representative Maryland a total of three times while on probation.

4. **Southern Cal '71 (24-2)** — Dynamite club unfortunately had to play in the shadows of mighty UCLA.

5. **La Salle '69 (23-1)** — Many fans outside the East might not remember the probation-bound Explorers, led by Ken Durrett and Larry Cannon, but they were tough as nails.

YOU CAN'T Always Get WHAT YOU WANT

You really had to feel for Chris Webber when he called for a timeout with 11 seconds remaining in last year's title game when Michigan was out of timeouts. That mistake prevented the Wolverines from having an opportunity to tie the score or take the lead against North Carolina. And you really have to admire the way Webber and his family have taken the embarrassment in stride and reacted to it in a positive way. That's what life's all about, turning negatives into positives.

"It's no big deal," Webber said shortly before he became the first pick in the 1993 NBA draft. "I'm not happy it happened. But I know it's going to help me in some way. It made me a man. It made me grow up a lot faster than if it hadn't happened."

Webber's father, Mayce, bought a vanity license plate that reads "Timeout." And Chris has formed the "Timeout Baby" foundation. His mom recommended to him that he invest some dollars to help innercity youngsters pursue an education if they really want to take a timeout in their life and get themselves together. I think that is fantastic.

Webber's ill-fated mistake wasn't the first mental meltdown or physical lapse in an NCAA Tournament game, and it won't be the last. It has happened frequently, and to some of the real PTP'ers. You can't go back and change history, but it's fun to think of what might have been.

For example, Hall of Famer Elgin Baylor shot over 50 percent from the floor in his college career. But in the 1958 championship game, he played with bruised ribs and hit just 9 of 32 field goal attempts. If he had hit his usual 50 percent, Seattle would have beaten Kentucky instead of losing, 84-72. To be fair, Baylor scored 49 more points than any other player in the tournament and Seattle wouldn't have had a prayer to reach the Final Four without him.

We could go on forever with these "what ifs." People struggle all the time to achieve their potential — that's life. I don't think any team should be labeled a "classic underachiever" as analyst Bill Walton called Michigan last year, particularly a team as young as the Wolverines were, but every tournament brings sub-par performances from standout players. Of course defense often has something to do with that. Anyway, here are some other thought-provoking scenarios from the last 20 years that demonstrate how exasperating the playoffs can be for coaches, players and fans alike:

- Forwards **Calbert Cheaney** and **Eric Anderson** shot better than 50 percent from the floor in their careers at Indiana. But they only hit 26.3 percent (5 of 19) in their 1992 Final Four loss to Duke, 81-78.

- Forward **Larry Johnson** and guard **Stacey Augmon** combined for 37 points per game on 61 percent field goal shooting in their two years together as teammates at UNLV. But they combined for only 19 points on 40 percent shooting (8 of 20) in the 1991 national semifinals, when the seemingly invincible Rebels lost to eventual champion Duke, 79-77.

- Guard **Kenny Anderson** averaged 27 points per game in his first four tournament contests as a freshman for Georgia Tech. But he scored just 16 in his fifth game, the 1990 national semifinal, as the Yellow Jackets squandered a seven-point halftime lead and lost to eventual champion UNLV, 90-81.

- Forward **Nick Anderson** (55.3 percent) and center **Lowell Hamilton** (53.4 percent) rank among the top five Illinois players in career field goal shooting. But they shot just 39.3 percent (11 of 28) in the 1989 national semifinals as the Illini lost to eventual champion Michigan, 83-81. The Wolverines also dodged a bullet against Seton Hall in the final, when they won 80-79 as Pirates forward **Andrew Gaze** was restricted to one field goal after contributing at least six baskets in each of the previous four playoff games.

- Forwards **Danny Ferry** and **Robert Brickey** and guard **Phil Henderson** combined to shoot 50 percent from the floor in their Duke careers. But they hit just 27.3 percent (9 of 33) in the 1988 national semifinals when the Blue Devils lost to Kansas, 66-59.

- Forward **Derrick Coleman** and guards **Stephen Thompson** and **Howard Triche** combined to shoot 51.6 percent from the floor for Syracuse in the 1986-87 season. If they had hit better than 33.3 percent (six of 18) in the 1987 championship game, **Keith Smart's** shot wouldn't have mattered. As it turned out, Indiana won, 74-73.

Forwards **Mark Alarie** and **David Henderson** and guard **Tommy Amaker** combined to make more than 50 percent of their field-goal attempts for Duke in the 1985-86 season. But they hit just 33.3 percent (12 of 36) in the 1986 championship game, when the Blue Devils lost to Louisville, 72-69.

 Center **Patrick Ewing** averaged just 13.2 points in six Final Four games with Georgetown, but has never averaged fewer than 20 points per game in his eight-year career with the New York Knicks. Just think if he had scored a few more points in the two championship games the Hoyas lost during his career — a 63-62 loss to North Carolina in 1982 and a 66-64 loss to Villanova in 1985. Then, the Hoyas would be sitting on three national titles instead of the one they won in 1984.

 Eventual top-six NBA draft choices **Sam Bowie**, **Melvin Turpin** and **Kenny Walker** combined to shoot 56.4 percent from the floor to help Kentucky register 51.5 percent field-goal accuracy as a team in the 1983-84 season. But do you remember what happened in the second half of their national semifinals game against Georgetown in 1984? Brick city, baby! It was unbelievable. The Wildcats hit just 9.1 percent (3 of 33) as they blew a seven-point halftime lead and lost, 53-40. Kentucky's starters missed all 21 of their field goal attempts after the break. The first-round starting frontcourt of Bowie, Turpin and Walker combined to shoot 25 percent from the floor (6 of 24) in the entire game.

 Houston swingmen **Clyde Drexler** and **Michael Young** and forward **Larry Micheaux** combined to score 47 points per game in the 1982-83 season. But they combined for just 14 points in the 1983 championship game when the Cougars lost to North Carolina State, 54-52.

 Guard **Rob Williams**, swingman **Michael Young** and center **Hakeem Olajuwon** combined to score 40.3 points per game for Houston in the 1981-82 season. But they scored just two points apiece in the 1982 national semifinals when the Cougars lost to eventual champion North Carolina, 68-63. Williams, the team leader in scoring with a 21.1-point average, missed all eight of his field goal attempts against the Tar Heels, but still finished as the tourney's leading scorer.

 Forwards **Kiki Vandeweghe**, **Mike Sanders** and **James Wilkes**, guards **Rod Foster**, **Michael Holton** and **Darren Daye**, and center **Darrell Allums** each shot at least 50 percent from the floor for UCLA in the 1979-80 season and were proficient enough to eventually play in the NBA. But they combined to hit just 38.6 percent (17 of 44) of their field goal attempts in the 1980 championship game, when the Bruins lost to Louisville, 59-54.

 The acclaimed Arkansas trio of guards **Ron Brewer** and **Sidney Moncrief** and forward **Marvin Delph** combined to shoot 55.7 percent from the floor in the 1977-78 season. They hit just 41.7 percent (15 of 36) in the 1978 national semifinals, when the Razorbacks lost to Kentucky, 64-59. The Wildcats were fortunate to overcome a five-point halftime deficit in their previous game, a 52-49 victory over Michigan State in the Mideast Regional final. The Spartans' point guard, a freshman by the name of **Magic Johnson**, hit just two of 10 field goal attempts and committed six turnovers.

Guards **Phil Ford** and **John Kuester** combined to score 28.4 points per game on 52.7 percent field-goal shooting for North Carolina in the 1976-77 season. But they managed just 11 points on 5 of 16 shooting (31.3 percent) in the 1977 championship game, which the Tar Heels lost to Marquette, 67-59.

Eventual NBA first-round draft choices **Leon Douglas** and **Reggie King** combined to score an average of 31.5 points per game for Alabama in the 1975-76 season. They had just 16 in the 1976 Mideast Regional semifinals, when the Crimson Tide lost to Indiana, 74-69. The Hoosiers also were fortunate when eventual NBA players **Butch Lee**, **Lloyd Walton** and **Jerome Whitehead** struggled from the floor for Marquette in the Mideast Regional final. Those three combined to hit 21.6 percent (8 of 37) of their field goal attempts in Indiana's 65-56 victory.

Kentucky had four regulars shoot better than 50 percent from the floor in the 1974-75 season — forward **Kevin Grevey**, guard **Jimmy Dan Conner**, and centers **Rick Robey** and **Mike Phillips**. But they combined to hit just 36.5 percent (19 of 52) in the 1975 championship game, when the Wildcats lost to UCLA, 92-85. Similarly, three Louisville regulars shooting better than 52 percent from the floor for the season (swingman **Junior Bridgeman**, center **Ricky Gallon** and guard **Phillip Bond**) combined to hit 25 percent (6 of 24) in a 75-74 loss against UCLA in the national semifinals. Adding insult to injury for the Cardinals was reserve guard **Terry Howard** missing the front end of a one-and-one free-throw opportunity in the closing seconds of overtime after he had converted all 28 of his foul shots that season. The Bruins led a charmed life throughout the playoffs that season in coach John Wooden's farewell. They won their opener in overtime after Michigan's **C.J. Kupec** missed a shot at the end of regulation, then defeated Montana by three points (67-64) in the West Regional semifinals when future pro standout **Micheal Ray Richardson** scored just two points for the Grizzlies.

Not that things *always* went right for UCLA. Two-time consensus first-team All-America forward **Keith Wilkes** shot better than 50 percent from the floor in his three varsity seasons with the Bruins, and hit half of his field goal attempts in a 12-year NBA career. But in the 1974 national semifinals he made just 29.4 percent (5 of 17) as UCLA lost to North Carolina State, 80-77, interrupting Wooden's incredible run of championships.

SCORERS WHO SIZZLE SOMETIMES FIZZLE

As you can see, great players sometimes come up short in the big games. Even guys who went on to outstanding professional careers have had to endure nightmares in the NCAA Tournament.

Remember Ralph Sampson? He was the NBA's Rookie of the Year in 1984 and the MVP of the league's all-star game in 1985. At Virginia, he was a consensus first-team All-America three years running. But he never led the Cavaliers to a national championship, as many people assumed he would. Virginia did reach the Final Four in 1981 when he was a sophomore, but Sampson had three mediocre playoff games of less than 12 points, including an 11-point outing in the national semifinals in a loss to North Carolina.

Chris Mullin, after averaging 25.5 points in St. John's first four playoff games in 1985, became the only national player of the year (UPI, USBWA and Wooden Award) to score less than 10 points when his school was eliminated in a Final Four contest. The Redmen were routed by Georgetown (77-59) in the national semifinals when Mullin was limited to eight points in 39 minutes. Here are the 15 different team-leading scorers to go more than 10 points below their season scoring average when their school lost in the national semifinals or final:

PLAYER, FINAL FOUR TEAM	SEASON AVERAGE	DEPRESSED POINT TOTAL IN FINAL FOUR SETBACK	DECREASE
Elvin Hayes, Houston '68	36.8 ppg	10 vs. UCLA in semifinals	-26.8
Rob Williams, Houston '82	21.1 ppg	2 vs. N. Carolina in semis	-19.1
O. Robertson, Cincinnati '60	33.7 ppg	18 vs. Cal in semifinals	-15.7
Jack Egan, St. Joseph's '61	21.9 ppg	8 vs. Ohio State in semis	-13.9
O. Robertson, Cincinnati '59	32.6 ppg	19 vs. Cal in semifinals	-13.6
Tom Sanders, NYU '60	21.4 ppg	8 vs. Ohio State in semis	-13.4
Phil Ford, North Carolina '77	18.7 ppg	6 vs. Marquette in final	-12.7
Danny Manning, Kansas '86	16.7 ppg	4 vs. Duke in semifinals	-12.7
Billy Donovan, Providence '87	20.6 ppg	8 vs. Syracuse in semis	-12.6
Danny Knight, Kansas '74	12.4 ppg	0 vs. Marquette in semis	-12.4
Burdette Haldorson, Colo. '55	21.0 ppg	9 vs. USF in semifinals	-12.0
Chris Mullin, St. John's '85	19.8 ppg	8 vs. Georgetown in semis	-11.8
Michael Young, Houston '83	17.3 ppg	6 vs. N.C. State in final	-11.3
Bob Cousy, Holy Cross '48	16.2 ppg	5 vs. Kentucky in semis	-11.2
Jerry Lucas, Ohio State '62	21.8 ppg	11 vs. Cincinnati in final	-10.8
Melvin Turpin, Kentucky '84	15.2 ppg	5 vs. Georgetown in semis	-10.2

COPING WITH A CURSE

Great scorers are fun to watch, but don't figure on them taking their teams to the Big Dance. More often than not, fans get stood up by them. Why? Hey, it's a team game, baby! Offense is fickle. Defense and rebounding are the constants that win for you night in and night out.

Remember, Pete Maravich, the greatest scorer in the history of college basketball, a guy who *averaged* 44.2 points over his three varsity seasons, never even got LSU into the the NCAA Tournament. And get this: In the last 13 years, no player who was the single-game scoring leader in the tournament played in the Final Four.

In fact, the only player ever to lead the nation in scoring during the regular season and play in the tournament's championship game was Clyde Lovellette, a huge, 6-foot-9 farm boy from Indiana who carried Kansas to the title in 1952. Lovellette, who averaged 28.4 points per game, was the first player to score more than 30 points in a Final Four game and the only player to crack the 30-point plateau in both Final Four games in the same season. He scored 33 against Santa Clara in the semifinals and 33 against St. John's in the final.

The only other player to lead the nation in scoring and play for a Final Four team was Oscar Robertson, who averaged 32.6 and 33.7 points, respectively, in leading Cincinnati to the national semifinals in 1959 and 1960. But the Bearcats were beaten both years by California. The Big O scored a total of 37 points in his two Final Four losses, hitting 9 of 32 shots from the floor.

Robertson, by the way, was involved in one of the most bizarre finishes in NCAA Tournament history when Cincinnati lost to Kansas State in overtime, 83-80, in 1958. The Bearcats trailed K-State by one point with one second remaining in regulation when Robertson was fouled.

"He hit the first (free throw)," said Oklahoma State coach Eddie Sutton, a player for the Cowboys in the same regional. "Then, he walked back to the center jump circle to converse with his teammates. When he turned around, the referee had put the ball on the free throw line and started counting. You have 10 seconds to shoot once he gives you the ball. Not knowing how many seconds had been counted off, Robertson ran to the line, scooped up the ball, took a quick jump shot and hit the heel of the rim. Robertson fouled out in the first minute or two of overtime."

Here's another argument against the value of big-time scorers. Of the eight teams to reach the Final Four with two or three 20-point scorers in the lineup, none won the championship. And of the 38 different players to score more than 225 points in the NCAA Tournament and/or average over 25 points per game in the playoffs over the course of at least six games, the only one to compile a losing record in postseason play was — you guessed it — the individual with the highest scoring average. Notre Dame guard Austin Carr averaged 41.3 points in seven tournament games from 1969 through 1971, but the Fighting Irish won just two of seven games during that span.

Of the more than 60 different players to score at least 2,500 points and/or rank among the top 25 in career scoring average through the 1992-93 season, just one player — Arizona's Sean Elliott — compiled a winning NCAA Tournament record in his career and had higher scoring, rebounding and field goal shooting averages in the playoffs than in the regular season — apparent proof that scorers tend to falter somewhere along the tournament trail. Elliott averaged 23.6 points and 6.8 rebounds and shot 57.5 percent from the floor to help the Wildcats win six of 10 NCAA playoff games from 1986-89. He averaged 19.2 points and 6.1 rebounds and shot 51.2 percent from the floor in his career.

Maravich, who scored 3,667 points at LSU from 1968-70, isn't the only scoring machine from a major college not to participate in the NCAA Tournament. Last year, Mississippi Valley State's Alphonzo Ford (3,165 points) and Tennessee's Allan Houston (2,801) joined Maravich, Portland State's Freeman Williams (3,249 from 1975-78), Texas Southern's Harry Kelly (3,066 from 1980-83) and Houston's Otis Birdsong (2,832 from 1974-77) as players to score more than 2,800 points in their major college careers but never participate in the NCAA Tournament.

Southwestern Louisiana guard Bo Lamar, who scored 3,493 points in his career, did play in the tourney, but he became the only player to take more than 40 field goal attempts in a playoff game and lose. Lamar was the nation's leading scorer as a junior with 36.3 points per game in 1972 when he connected on just 14 of 42 shots from the floor and one of three free throws in an 88-84 defeat to Louisville in the Midwest Regional semifinals.

So if your favorite team ever gets a big scorer who fills it up, look out! It doesn't mean you're going to the Final Four; probably just the opposite.

BOTTOM OF THE BARREL

"No, you never get any fun out of the things you haven't done."
— Ogden Nash

Sometimes it might seem like it's not that difficult to get into the NCAA Tournament. Hey, 64 teams go, right? And a lot of them don't look like world-beaters.

But Ogden Nash knew what he was talking about. Out of 301 Division I members eligible to compete in the tournament, 68 have never gone. Last year, two schools received their first-ever invitation to the tournament, Tennessee State and Wright State. Here's an alphabetical list of the remaining playoff wannabees, with the first season they became eligible to participate in the tournament in parentheses:

Alabama State ('83), American ('67), Arkansas State ('71), Army ('48), Bethune-Cookman ('81), Buffalo ('74-77 and '92), Cal State Northridge ('92), Centenary ('60), Central Connecticut State ('87), Central Florida ('85), College of Charleston ('92), Charleston Southern ('75), Chicago State ('85), The Citadel ('48), Colgate ('48), Delaware State ('74), Eastern Washington ('84), Florida A&M ('79), Florida Atlantic ('94), Florida International ('88), Gonzaga ('53), Grambling State ('78), Hartford ('85), Illinois-Chicago ('82), Jackson State ('78), Kent ('52), Liberty ('89), Loyola, Md. ('82), Maine ('62), Maryland-Baltimore County ('87), Maryland-Eastern Shore ('82), Missouri-Kansas City ('90), Monmouth ('84), Morgan State ('85), Mount St. Mary's ('89), New Hampshire ('62), Nicholls State ('81), UNC Asheville ('87), UNC Greensboro ('93), UNC Wilmington ('77), Northeastern Illinois ('91), Northern Arizona ('72), Northwestern ('48), Northwestern (La.) State ('77), Prairie View A&M ('81), Radford ('85),

Sacramento State ('92), St. Francis, N.Y. ('48), Samford ('73), Sam Houston State ('87), Southeastern Louisiana ('81), Southeast Missouri State ('92), Southern Utah State ('89), Southwest Texas State ('85), Stephen F. Austin State ('87), Stetson ('72), Tennessee-Martin ('93), Texas-Arlington ('69), Texas-Pan American ('69), Troy State ('94), Valparaiso ('48-58 and '77), Vermont ('62), Wagner ('77), Western Carolina ('77), Western Illinois ('82), William & Mary ('48), Winthrop ('87), Wisconsin-Milwaukee ('74-80 and '91), Youngstown State ('82).

The most recognizable school never to appear in the NCAA tourney is Northwestern, where new coach Ricky Byrdsong, who coached at my old school, Detroit, will discover how difficult it is to survive in the Big Ten. In the past, the Wildcats seem to have been content with the rare upset or near-upset of a nationally-ranked team. Get ready for lots of "L"'s, Ricky baby!

But it won't be his fault if they don't win. Northwestern's hierarchy should decide to get out of the Big Ten if they are not going to make a commitment to give their young athletes a chance to win in the revenue-producing sports of football and basketball. By that, I mean spending the money to improve their facilities and make the commitments other major college programs make. It's not fair to the young people to get pounded week in and week out. If the administration doesn't want to make that commitment, they should say bye-bye and find another conference to play in. There's nothing wrong with playing in conference with smaller schools, where everybody plays under the same guidelines.

Other Division I schools have competed in the NCAA Tournament, but never won a game there. The following list includes 10 institutions to go winless in the first 55 years of the tournament despite playing in a major conference where at least one current member has won a national title:

School (Conference)	NCAA Playoff Appearances
Air Force (member of WAC)	lost two games (1960 and 1962)
UC Irvine (Big West)	never participated
Hawaii (WAC)	lost one game (1972)
Miami, Fla. (Big East)	lost one game (1960)
Mississippi (SEC)	lost one game (1981)
Nebraska (Big Eight)	lost four games (1986, 1991, 1992 and 1993)
Northwestern (Big Ten)	never participated
*San Diego State (WAC)	lost three games (1975, 1976 and 1985)
*San Jose State (Big West)	lost two games (1951 and 1980)
Southern Mississippi (Metro)	lost two games (1990 and 1991)

*San Diego State and San Jose State have also never won an NIT game.

NOTES: Four of the 10 winless schools in NCAA playoff competition from prominent leagues didn't start playing major college basketball permanently until the last 25 years — UC Irvine (moved up to Division I in 1978), Hawaii (1971), San Diego State (1971) and Southern Mississippi (1973).... Texas-El Paso won the national title four years before joining the Western Athletic Conference in 1970.

20/20

Army never has participated in the NCAA Tournament, but it has contributed to it in a major way. In 1968, the military academy made one of its eight NIT appearances after earning a ranking in a final UPI poll for the only time (16th). The school's coach in that 20-5 season was Bob Knight, and the roster included a junior guard by the name of Mike Krzyzewski. Knight or Krzyzewski, or both, coached teams to seven consecutive Final Fours from 1986-92 and rank among the six winningest coaches in NCAA Tournament history. It has been reported that Knight and Krzyzewski had a falling out after Duke beat Indiana in the 1992 Final Four, but I think that's been blown out of proportion.

Lately, it seems as if the same group of schools contends for the championship every year. It's difficult for a smaller program without much tradition to break through and challenge the big boys; that's why it's so exciting when a Western Kentucky or Santa Clara advances in the tournament, as they did last year.

You would be surprised at some of the schools that once were considered powers. Here's 10 that haven't competed in the tournament for at least 20 years, but once were ranked among the Top 20 in a wire service poll (the last NCAA Tournament appearance is in parentheses): Bowling Green State (1968), Canisius (1957), Colorado (1969), Columbia (1968), Drake (1971), Miami, Fla. (1960), Niagara (1970), Rice (1970), St. Louis (1957) and Tennessee Tech (1963).

Five of those schools finished in the Top 10: Bowling Green State, with the great center Nate Thurmond, in 1962; Colorado in 1963; Columbia, with Jim McMillian, in 1968; Miami in 1960; and St. Louis in 1957.

That's the great thing about basketball. One or two great players, if they're surrounded by the right people, can make a team a contender.

Some smaller schools, though, wonder what they have to do to win the favor of the tournament's selection committee. Several schools have won 20 or more games in recent years but had to sit home at tournament time, mainly because the selection committee wasn't impressed with the strength of their schedules.

In 1992, for example, 28 schools eligible for the tournament won 20 or more games, but got stood up by the Big Dance committee. Five of those schools (Ball State, Louisiana Tech, Penn State, Rhode Island and Richmond) had won at least one NCAA playoff game in the previous four seasons and another, Wisconsin-Green Bay had been a last-second loser to Michigan State in the 1991 tourney. Excluding schools on probation, an average of almost eighteen 20-win teams have fallen through the cracks annually since the playoff field was expanded to 64 teams in 1985.

The winningest eligible team to sit home during the NCAA Tournament was Southern Illinois, which was 26-7 in 1990. The most snakebitten school seems to be New Mexico, which averaged 21 victories a season from 1984 through 1992. The Lobos received just one invitation from the NCAA during that period (1991) before earning an automatic bid in 1993 by winning the WAC Tournament.

But at least New Mexico got to play in the NIT in those years. Idaho wasn't invited to either the NCAA or NIT in 1993, despite a 24-8 record. The winningest school not to get to play in either the NCAA or NIT tournaments since 1985 is Howard, which was 25-5 in 1987. And take pity on Texas-San Antonio. The Roadrunners sat at home in the postseason three consecutive years from 1990 through 1992 despite winning more than 20 games each season. Wisconsin-Milwaukee was bypassed despite compiling a 43-12 record in its last two seasons as an independent before joining the Mid-Continent Conference this season.

Here is a look at the ample number of 20-win teams at the end of conference tournament competition from 1985-93 to not be invited to the NCAA playoffs (schools also shunned by the NIT denoted in parentheses):

1985 — 15 (7); 1986 — 17 (7); 1987 — 15 (3); 1988 — 20 (6); 1989 — 16 (4); 1990 — 18 (6); 1991 — 12 (4); 1992 — 28 (12); 1993 — 18 (9).

THE EMPIRES STRIKE OUT

You might think being a traditional power would almost guarantee success in the NCAA Tournament. But many teams with first-rate merchandise entering the postseason get dime-store results.

For instance, Syracuse was eliminated seven times in 13 years from 1979 through 1991 by teams seeded fifth or worse. And Irish eyes are crying at Notre Dame, which is on a downward spiral. I feel very strongly about Notre Dame needing to join a conference. Competing as an independent doesn't excite the blue-chip recruit any longer. Football is different at Notre Dame. They have the magical Golden Dome and that incredible tradition, so they can thrive as an independent. But Irish basketball needs to be part of the excitement of regular-season competition leading up to postseason play.

Here is a list of schools, including Notre Dame and Syracuse, that have never won an NCAA championship despite finishing in the Associated Press Top 10 at last seven times since the wire service's first poll in 1949:

SCHOOL	ASSOCIATED PRESS TOP TEN FINISHES	FINAL FOURS
*Notre Dame	12 (1953-54-58-70-74-76-77-78-79-80-81-86)	one (1978)
Syracuse	10 (1975-77-79-80-86-87-88-89-90-91)	two (1975-87)
Bradley	8 (1949-50-51-54-59-60-61-62)	two (1950-54)
*DePaul	8 (1964-78-79-80-81-82-84-87)	two (1943-79)
St. John's	8 (1950-51-52-53-69-83-85-86)	two (1952-85)
*Arkansas	7 (1978-79-83-84-90-91-92)	four (1941-45-78-90)
*Illinois	7 (1949-51-52-56-63-84-89)	four (1949-51-52-89)

*Never reached an NCAA playoff championship game.

NOTES: Maryland is the only school to finish in an AP Top 10 at least five times (6th in 1958, 8th in 1973, 4th in 1974, 5th in 1975 and 8th in 1980) and never reach the Final Four.... Arkansas, Illinois, Notre Dame and Syracuse have also never won the NIT.

Not Good, But Good Enough

I believe money generated by the tournament should be spread among all the Division I schools. And I like to see as many worthy teams as possible from a variety of leagues earn invitations to the playoffs. But I don't like to see a team with a losing record participate. Last year, East Carolina became the eighth school with a losing record to appear in the NCAA Tournament. Needless to say, they were immediately eliminated by North Carolina.

The only one of the eight sub-.500 schools to win an NCAA playoff game was Bradley. The Braves won twice in the 1955 tournament (69-65 over Oklahoma City and 81-79 over Southern Methodist) after losing 14 consecutive contests during one stretch in the regular season. Despite the pair of playoff victories, they finished with their worst overall record (9-20) in a 53-year span until going 8-20 in the 1990-91 season.

In 1950, Bradley won two games apiece in both the NCAA Tournament and NIT to reach the championship game of both events. The Braves lost against CCNY in each final to finish the season with a 32-5 record under coach Forddy Anderson. Bradley's coach in 1955 was Bob Vanatta. He was in his first of two seasons at the school after succeeding Anderson, who departed for Michigan State after guiding the Braves to a national second-place finish in 1954.

Texas, winner of just one non-conference game in the 1973-74 season, is the only school with a losing overall record to secure an automatic bid by winning a regular season league title. Here is a list of the eight schools to denigrate the NCAA playoffs by entering the tourney with a losing record:

School	W-L	Pct.	Coach	How Team Qualified
Bradley '55	7-19	.269	Bob Vanatta	Independent*
Oklahoma City '55	9-17	.346	Doyle Parrack	Independent*
George Washington '61	9-16	.360	Bill Reinhart	Won SC Tournament
Lehigh '85	12-18	.400	Tom Schneider	Won ECC Tournament
East Carolina '93	13-16	.448	Eddie Payne	Won Colonial Tournament
Texas '74	12-14	.461	Leon Black	SWC regular-season title
Montana State '86	14-16	.466	Stu Starner	Won Big Sky Tournament
Missouri '78	14-15	.482	Norm Stewart	Won Big Eight Tournament

*District 5 committee restricted to District 5 independents (only two in the district) to fill out bracket; this rule was changed for the 1956 playoffs.

NOTES: Regular-season league records of five conference tournament champions: George Washington '61 (3-9 in Southern before defeating #2 seed Virginia Tech, #3 The Citadel and #4 William & Mary); Missouri '78 (4-10 in Big Eight before defeating #2 seed Iowa State, #3 Nebraska and #4 Kansas State); Lehigh '85 (6-8 in ECC before defeating #3 seed Drexel, #7 Hofstra and #1 Bucknell); Montana State '86 (6-8 in Big Sky before defeating #4 seed Nevada, #1 Northern Arizona and #2 Montana); East Carolina '93 (4-10 in Colonial before defeating #2 seed Old Dominion, #6 UNC-Wilmington and #1 James Madison).

Final Four Futility

I've been nominated several times for an Ace Award, the equivalent of the Emmy for cable excellence, but I've never been to the winner's circle. My role model is Duke, which kept plugging away until it finally won the championship.

The Blue Devils made it to the Final Four nine times until finally winning their first national title in 1991. That was a distinction they were more than happy to relinquish, and left these seven schools as those appearing in the Final Four the most times without ever winning the championship:

5 — Houston (1967, 1968, 1982, 1983 and 1984/finished runner-up twice)

4 — Arkansas (1941, 1945, 1978 and 1990/never reached NCAA title game)

4 — Illinois (1949, 1951, 1952 and 1989/never reached NCAA title game)

4 — Kansas State (1948, 1951, 1958, and 1964/finished runner-up once)

3 — Iowa (1955, 1956 and 1980/finished runner-up once)

3 — LSU (1953, 1981 and 1986/never reached title game)

3 — Oklahoma (1939, 1947 and 1988/finished runner-up twice)

But there's always someone worse off than you are, especially when it comes to the NCAA Tournament. At least those schools have made it to the semifinals. Five more have qualified for the tournament at least 12 times, but never reached the Final Four (the closest they came to national semifinals is in parentheses):

School	Years without Final Four Appearance
Brigham Young	17 years (11-20 record/lost regional final in 1981)
Connecticut	16 years (10-17/lost regional finals in 1964 and 1990)
Missouri	14 years (9-14/lost regional final in 1976)
Miami of Ohio	13 years (3-15/never won more than one game in a tourney)
Alabama	12 years (13-12/never reached regional final)

Miami of Ohio has been hailed as the cradle of coaches in football, but it is the only school to have as many as six different basketball coaches compile losing NCAA playoff records. Four other colleges have had five coaches participate in the tournament without compiling a winning playoff record for that school — Idaho State, New Mexico State, Pepperdine and Southern Cal. I ache for USC's George Raveling, the only coach to register losing NCAA playoff records at three different schools — Washington State (1-2), Iowa (0-2) and USC (1-2).

Four coaches have gaping holes in their Final Four records, losing at least three more games than they've won: Jack Gardner (1-7 with Kansas State and Utah), Slats Gill (0-4 with Oregon State), Ted Owens (0-4 with Kansas) and Tex Winter (0-4 with Kansas State).

First-Round Flops

I know about failure in front of an audience. I was at a nightspot in Jersey in 1970 when a dynamite redhead turned me down twice for a dance. You can't imagine the grief I caught from my coaching buddies. But I hung in there and not only got a dance that night with the lady named Lorraine, but wound up marrying her less than a year later. Hey, I was a great recruiter!

The Southeastern Conference needs to have that kind of persistence, because it's had more tournament frustrations than any other major conference. Despite having an average of three first-round NBA draft choices annually in 15 years from 1979 through 1993, no current member of the 12-team SEC reached the NCAA Tournament championship game in that span, although every school participated in the playoffs at least once.

Kentucky is the only SEC school to appear in an NCAA Tournament championship game. Six others have never made it to a regional final in the 55-year history of the national tourney: Alabama, Florida, Mississippi, Mississippi State, South Carolina and Tennessee. In contrast, only three of the total of 55 current members from the ACC, Big East, Big Eight, Big Ten, Great Midwest and Pacific-10 have failed to advance to a regional final — Miami (Big East), Nebraska (Big Eight) and Northwestern (Big Ten).

The SEC posted the worst composite conference record in any one year of the NCAA playoffs in 1989, when all five league entrants lost their first-round game — four of them by more than 10 points. In 1991, the SEC had four first-round losers.

LSU, the only SEC school to compile a winning league record in each of five seasons from 1988 through 1992, was the only school in the country to have a consensus first-team All-America each of four years from 1989 through 1992 (guard Chris Jackson in 1989 and 1990 before center Shaquille O'Neal in 1991 and 1992). But the Tigers gave their fans achy breaky hearts by posting a paltry 2-5 playoff mark from 1989-93, with three of the defeats by double-digit margins. Remember, stars don't win basketball games, teams do!

The SEC also is the only league to have a team lose in the first round of the NCAA playoffs by more than 20 points to a lower-rated squad seeded 10th or worst. And that's happened to four different schools! Perhaps the biggest SEC disappointment was LSU in 1985. The Tigers were seeded fourth in the Southeast Regional with a roster including eventual NBA first-round draft picks John Williams and Jerry Reynolds, and six other players who became NBA draft choices. But they became the only top-four seed to lose a first-round game by more than 20 points when they were trounced by Navy, as David Robinson collected 18 points and 18 rebounds.

Here is a capsule look at the four embarrassing SEC first-round defeats since the field was expanded to at least 52 teams:

Year	SEC Opening-Round Debacle (Score)	Regional
1983	#11 seed Lamar over #6 Alabama (73-50)	Midwest
1985	#13 Navy over #4 Louisiana State (78-55)	Southeast
1989	#10 Colorado State over #7 Florida (68-46)	Midwest
1991	#12 Eastern Michigan over #5 Mississippi State (78-56)	East

NOTES: The only one of these four winning teams to win a second-round game was Eastern Michigan.

All Dressed Up with No Place to Go

UNLV is eligible for the NCAA Tournament again this season, but just think what could have been if the Runnin' Rebels had not been ineligible in 1992 and '93? The Rebels, winner of 20 NCAA playoff games in the previous six years, had a 26-2 record in '92, won their 10th Big West Conference crown in as many seasons and had leveled LSU, which was in the tournament, by 21 points during the regular season — but they were sitting home.

Of course, there was no guarantee UNLV would reach the national semifinals for the third consecutive season in 1992. But if it had, it would have joined the list of Final Four teams to have its participation voided because of various infractions ruled on after the schools advanced that far — St. Joseph's (3rd in 1961), Villanova (2nd in 1971), Western Kentucky (2nd in 1971), UCLA (2nd in 1980) and Memphis State (tied for 3rd in 1985).

Kansas won the championship in 1988, but was declared ineligible for the tournament by the NCAA the following season, becoming the only champion unable to defend its title. The Jayhawks finished 19-12 that year under first-year coach Roy Williams. Other marginal teams likely to have received at-large bids in recent years if they hadn't been banned by the NCAA because of various infractions include Syracuse '93 (20-9 mark), Illinois '91 (21-10), North Carolina State '90 (18-12), South Carolina '88 (19-10) and Virginia Tech '88 (19-10).

While it's doubtful any of those six trespassers would have had a significant impact on the playoffs, NCAA Tournament history probably would be quite a bit different if some of the great teams in the last 40 years hadn't been ruled ineligible for the tournament. Florida State, Kansas, Kentucky, North Carolina State and Wichita State are among the schools who have been ineligible for tournament play at least twice. They, among others, probably could have made some noise in the tournament if they had been eligible. Here are 20 outstanding teams that had to stay home at tourney time:

SCHOOL	RECORD	COACH	KEY PLAYER(S)
Kentucky '53	DNP	Adolph Rupp	Cliff Hagan, Frank Ramsey

Comment: After a one-year schedule boycott, the Wildcats' undefeated squad in 1954 declined a bid to the NCAA playoffs.

N.C. State '55   28-4   Everett Case   Ronnie Shavlik, Vic Molodet

Comment: ACC regular-season and tournament champion Wolfpack defeated eventual national runner-up La Salle.

N.C. State '59   22-4   Everett Case   John Richter, Lou Pucillo

Comment: ACC regular-season co-champion and tournament kingpin Wolfpack defeated Final Four teams Louisville and Cincinnati.

Seattle '59   23-6   Vince Cazzetta   Charley Brown

Comment: Despite losing All-America Elgin Baylor to the NBA, this independent twice defeated NCAA playoff first-round winner Idaho State.

No. Carolina '61 19-4   Frank McGuire   York Larese, Doug Moe

Comment: ACC regular-season champion Tar Heels defeated league NCAA representative Wake Forest twice by a total of 24 points.

Utah '62   23-3   Jack Gardner   Billy McGill

Comment: The Utes won by nine points at UCLA, but the Bruins won their conference title and advanced to the Final Four.

Miami (Fla.) '65   22-4   Bruce Hale   Rick Barry

Comment: The Hurricanes defeated NCAA playoff first-round winners Houston and Oklahoma City by a total of 35 points.

La Salle '69   23-1   Tom Gola   Ken Durrett, Larry Cannon

Comment: The Explorers defeated NCAA Tournament entrants Villanova, St. Joseph's and Duquesne by a total of 38 points.

Fla. State '70   23-3   Hugh Durham   Dave Cowens, Skip Young

Comment: The Seminoles split two games with national runner-up Jacksonville, losing at JU by just four points.

N.C. State '73   27-0   Norm Sloan   David Thompson, Tom Burleson

Comment: ACC regular-season and tournament champion Wolfpack defeated league NCAA representative Maryland a total of three times.

SCHOOL	RECORD	COACH	KEY PLAYER(S)
Centenary '74	21-4	Larry Little	Robert Parish

Comment: Playing an independent schedule, the Gents won at Texas, the Southwest Conference champion.

Clemson '77	22-6	Bill Foster	Tree Rollins, Stan Rome

Comment: ACC regular-season runner-up Tigers defeated league champion and national tournament runner-up North Carolina by 20 points.

Minnesota '77	24-3	Bill Musselman	M. Thompson, Ray Williams

Comment: Big Ten runner-up Gophers (behind top-ranked Michigan) defeated national champ Marquette on the Warriors' home court.

San Francisco '80	22-7	Dan Belluomini	Quintin Dailey

Comment: WCC co-champion Dons compiled a 4-1 record against three different NCAA Tournament teams.

UCLA '82	21-6	Larry Farmer	Mike Sanders, Rod Foster

Comment: Pac-10 runner-up Bruins defeated Midwest Regional No. 1 seed DePaul by 12 points for the Blue Demons' only regular-season loss.

Wichita St. '82	23-6	Gene Smithson	Antoine Carr, Cliff Levingston

Comment: Missouri Valley runner-up Shockers (behind eventual NIT champion Bradley) beat Mideast Regional runner-up UAB by 15 points.

Wichita St. '83	25-3	Gene Smithson	Antoine Carr, Xavier McDaniel

Comment: Missouri Valley champion Shockers won at Alabama-Birmingham, the Sun Belt Conference Tournament champion.

Memphis St. '87	26-8	Larry Finch	Vincent Askew, Sylvester Gray

Comment: Metro runner-up Tigers lost by just three points against UNLV, a Final Four team ending the season with a glittering 37-2 record.

Kentucky '91	22-6	Rick Pitino	Reggie Hanson, Jamal Mashburn

Comment: SEC regular-season champion Wildcats defeated Big Eight co-champion Kansas, the national runner-up, by 16 points.

Missouri '91	20-10	Norm Stewart	Anthony Peeler, Doug Smith

Comment: Big Eight Tournament titlist Tigers lost close early-season game against eventual Southeast Regional No. 1 seed Arkansas when Peeler was sidelined because of academic woes.

FALSE STARTS

North Carolina A&T has appeared in the NCAA playoffs the most times (seven) without winning a tournament game. Northeast Louisiana is runner-up with an 0-6 record. Two schools are tied for third place in this dubious category with 0-5 records — Eastern Kentucky and Marshall. Nebraska and Yale are next at 0-4. But these six winless universities still have a long way to go to join the ranks of the five "quick exit" schools, four from the East, with at least 10 opening-round defeats.

Connecticut, after absorbing nine opening-round losses in 17 years from 1951-'67, had the most opening-round setbacks for years. But the Huskies haven't lost in the first round since 1979, while Princeton and West Virginia passed them up in this category with four such defeats apiece in the last 10 years. St. John's suffered eight opening-round losses in a 20-year stretch from 1973-'92.

It's amazing when you think about Princeton having the most opening-round defeats. Anybody around basketball knows that one of the consistently great jobs in all of college coaching is done by Princeton's Pete Carril. To me, coaching is the ability of an individual to get the most out of his personnel. Who could ever forget that dramatic 1989 East Regional first-round game when Princeton's poise and patience challenged mighty Georgetown before the Hoyas escaped with a 50-49 victory? Even Georgetown coach John Thompson graciously said he had been outcoached. There aren't many who do it better than Carril, although it might not be reflected by looking at their NCAA playoff record over the years.

The only school to incur at least 10 NCAA Tournament defeats but never absorb an opening-round loss is Maryland. The Terrapins have a 13-10 record overall. Here is a list of the five schools most prone to sustaining an opening-round defeat:

SCHOOL (PLAYOFF LOSSES)	NCAA TOURNAMENT OPENING-ROUND DEFEATS
Princeton (22)	12 (1952-55-60-63-69-76-77-81-89-90-91-92)
West Virginia (17)	11 (1955-56-57-58-62-65-67-83-86-87-92)
Connecticut (17)	10 (1951-54-57-58-59-60-63-65-67-79)
Miami of Ohio (15)	10 (1953-55-57-66-71-73-84-85-86-92)
St. John's (24)	10 (1961-68-73-76-77-78-80-84-88-92)

HOW THE WEST HAS LOST

Lute Olson, the Cary Grant of college coaches, must be a great actor. He looks so unruffled by Arizona 's first-round exits the past two tourneys. They would have had to put me in a padded cell.

Arizona's five first-round defeats in the last 10 years are a symptom, but the entire West has struggled in the NCAA Tournament. For example, only two schools west of the Mississippi River have won the national title since UCLA's last championship in 1975: Kansas (1988) and UNLV (1990).

Furthermore, Wyoming is the only former national champion (1943) to compile an all-time NCAA playoff record at least two games below .500 (8-18). Holy Cross (1947 titlist) is 7-8 in the tournament and Utah (1944) is 19-19.

Everett Shelton, coach of Wyoming's titlist in 1943, is the only championship team coach to finish with a non-winning playoff record, and is more games under .500 in NCAA Division I Tournament competition than any coach in history. The six coaches at least six games under the .500 mark include Shelton (4-12 with Wyoming from 1941-58), Pete Carril (3-10 with Princeton from 1969-92), Don Corbett (0-7 with North Carolina A&T from 1982-88), Hugh Greer (1-8 with Connecticut from 1951-60), Ralph Miller (5-11 with Wichita State, Iowa and Oregon State from 1964-89) and Stan Watts (4-10 with Brigham Young from 1950-72).

Wyoming, Brigham Young and Oregon State are three of the six Western schools among the nation's 10 universities to compile NCAA Tournament records at least seven games below .500. Three of the following 10 institutions in this languid category are located in Utah (Brigham Young, Utah State and Weber State):

SCHOOL	PLAYOFF RECORD	GAMES BELOW .500 MARK	LAST NCAA TOURNAMENT VICTORY
Miami of Ohio	3-15	minus 12	'78 Mideast Regional 1st round
Princeton	11-22	minus 11	'83 West Regional 1st round
Wyoming	8-18	minus 10	'87 West Regional 2nd round
Brigham Young	11-20	minus 9	'93 Midwest Regional 1st round
Utah State	5-13	minus 8	'70 West Regional semifinals
Oregon State	12-19	minus 7	'82 West Regional semifinals
Connecticut	10-17	minus 7	'92 Southeast Regional 1st round
Pepperdine	4-11	minus 7	'82 West Regional 1st round
Weber State	4-11	minus 7	'79 Midwest Regional 1st round
North Carolina A&T	0-7	minus 7	winless in the NCAA playoffs

OUT OF SIGHT, OUT OF MIND

If I would have stayed in college coaching, I would have been obsessed with reaching the Final Four. But I couldn't take it physically; I was diagnosed with a bleeding ulcer on three occasions. You think I'm wacko now, you should have seen me as a coach! To this day, I'm still on medication.

I bet there's a lot of coaches out there today who also are on medication, or at least should be. Like Norm Stewart and Lefty Driesell, maybe. They've made the most appearances in the NCAA playoffs without reaching the Final Four. Thirteen Stewart-coached teams at Missouri from 1976-93 played in the tournament, but failed to reach the Final Four, although Stewart wasn't with the Tigers' squad in 1989 because of illness. Driesell, now at James Madison, made 11 NCAA playoff appearances with Davidson and Maryland from 1966-86.

Three other active coaches with more than 400 victories at the major college level who, like Stewart and Driesell, probably will never receive the accolades they deserve until they direct a team to the Final Four are Princeton's Pete Carril, West Virginia's Gale Catlett and Iowa's Tom Davis.

In the 1993-94 season, Driesell and Stewart probably will join the list of coaches to never reach the Final Four despite compiling more than 625 major college victories. Previous coaches with such a dubious distinction include Ed Diddle (759 with Western Kentucky), Ralph Miller (657 with Wichita State, Iowa and Oregon State) and Marv Harshman (642 with Pacific Lutheran, Washington State and Washington). Diddle (3-4), Miller (5-11) and Harshman (2-3) each posted a losing NCAA playoff record.

Driesell coached one of the six eligible teams ranked among the top five in the AP and/or UPI final polls to not participate in either the NCAA Tournament or the NIT in the days before teams other than the conference champion could be chosen to the NCAA playoffs as at-large entrants. Here is a chronological list of these six highly-ranked teams that weren't on NCAA probation, but are somewhat forgotten because they didn't appear in national postseason competition:

SCHOOL (RECORD)   **COACH**   **KEY PLAYERS**
Kansas State '52 (19-5) Jack Gardner Jim Iverson, Dick Knastman, Jesse Prisock

Comment: Finished runner-up in the Big Seven Conference to NCAA champion-to-be Kansas, a team the Wildcats defeated at home in Manhattan by 17 points. K-State, ranked 3rd by AP and 6th by UPI after finishing as national runner-up to Kentucky the previous year, lost another matchup against the Jayhawks on a neutral court in overtime.

Kentucky '54 (25-0)   **Adolph Rupp**   **Cliff Hagan, Frank Ramsey, Lou Tsioropoulos**

Comment: After a schedule boycott in the 1952-53 season stemming from an NCAA probation, the Wildcats' undefeated squad declined a bid to the 1954 NCAA playoffs. They defeated eventual national champion La Salle by 13 points in the UK Invitation Tournament final on their way to being ranked 1st by AP and 2nd by UPI.

Alabama '56 (21-3)   **Johnny Dee**   **Jerry Harper, George Linn, Dennis O'Shea**

Comment: The last team to compile a perfect SEC record (14-0) was ranked 5th by AP and UPI but didn't participate in the NCAA playoffs because of a rules technicality stemming from varsity participation as freshmen by some of the "Rocket Eight" star players in 1953. Alabama's squad, dominated by Midwest recruits who didn't survive tryouts to receive scholarships from Notre Dame, became the first squad to score 100 points against Kentucky. The 20-6 Wildcats, the league's representative to the NCAA Tournament, were whipped by 24 points (101-77) as 'Bama finished the season with 16 consecutive victories. The Crimson Tide's defeats — at North Carolina and St. John's and against Notre Dame on a neutral court — were in a span of four games. As incredible as it seems today, Dee left Alabama after that season to coach an amateur team sponsored by the Denver-Chicago Trucking Company. An Alabama team didn't receive an NCAA bid until 1975. Dee later coached Notre Dame for seven seasons from 1965-71, compiling a 2-6 NCAA playoff record in four appearances with the Fighting Irish.

**Kansas State '62 (22-3)   Tex Winter   Mike Wroblewski, Pat
                                              McKenzie, Gary Marriott**

Comment: The Wildcats, ranked 5th by UPI and 6th by AP the year after being eliminated from the NCAA Tournament by eventual champ Cincinnati, finished runner-up in the Big Eight to Colorado. Their three defeats were in road games to Colorado, Kentucky and Oklahoma State.

**Southern Cal '71 (24-2)   Bob Boyd   Dennis Layton, Ron Riley,
                                              Paul Westphal**

Comment: Both of the Trojans' defeats were by a single-digit margin in Pacific-8 Conference competition against eventual national champion UCLA. USC ranked 5th in both polls. Boyd didn't direct the Trojans to the NCAA Tournament until his 13th and final year at the school in 1979.

**Maryland '74 (23-5)   Lefty Driesell   Len Elmore, John Lucas,
                                              Tom McMillen**

Comment: The Terrapins, ranking 4th in both polls, lost to eventual NCAA champion North Carolina State in the ACC Tournament final (103-100 in overtime) in what some believe might have been the greatest college game ever played. Maryland lost by one point at UCLA in its season opener before dropping both regular-season games to N.C. State by six points and bowing at North Carolina to finish in a tie with the Tar Heels for second place in the ACC.

FROM FANTASTIC 4 TO FORLORN 14

Here's another inside scoop for you to test your hoop junkie friends. What four players were a member of an NCAA title team one year and an NBA champion the next season as a rookie?

Here they are: Bill Russell (San Francisco '56, Boston Celtics '57); Henry Bibby (UCLA '72, New York Knicks '73); Magic Johnson (Michigan State '79, Los Angeles Lakers '80), and Billy Thompson (Louisville '86, Lakers '87). Johnson was the only one of this quartet to be named Final Four Most Outstanding Player and NBA Finals Most Valuable Player in back-to-back seasons.

Some of the players who excelled in the NBA never got the chance to compete in the NCAA Tournament, such as Massachusett's Julius Erving (above), Providence's Lenny Wilkens (left) and Indiana's Walt Bellamy (top left).

Many of the all-time NBA greats didn't fare too well in the NCAA Tournament, however. Three of the top 10 scorers in NBA history — Wilt Chamberlain (2nd), Jerry West (8th) and Elgin Baylor (10th) — were teammates with the Los Angeles Lakers for all or parts of five seasons and combined for 27 All-NBA first team selections. But they were linked by a dubious college streak in the late 1950s when they were on the losing end of three consecutive NCAA championship games. Kansas (with Chamberlain) lost to North Carolina in 1957, Seattle (Baylor) lost to Kentucky in 1958 and West Virginia (West) lost to California in 1959.

Another Final Four fallen star was Oscar Robertson, the fifth-leading scorer in NBA history and an All-NBA first-team pick his first nine seasons in the league. Robertson averaged 33.8 points per game in his college career, but was held under 20 points by California in back-to-back national semifinal defeats in 1959 and 1960.

Pete Maravich is another prime case regarding the specter of tourney trials. Maravich's star, shining so brightly as the NCAA's all-time leading scorer (3,667 points), faded as cynics questioned whether he was a team player because LSU was just two games above .500 against SEC competition and didn't participate in the NCAA Tournament while he was there. He is the only three-time first-team All-America to fail to appear in the NCAA playoffs. Tennessee's Allan Houston, runner-up to Maravich as the SEC's all-time leading scorer and a 1993 first-round draft choice of the Detroit Pistons, also didn't play in the NCAA Tournament.

Hall of Famer Julius Erving is the only former major-college player to become NBA Most Valuable Player (1980-81 with the Philadelphia 76ers) after never participating in the NCAA tourney. Although many of the pro stalwarts resembled Erving and participated in the NIT, following are 14 of the highest scorers in NBA and ABA history to play at least two years of varsity basketball at a major college but never appear in the NCAA Division I playoffs:

PLAYER, COLLEGE (VARSITY SEASONS)	COLLEGE W-L MARK	NIT W-L	POINTS AS PRO
Julius Erving, Massachusetts ('70-'71)	41-11	0-2	30,026
Rick Barry, Miami, Fla. ('63-'64-'65)	65-16	1-2	25,279
*Dominique Wilkins, Georgia ('80-'81-'82)	52-37	4-2	22,096
*Robert Parish, Centenary ('73-'74-'75-'76)	87-21	DNP	21,628
Walt Bellamy, Indiana ('59-'60-'61)	46-24	DNP	20,941
Chet Walker, Bradley ('60-'61-'62)	69-14	3-1	18,831
Lou Hudson, Minnesota ('64-'65-'66)	50-22	DNP	17,940
Lenny Wilkens, Providence ('58-'59-'60)	62-18	5-3	17,772
Bailey Howell, Mississippi State ('57-'58-'59)	61-14	DNP	17,770
Kevin McHale, Minnesota ('77-'78-'79-'80)	73-40	4-1	17,335
Billy Cunningham, North Carolina ('63-'64-'65)	42-27	DNP	16,310
Pete Maravich, Louisiana State ('68-'69-'70)	49-35	2-2	15,948
Jack Twyman, Cincinnati ('52-'53-'54-'55)	54-47	2-1	15,840
Dick Van Arsdale, Indiana ('63-'64-'65)	41-31	DNP	15,079

*Career point totals for the two active NBA players on the list are through the conclusion of the 1992-93 season.

NOTES: Guards Bill Sharman (Southern Cal) and John Stockton (Gonzaga) join Erving, Barry and Wilkins on the list of major-college players to never appear in the NCAA Tournament before selection to an All-NBA Team at least six times.... Walker-led Bradley won the 1960 NIT with an 88-72 title game victory over Wilkens-led Providence.... Cincinnati (first NCAA Tournament appearance in 1958), Georgia (1983), Minnesota (1972), Mississippi State (1963) and Providence (1964) didn't reach the NCAA playoffs for the first time until the college playing careers of Twyman, Wilkins, Hudson, Howell and Wilkens had ended, respectively.... Erving (Philadelphia 76ers '83), Barry (Golden State Warriors '75), Parish (Celtics '81, '84 and '86), Walker (76ers '67), Howell (Celtics '68 and '69), McHale (Celtics '81, '84 and '86) and Cunningham (76ers '67) played on NBA championship teams.... The only player to become NBA Rookie of the Year and Most Valuable Player who participated in the NCAA Tournament but never won an NCAA playoff game was Dave Cowens, who managed just 11 points and four rebounds as a sophomore for Florida State in 1968 when the Seminoles lost a first-round game to East Tennessee State (79-69).... Spencer Haywood (1968-69 with Detroit) and George McGinnis (1970-71 with Indiana) both scored more than 17,000 points in the pros after averaging at least 30 points per game in their only year in college before entering the ABA.... Bellamy, McGinnis, Van Arsdale and Van Arsdale's twin brother, Tom, combine to make Indiana the only school to have as many as four of its players score more than 14,000 points in the pros after never appearing in the NCAA playoffs or NIT. Tom Van Arsdale, finishing his 12-year pro career with 14,232 points after playing for five different teams, is the highest scorer in NBA history to never participate in the NBA playoffs.

NOWHERE TO HIDE

The average championship team coach has almost 17 years of head coaching experience. Recently retired Glenn Wilkes had a distinguished 36-year career at Stetson, the last 22 seasons after the school moved up to Division I. But Wilkes is the only major-college coach to finish with more than 500 victories and never participate in the NCAA playoffs.

Many highly-respected coaches simply don't have the budgets or player talent to challenge the big guys in postseason play. For example, Holy Cross' George Blaney is winless in the NCAA playoffs but is held in such high esteem by his colleagues that he is president of the National Association of Basketball Coaches this season. Blaney is among the following seven active coaches to have attended the Big Dance, but never win a game despite at least 17 years of experience:

COACH, CURRENT SCHOOL	SEASONS OVERALL	DIVISION I EXPERIENCE	PLAYOFF RECORD
George Blaney, Holy Cross	26	24 years	0-3
Hank Egan, San Diego	22	22 years	0-1
Tom Apke, Appalachian State	19	19 years	0-3
Paul Lizzo, Long Island University	22	18 years	0-2
Stan Morrison, San Jose State	18	18 years	0-3
Charlie Woollum, Bucknell	18	18 years	0-2
M.K. Turk, Southern Mississippi	17	17 years	0-2

NOTES: Apke (seven years at Creighton and five at Colorado), Blaney (three at Dartmouth), Egan (13 at Air Force) and Morrison (seven at Pacific and seven at Southern Cal) previously coached other Division I colleges. Apke lost all three of his playoff games with Creighton while Morrison was 0-1 with Pacific and 0-2 with Southern Cal.

BEHIND THE SCENES

Did you know . . . ?

 The only schools to compile a losing record as defending NCAA champion were 1942 titlist **Stanford** (10-11 in the 1942-43 season) and 1979 titlist **Michigan State** (12-15 in 1979-80). The last time both championship game teams from one year failed to appear in the NCAA playoffs the next season was 1980, when Michigan State and runner-up **Indiana State** lost **Magic Johnson** and **Larry Bird** to the NBA, respectively.

Michigan's 37.9 percent field goal shooting (22 of 58) in the 1992 championship game defeat against **Duke** was the lowest in a national final since UCLA hit 36.5 percent (19 of 52) in a 59-54 setback against **Louisville** in 1980. The last eight national runners-up each hit under 50 percent from the floor in the final, shooting a cumulative 43.1 percent (217 of 503).

The only team to fail to have at least one player score in double figures in the championship game was **Georgetown**, a 46-34 loser against **Wyoming** in 1943.

The four teams to have 10 different players score in a title game all lost the NCAA final — **Kansas State** '51, **Duke** '64, Duke '90 and **Kansas** '91.

Guy Lewis won more NCAA playoff games (26) and made more Final Four appearances than any coach without winning the national title. Lewis directed **Houston** to the Final Four on five occasions from 1967-'84 and came back empty-handed each time.

Wimp Sanderson, a loser in all six of his regional semifinal games with **Alabama** (1982-85-86-87-90-91), is the only one of 17 former college coaches with at least 20 NCAA Tournament decisions to fail to reach the Final Four.

The only player to score 40 or more points in a Final Four contest and not eventually play in the NBA was **St. Joseph's** forward **Jack Egan**, who scored 42 points in a four-overtime, 127-120 triumph against **Utah** in the 1961 national third-place game. Egan was a third-round draft choice of Philadelphia that year but forfeited the opportunity to play in the league when he was implicated in a game-fixing scandal. Egan was susceptible to such shenanigans inasmuch as he was the father of two children and his wife had suffered a miscarriage just before the season started.

The only player to lead a single tournament in scoring with more than 120 points and not eventually play in the NBA was guard **Rick Mount**, who scored 122 points in four games for **Purdue** in the 1969 playoffs before playing five seasons in the ABA with four different franchises. The three players other than Mount to lead a tourney in scoring since 1947 but not play in the NBA or ABA were **Syracuse** guard **Jim Lee** (119 points in five games in 1975), **North Carolina State** guard **Dereck Whittenburg** (120 points in six games in 1983) and **Dayton** forward **Roosevelt Chapman** (105 points in four games in 1984). Two players other than Chapman led an NCAA Tournament in scoring although they did not participate in the Final Four — **Austin Carr** scored 158 points in three games for **Notre Dame** in 1970 and **Chet Palmer** scored 43 points in two games for **Rice** in 1942 (tying **Jim Pollard** of champion **Stanford**).

The only player since 1957 to lead a tournament in rebounding and not eventually play in the NBA was forward **Daryll Walker**, who grabbed a total of 58 rebounds in six games for 1989 runner-up **Seton Hall**.

The only individuals to be named national player of the year by both AP and UPI and not play that season in either the NCAA Tournament or NIT were **North Carolina State** forward **David Thompson** and **Ohio State** center **Gary Bradds**. Thompson averaged 29.9 points and 8.2 rebounds per game in 1974-75 when the Wolfpack finished in a three-way tie for second place in the ACC standings. N.C. State chose to bypass the NIT after losing against **North Carolina** (70-66) in the ACC Tournament final when Thompson hit just 7 of 21 field-goal attempts. Bradds averaged 30.6 points and 13.4 rebounds per game for the Buckeyes in 1963-64 when they compiled a 16-8 record and finished in a first-place tie with **Michigan** in the Big Ten Conference. The Wolverines went on to win the national third-place game in the NCAA playoffs. Bradds was the only national player of the year in an 11-year span from 1959 through 1969 to not appear at the Final Four. AP didn't start naming a player of the year until 1961. UPI, introducing its award in 1955, honored **Columbia** guard **Chet Forte** in 1957. Forte, who became a network TV executive, averaged 28.9 points per game for an 18-6 Lions team failing to appear in either national postseason tourney.

So many notable people have been associated with the NCAA Tournament in one form or other that it's impossible to work them all in. But here's a few stray photographs you might be interested in seeing. Everett Dean (top left) coached Stanford to the 1942 NCAA Tournament championship, and was a successful baseball coach there as well. He passed away last fall at the age of 95. Bud Foster (top right) played at Wisconsin and later coached the Badgers to the 1941 championship. Wes Unseld (bottom right) was nearly svelte when he played for Louisville's tournament team. He later played for the Washington Bullets' NBA championship team and now coaches them. And you know I couldn't forget Lou Henson (bottom left), who coached New Mexico State into the Final Four in 1970. As you can see, he had the Lou-do going even then.

DICK'S DICTIONARY

ALL-AIRPORT	A player who looks good in airports, but gets no playing time.
ALL-KODAK	A player who doesn't move enough; he might as well be taking pictures.
ALL-RIP VAN WINKLE	A player who is a "sleeper," or unnoticed.
ALL-ROLLS ROYCE	A player or coach who is among the best.
ALL-THOMAS EDISON	A creative and innovative player, usually a point guard.
BRICK CITY	When a player or team shoots poorly.
DIAPER DANDY	A great first-year player.
GET A T.O., BABY!	Call a timeout.
CREAM PUFF	An easy opponent or schedule.
THE ROCK	The ball.
DOUGHNUT OFFENSE	A team without a center.
DOW JONESer	An up-and-down, or inconsistent, player.
ISOLATION MAN	A great one-on-one player.
M&Mer	A mismatch.
MR. PAC MAN	A great defender who eats up offensive players.
N.C.	No contest.
N.B.N.	A shot that swishes through the net, hitting Nothing But Nylon.
P.T.	Playing time.
P.T.P.er	Prime Time Player.
RIP AND RUN	Fastbreaking transition game.
SKY WALKER	A great leaper.
SPACE EATER	Big player.
SURF-AND-TURFER	A superstar.
3-D MAN	A player who drives, draws (the defense) and dishes the rock.
3-S MAN	A scintillating, sensational, super player.
UNCLE MO	Momentum, which swings back and forth.
WINDEX MAN	A strong rebounder who "wipes the glass."

INDEX

PLAYERS

INDEX

INDEX

INDEX

COACHES

INDEX

INDEX

SCHOOLS

INDEX

INDEX

5-30
4201-36

4261-36
5-30